CATHY GLASS

THE MILLION COPY BESTSELLING AUTHOR

Please Don't Take My Baby

A pregnant teenager, lost and
alone. A foster carer with room
in her heart for two.

HarperElement
An imprint of HarperCollins*Publishers*
1 London Bridge Street
London SE1 9GF

www.harpercollins.co.uk

First published by HarperElement 2013

14

A catalogue record of this book is
available from the British Library

ISBN 978-0-00-751491-5

Printed and bound in Great Britain by
Clays Ltd, St Ives plc

MIX
Paper from
responsible sources
FSC www.fsc.org **FSC** C007454

Please Don't Take My Baby

Acknowledgements

A big thank-you to my editor, Anne; my literary agent Andrew; and Carole, Vicky, Laura and all the team at HarperCollins.

Author's Note

E ngland has one of the highest teenage pregnancy rates in the developed world. Last year nearly 40,000 teenage girls gave birth and nearly 60,000 terminated a pregnancy. These figures are truly shocking. And while some of the girls' stories have happy endings, many do not.

Please Don't Take My Baby

Chapter One

stranger at the Door

We'd just sat down to our evening meal when the door-bell rang. I sighed. Why did salespeople always manage to time their calls with dinner? Double glazing, cavity-wall insulation, religion, new driveway, landscape the garden or fresh fish from Grimsby: whatever they were selling, 6.00 p.m. seemed to be the time they called, I supposed because most people are home from work by then and it isn't so late that people won't answer their front doors.

'Aren't you going to see who it is, Mum?' Paula, my eight-year-old daughter, asked, as I didn't immediately leave the table.

'Yes,' I said as the bell rang for a second time.

Standing, I swallowed my mouthful of cottage pie and went down the hall to the front door, ready to despatch the salesperson as quickly as possible.

'And don't be rude!' Adrian called after me.

As if I would! Although it was true I usually sent away cold callers efficiently and effectively, which to Adrian, aged twelve, could be seen as rude and certainly embarrassing.

'Don't be cheeky,' I returned, as I arrived at the front door.

It was dark outside at six o'clock in January and, as usual, before answering the door at night, I checked the security

1

spyhole, which allowed me to see who was in the porch. The porch was illuminated by a carriage lamp and gave enough light for me to see a lady in her early thirties, dressed smartly in a light-grey winter coat, and whom I vaguely recognized from seeing in the street. I guessed she was collecting either money for a charity or signatures for a petition on a local issue: traffic calming, crossing patrol, noisy pub in the high road, etc.

'Hello,' I said with a smile as I opened the door. The cold night air rushed in.

'I'm sorry to trouble you,' she began. 'You're Cathy Glass, aren't you?' I saw she wasn't carrying a charity-collection tin or a clipboard with a petition to sign.

'Yes,' I said, surprised she knew my name. I certainly didn't know hers.

'I'm sorry to disturb you. My name's Meryl Dennis. I work at Beachcroft School. I'm the games mistress – I teach PE. I expect you've seen me around? I live at number 122.'

'Oh yes,' I said. Number 122 was at the very bottom of the street.

I smiled politely and wondered why she was telling me who she was and about her school, which was on the other side of the county. Adrian, who'd started secondary school the previous September, attended a local school and Paula was still at our local primary school. I smiled again and waited, aware that the cold air was chilling the house and my half-eaten dinner was on the table going cold.

'You foster, don't you?' Meryl asked a little nervously.

'Yes. Although I don't have a child at present.'

'I thought not. I pass your house in my car on the way to work and I used to see you setting off on your school run. I thought your routine had changed.'

I smiled again and nodded, and continued to look at Meryl, still with no inkling as to why she was here or why she'd taken such an interest in my routine. Donna, the girl whose story I told in *The Saddest Girl in the World*, had left us in November and I'd taken Christmas off and was now waiting for another foster child to arrive. I didn't yet know who it would be. But what any of that had to do with Meryl I had no idea.

'Is it possible for me to come in for a few moments?' Meryl asked. 'What I have to say is confidential. I'm so sorry to trouble you like this.'

'Well, yes,' I said, slightly taken aback but intrigued. 'Come in.'

Grateful to be able to close the door against the cold night air, I led the way down the hall.

'Who is it?' Paula called from the dining table, having heard our footsteps.

'A lady who lives down our road,' I said. 'Finish your dinner, please.'

'Oh, I'm sorry,' Meryl said. 'I've interrupted your meal.'

'Don't worry. It will save. Let's go through here to talk.' I showed her into the sitting room and pushed the door to. Adrian and Paula knew where I was if they needed me.

Meryl had the authoritative air of a teacher. She sat on the sofa, unbuttoned her coat and, slipping it off, folded it on to the sofa next to her. 'I'm sorry to barge in on you like this,' she apologized again. 'But I need to ask you a favour – to help me out.'

It was then I thought she was probably looking for a child-minder – hence her comments about me not having a child; possibly someone to look after her child or children before or after school. I'd been approached before by neighbours who knew I fostered and asked if I could mind their children. If this was why Meryl was here I'd have to politely refuse, for as a foster carer I'm not allowed to childmind as well, although I am allowed to help out a friend, for example, by looking after their child for a couple of hours while they go to the dentist or similar.

Meryl now looked at me very seriously as she spoke. 'As well as teaching PE at Beachcroft I'm mentor for the girls in years twelve and thirteen. You know, what used to be known as the sixth form.' I nodded. 'The girls come to me with their problems, usually about studying and exams; or they have boyfriend problems, or they're not getting on with their parents. I listen to them and do what I can to help. However, I have one girl in year twelve who is pregnant. She telephoned me half an hour ago to say her mother has thrown her out. She's at a friend's now but can't stay there tonight. Can she come here?'

I was completely taken aback by the directness of the question, although the answer was simple: no. But I could see how passionate Meryl was in her desire to help the girl, so I thought she deserved a fuller explanation.

'I can't, I'm afraid. Although I'm a foster carer I can't take any child I choose. The way the system works is that when a social worker at the local authority decides to bring a child into care they first check their lists to see if they have a suitable foster carer free; if they haven't, they send a referral to the independent fostering agencies in the area to see if they have anyone suitable. The agency I foster for, Homefinders, receives the referral together with other agencies and if they think I'm suitable they contact me. Different foster carers have different expertise and specialities. I don't foster pregnant teenage girls, but some foster carers do. The social services will be able to find somewhere for this girl. Have you contacted them?'

'Jade doesn't want them involved,' Meryl said.

I paused and thought. 'I think they need to be involved,' I said.

'I think they know about Jade,' Meryl said. 'I understand there's a social worker already working with Jade's mother on other issues. Jade has younger brothers and sisters. But Jade told the social worker she didn't want her help – or words to that effect.' Meryl shrugged.

'I see. Well, I'm sorry but as a foster carer I can't take a child unless the referral has come through the proper channels, and they won't place Jade with me. I take younger children and often those with special needs or challenging behaviour.'

'Couldn't we have a private fostering arrangement?' Meryl asked, clearly having done some research into the matter. 'It's not as though Jade is a small child. She can look after herself.'

'I can't become involved in a private fostering arrangement,' I said. 'Not while I work for a fostering agency. Also the law is clear: if someone who is not a relative of a child looks after a child who is under the age of sixteen for more than twenty-eight days, then they have to be assessed and become a registered foster carer. It's for the child's good. Foster carers are trained and regularly monitored.'

'Jade's just seventeen.'

'I'm sorry, it doesn't make any difference. I still can't take her. I suggest you telephone the duty social worker now and explain the situation and that Jade has just become homeless. The social services will find her a bed for the night. At seventeen she's still a minor, so the social services have a legal duty of care towards her. They'll place her with a teen carer who can best take care of her needs.'

Meryl sighed and looked downcast. I felt sorry for her. She clearly wanted to help Jade and I think she really believed I could offer Jade a home, or at least a bed for the night. But it wasn't that simple. Even if I'd been registered as a teen carer and had a spare bedroom, the referral would still have had to go through the social services who, if necessary, would pass it on to the independent fostering agencies (which are charitable trusts that came about as a result of the local authorities never having enough foster carers). As I looked at Meryl I thought how nice it was of her to be so conscientious and caring in her role as the girls' mentor.

'Do you know anyone else with a spare bedroom who could put Jade up for a few nights?' Meryl asked. 'Just until I get something else sorted out?'

'No. I'm sorry, I don't,' I said. Although I knew some of my neighbours had spare bedrooms, I wasn't going to get them involved in what could have been a difficult and embarrassing situation. I didn't know Jade and I didn't know those neighbours that well either. 'All I can suggest is that you call the duty social worker,' I said again.

'Or perhaps I'll give Jade my bed for tonight,' Meryl said.

I looked at her, surprised. Clearly it was her decision to take Jade in but I wasn't sure it was the right one professionally. Meryl was, after all, a teacher at Jade's school and I wasn't sure it was a good idea to blur the boundaries between teacher and pupil for either of their sakes.

'I know I'm becoming too involved,' Meryl suddenly said, as though reading my thoughts. 'But you see, I can identify with Jade. I didn't have the best start in life and when I was Jade's age I went completely off the rails. It was a teacher at my school who helped me get my life back on track. I'll always be grateful to her for going that extra mile for me and I'd like to do the same for Jade.' Which explained a lot.

'Will she keep the baby?' I asked, mindful of the huge responsibility she'd be undertaking if she did.

'She wants to. And I'm trying to help her keep her studies going, although she won't be attending school for much longer.'

'Hopefully her parents will give her some support when they get over the shock,' I offered.

'Maybe, but I'm not counting on it. Jade's mother has problems of her own, and her other kids to look after. And as far as I'm aware Jade's father isn't around much. Anyway, I've taken up enough of your time,' Meryl said, now standing and putting on her coat. 'Thanks, and sorry to interrupt your dinner.'

'That's all right. I'm just sorry I couldn't help you.'

I went with Meryl down the hall, wishing I could have done more, but as I'd explained to Meryl I couldn't just take in any child, apart from which there were reasons I didn't foster teenagers: they were very hard work. They often went missing and required a great deal of emotional support. I felt I had enough responsibility looking after Adrian, Paula and a foster child, as well as coming to terms with being newly divorced, and I didn't feel I could offer support to a teenager at present.

Chapter Two

New Arrival

'Hi. How are you? Have you enjoyed your rest?' Jill, my support social worker from Homefinders, asked the following day.

It was mid-morning and I'd just returned from taking Adrian and Paula to school, having stopped off at the shops on my way home. I'd answered the telephone in the hall. 'I'm fine, thanks, Jill,' I said. 'Very rested. Donna telephoned at the weekend and she's doing well.'

'Good. I'm pleased. She's a nice kid. So you're ready for your next placement? Raring to go?'

I smiled. 'Yes, I am.' For although I enjoyed a short break between fostering placements, I was always ready to welcome the next child. I foster because I want to; it's what I do and love.

'Great,' Jill said. 'How would you like a teenager who is seven months pregnant?'

I fell silent. I didn't know how far into her pregnancy Jade was – Meryl hadn't said – but surely this was too much of a coincidence? 'She wouldn't be called Jade, would she?' I asked.

'That's right. The very same. I understand a teacher from her school has taken Jade under her wing and visited you last night.'

'Yes, Meryl. I told her I couldn't help her and she should telephone the duty social worker.'

'She did. First thing this morning. Jade's family is already known to the social services, and Meryl asked the family's social worker if Jade could stay with you. She thinks you'll take good care of her, and living in the same street she feels she'll be able to offer some support, which may be a help or a hindrance. I've told the social worker that although you're approved to foster teenagers you don't normally do so – you've enough to cope with, and you certainly wouldn't want a mother-and-baby placement.' Jill, as always, was forthright in her manner and, as my support social worker, could be relied upon to have my best interest at heart.

'Thank you,' I said.

'However,' Jill continued, 'Jade's social worker is asking if you can look after Jade until they find a mother-and-baby placement: four weeks at the most. She'll be moved before she has the baby. Jade won't be going to school any more but they're hoping to arrange some home tutoring. I said I'd ask you, but clearly it's your decision, Cathy. Feel free to say no.'

'I see,' I said thoughtfully. 'Just for a month?'

'Yes.'

'Can I think about it?'

'Unfortunately no. They need a decision straightaway. Jade's mother has thrown her out and Jade spent last night in Meryl's bed while Meryl slept on the sofa. But Meryl's husband is back tonight from a business trip and they don't have a spare bedroom.'

'I see,' I said again. I felt sorry for Jade: it was bad enough to be pregnant at seventeen but to have no family support must be devastating. 'And the social services will have found her a mother-and-baby carer before the baby is born?'

'Yes. Absolutely.'

'All right then, Jill,' I said with a small flush of relief. 'I'll do what I can to help her. I'll be pleased to.'

'Great. I'll tell Rachel, her social worker.'

'I thought Meryl said Jade wasn't having anything to do with the social services?' I queried.

'To be honest, Jade hasn't got much choice,' Jill said. 'Rachel is already involved with the family and although Jade is adamant she wants to keep the baby, she's going to have to prove she can look after it properly. Otherwise it will be taken into care.'

While this seemed harsh, it was in the best interest of the baby; babies are fragile, vulnerable little beings and if parenting goes badly wrong there is often no second chance.

'Jade needs to start cooperating with the social services,' Jill added. 'She also needs their help. I think she's starting to realize that.'

'Good. So when do I meet Jade?'

'I'll phone Rachel now and tell her you've agreed to look after her, and then I'll get back to you with more details. I think we'll probably move Jade in late this afternoon or early evening. I want to be there and obviously Rachel will need to be there too. Are you in today, apart from the school run?'

'Yes. I can be.'

'I'll phone you as soon as I've spoken to Rachel, then. Thanks, Cathy.'

'You're welcome.'

We said goodbye and as I replaced the receiver I felt a frisson of excitement: a new child and a new challenge. Although

Jade wasn't exactly a child, and she would only be staying with me for a short while, I would do all I could to help her. I felt sure she would benefit from some stability in her life and my TLC (tender loving care), which I prided myself on offering to all the children I looked after, and wouldn't go amiss even with a teenager. A wiser, more experienced teen carer might have asked some appropriate questions – for example, about Jade's boyfriend, the father of her unborn baby, and what involvement, if any, he would be having in Jade's life. But for me at that moment, elated by the prospect of doing all I could to help Jade, such questions never crossed my mind.

Leaving the hall, I jogged up the stairs and to the spare bedroom to make some last-minute changes so that it was suitable for when Jade arrived and she felt comfortable. I didn't think she'd mind the soft toys dotted around the room, but I removed the toy box. Then I changed the duvet cover and pillowcase, replacing the pictures of Batman with plain pale yellow. Satisfied the room was clean and welcoming, I returned downstairs. As a foster carer and an individual I try not to be judgemental, and if I thought Jade was far too young to be having a baby and that she should have been more careful I didn't dwell on it. Who knew what past experience had brought Jade to this point in her life and self-righteous recrimination is never helpful. My role was to look after Jade and her unborn baby, which I intended to do to the best of my ability, and if she left me feeling less alone and better able to face the world then I would be delighted.

Jill telephoned again two hours later, by which time I had vacuumed the carpets, dusted the shelves, tidied the house and begun the preparation of the spaghetti bolognese for dinner.

Although it was only lunchtime, I knew from experience that when a new child arrives time evaporates; I'd been caught out before by suddenly finding it was seven o'clock and no dinner was ready. Now, having been fostering for eleven years, I was better prepared. However, the only news Jill had was that she didn't know when Jade would be arriving, as Rachel hadn't been able to contact her. Apparently Jade wasn't in school and Meryl didn't know where she was.

'I'll phone as soon as I know more,' Jill said.

Such uncertainty isn't unusual in fostering, so I wasn't fazed. Plans change and I knew enough about teenagers to know that their timekeeping was fluid and their appointment keeping variable.

As the afternoon was cold but bright I put the washing on the line to dry, and then with some time to spare I began a new fostering folder in preparation for Jade's arrival. In this would go the forms the social worker would bring with her, as well as the daily record all foster carers have to keep of the child they are looking after. This includes medical, education and social-care appointments, any significant events, details of contact and the child's general disposition. This record keeping allows the child's progress to be monitored so that additional help can be accessed if necessary. The notes are confidential and when the child leaves the foster carer they are placed on the child's file at the social services. Even though Jade would be with me for only a short while I had to start a file, although I couldn't include much at present other than her name, age and today's date. More information would follow with the social worker when she placed Jade.

Having heard no more from Jill that afternoon, I left the house at 3.00 to collect Paula from school. Adrian, as normal, would make his own way home from secondary school; usually he walked with his friends. I knew I needed to prepare both children for Jade's arrival. Although they were used to children suddenly appearing and starting to live with us, a heavily pregnant teenager was something different – as new to them as it was for me.

I took the opportunity to talk to Paula on the way home. Once she'd finished telling me her news from her day at school, I said: 'Jill phoned today and she's asked us if we can look after a teenage girl for about a month.'

'Good, I'm pleased we're having a girl,' Paula said. She always preferred fostering girls so that she had someone to play with, while Adrian preferred boys for the same reason, although in the end they usually all played together, and of course we had no choice as to which sex the child would be: it was a matter of which child needed a foster home.

'Yes, a big girl,' I said. 'She's seventeen.'

'Will she still want to play with me?' Paula asked.

'I am sure she will sometimes, although she'll need a lot of rest. She's expecting a baby.'

Paula went quiet for a moment and I could almost hear her thought processes ticking. I would wait for her next question rather than rush in.

'Is the daddy coming to live with us too?' Paula asked. Aged eight, Paula knew that babies had daddies, although they didn't always live with their child.

'No. It will just be Jade,' I confirmed.

'And the baby is still in her tummy?'

'Yes. That's right.'

'Will it come out while she's living with us?' Paula asked, pulling a face. She also knew where babies came from and that giving birth was a messy business, from seeing baby rabbits being born.

'No. Jade will leave us before the baby is born,' I said. 'Although there's nothing to be squeamish about. Giving birth is perfectly natural.'

'I'd rather be a bird and lay eggs,' Paula said.

I smiled. 'And have to build a nest each year? And then sit on the eggs until they hatch?'

Paula laughed and then fell silent again. I could see she was thinking again. 'Do teenagers normally have babies?' she asked. 'Our teacher said you had to be an adult.'

'It's best to be an adult,' I said, 'although a teenager can have a baby. But it's a big responsibility, so it's much better to wait until you are older and have a nice home and a husband to help you.' It might have sounded as though I was lecturing Paula, but I thought it was important she knew what was generally considered the better option. Paula was young and impressionable and looked up to older girls. I didn't want her using Jade as a role model; pregnant at seventeen with nowhere to live – what mother would?

We'd just got home when the telephone rang. It was Jill. She said that Jade had been found and was now with her social worker, Rachel, and they would be with us at about five o'clock. Jill also said she was aiming to be with us just before then. As my support social worker, whenever possible she was present when a child was placed – to check the paperwork and that I had everything I needed to look after the child, and generally to be supportive and give advice where necessary.

Adrian arrived home at 4.30, and as he helped himself to a glass of milk and a banana I quickly brought him up to date.

'Is that the girl that teacher wanted us to have?' he asked. After Meryl had left the evening before, Adrian and Paula had asked what she'd wanted and I'd briefly told them.

'Yes, the same one,' I said. 'Meryl – the teacher – phoned the social services first thing this morning. I've said we'll look after Jade just for a month, until they've found her somewhere else to live.'

Adrian nodded and, having finished his snack, went off to play with his Nintendo in his room, which was far more interesting than a teenage girl coming to stay. Paula watched some children's television. Then at 4.50 the doorbell rang and it was Jill. Paula knew we would need the sitting room and scampered off upstairs to play – either with Adrian or in her own room. Jill called hi to her and then came with me into the kitchen while I made her a cup of coffee.

Jill didn't have any more details about Jade, so we'd have to wait until Rachel arrived with Jade. We went through to the sitting room with the coffee and Jill commented that snow was forecast, and also that it was good of Meryl to take such an interest in Jade. I agreed, although I didn't tell Jill that Meryl's interest was partly due to her having experienced something similar, as I thought she'd told me that in confidence.

At just gone 5.00 the doorbell rang and, feeling a little nervous and apprehensive, I left the sitting room and went down the hall to answer it. As I opened the front door the cold air rushed in.

'Hello.' I smiled. 'I'm Cathy.'

'Hello, I'm Rachel,' the social worker said, shaking my hand and stepping into the hall first. 'This is Jade, and this is Tyler, Jade's boyfriend.'

'It's nice to meet you.' I smiled again. Then, without thinking, I added to Tyler: 'I wasn't expecting you.'

'No, neither was I,' Rachel said pointedly.

'I wanted him here,' Jade put in a little grumpily.

'OK,' I said. 'Welcome.'

'He'll just be here for a short while,' Rachel said. 'So he knows Jade is all right, and then he'll be leaving.'

Tyler looked about aged twelve and beside Jade looked more like her son than boyfriend. Not only was she taller than him by a good two inches, but she was also about twice his width and matronly. I thought she'd probably been a bit overweight before her pregnancy but now with her stomach distended she was certainly a big girl and, to use a saying, looked as though she could have eaten him for dinner. She was plain but not unattractive, with chin-length brown hair. She was dressed in black leggings and a long jumper, which was stretched tightly over her bump.

Tyler was carrying a zipped holdall, which I assumed contained Jade's belongings, and I suggested he left it in the hall. I then showed the three of them through to the sitting room, where Jill stood to greet them. I asked Rachel, Jade and Tyler if they would like something to drink but they didn't want anything. Jade and Tyler sat close together at one end of the sofa and Rachel sat at the other, while Jill and I took the single chairs. Rachel was tall and slender and I guessed in her late twenties. She had a pleasant manner, warm and vibrant, although I thought she could be firm when necessary.

'Thank you for agreeing to take Jade,' Rachel said, removing a wodge of papers from her large bag-cum-briefcase. 'She's promised me she's going to behave herself.' Which suggested she might not have behaved herself in the past.

I smiled at Jade. She linked her arm through Tyler's but didn't smile back and concentrated on the carpet.

'I'm pleased to be able to help,' I said brightly. 'I'm sure Jade and I will get along fine. I'm looking forward to having a teenager in the house.'

Tyler glanced at me, while Jade continued staring at the carpet.

'Everything you need should be in here,' Rachel said, passing a set of paperwork to me and then another to Jill. 'Essential information and consent form – for the fostering. I've run through the contents with Jade and at her age she'll sign the consent as well.'

I nodded and quickly flicked through the papers, which included the contact details of the social services; Jade's mother's address, which Jade had given as her permanent home; the names and dates of birth of Jade's siblings; and the names and date of birth of the baby's father, from which I quickly calculated Tyler to be only sixteen. Jill was also glancing through the paperwork.

'Cathy,' Rachel said after a moment, 'I would like you to make sure Jade attends her antenatal appointments. She's missed some in the past and they are important.'

'Absolutely,' I said. 'When is the next one due?'

'Next week,' Rachel said. 'She attends the Lakeview Health Centre for her antenatal care.'

'I want Tyler to come too,' Jade said, finally raising her eyes from the floor to look at Rachel.

'That's fine,' Rachel said, 'as long as he doesn't miss school. You've got exams this year, haven't you?'

Tyler shrugged. 'Maybe. Dunno. I'm leaving school as soon as I can.'

'When exactly is the appointment?' Jill now asked.

'Jade has the appointment card in her bag,' Rachel said.

'It's in the hall. I'll get it later,' Jade said.

'Make sure you tell Cathy the date in plenty of time,' Jill said to Jade. 'Cathy has two children and she has to work around their commitments too.'

Jade nodded sullenly, but I appreciated she had a lot to cope with and how difficult all this must be for her.

'Jade has some of her clothes with her,' Rachel said, moving on, 'enough for tonight and a couple of days, but she's hoping to collect some more of her belongings from home tomorrow. Aren't you, Jade?'

Jade nodded.

'Jade won't be attending school any more,' Rachel continued, looking at me, 'so perhaps the two of you could go to her home tomorrow and pick up her things? Jade has a front door key if no one is in.'

'That's fine with me,' I said. 'We'll go in my car.'

'Will Jade's mother be home?' Jill asked, mindful that some parents are angry towards the foster carer when their child is taken into care.

Rachel looked at Jade, who shrugged. 'Dunno,' she said.

'Jade's mother works part time,' Rachel said. 'But she's all right with me, so there shouldn't be a problem meeting you. She's happy for Jade to visit whenever she wants to.'

'Are you comfortable going?' Jill asked me.

'Yes,' I said. I was usually able to work with the parents whose children I fostered. However, I was becoming increasingly aware of just how different it was going to be fostering a teenager compared to a younger child; for example, children in care normally only see their parents at supervised contact, whereas Jade could go and see her mother any time. Another reminder followed quickly, as Rachel said: 'I've told Jade that this placement is for her only. She can see Tyler but he is not to stay here overnight.'

Chapter Three

Awkward

'So where can he sleep?' Jade asked, somewhat disgruntled.

'My mum says if I'm not staying at your place I have to go home,' Tyler said.

'Very sensible,' Rachel said. 'That solves the problem.' Then, addressing Jill and me, Rachel explained: 'Tyler has been sleeping at Jade's house for some time but it was very overcrowded.'

'No it wasn't,' Jade said. 'He slept with me – in my room.'

Jill and I exchanged a glance, for it would appear that Jade's mother had actively encouraged her seventeen-year-old daughter to sleep with her sixteen-year-old boyfriend and now she was pregnant had thrown her out.

Rachel didn't respond to Jade's comment but continued with the paperwork, checking through her copy and pointing out details that were relevant to me looking after Jade, while Jill and I followed on our copies. I read that Jade was the eldest of five children and she and the two elder siblings had the same surname, while the younger two had a different surname. Jade's mother's date of birth made her thirty-five, so she must have been eighteen when she'd had Jade. Jade's father's name and date of birth were given – he was the same age as Jade's mother – but he didn't live with Jade's mother, and there was no contact address for him. In the section headed 'health of young person' it stated that Jade was pregnant – approximately thirty weeks – and her emotional and developmental health was age appropriate. Under 'education' it showed that Jade had gained six GCSEs the summer before and that she was part way through an A-level course, which she hoped to continue after her baby was born.

'You mentioned that Jade might be receiving some home tuition,' Jill asked Rachel.

'We've decided to leave it until after the baby is born,' Rachel said. 'Jade felt she wouldn't be able to concentrate at present with everything else.' Which I fully appreciated, although I wondered how she would be able to concentrate on studying with a young baby to look after. 'Perhaps you could teach Jade some home-care skills?' Rachel asked me. 'Basic cooking, for example, to help prepare her for when she lives independently.'

'Yes, I'd be pleased to,' I said, again smiling at Jade.

'I can cook already,' Jade said a little dourly.

'Great. You can help me, then,' I said lightly, throwing her another smile.

Rachel ran through the rest of the forms and then the four of us signed the last page, which formed the contract: Jade was signing to give her consent to being in care, Rachel signed as the social worker responsible, Jill signed as the representative of the fostering agency and my support social worker, and I signed to agree to the terms of looking after Jade. If I wanted to end a placement early I had to give the social services and Homefinders twenty-eight days' notice in writing, but that hadn't happened yet.

'So what are you going to do this evening, then?' Rachel asked Jade as she packed away her copy of the papers.

Jade shrugged.

'We'll be having dinner soon,' I said, for I noticed it was nearly half past six.

'That sounds good,' Rachel said. 'What are you going to have?'

'Spaghetti bolognese,' I replied.

'Lovely. I expect you're hungry,' Rachel said to Jade as she closed her briefcase.

Jade shrugged. 'Can Ty stay for dinner?'

'That will be up to Cathy,' Rachel said decisively.

Jade and Tyler now looked at me expectantly. 'Yes, there's plenty,' I said.

'Excellent. What time does your mother want you home?' Rachel asked Tyler. The contrast between the man (who'd created a baby and was shortly to be a father) and the boy (whose mother wanted him home at a set time) was not lost on Jill and I saw the briefest of smiles flicker across her face.

'After dinner, I guess,' Tyler said easily.

'I think we should set a time for Tyler to leave,' Jill said. Tyler was settled so comfortably on my sofa that he looked as though he was there for the night. 'What time do you think is reasonable?' Jill asked.

While I wanted Jade to feel welcome in what would be her home for the next month, I thought that it could be quite disruptive to the household routine and to Adrian and Paula if Tyler was here every evening until late. 'I have to see to my daughter, Paula,' I said. 'And Adrian has homework to do, so is eight o'clock on a weekday all right? Later at weekends.'

'That seems reasonable to me,' Rachel said. 'And Jade needs to establish a routine.' Then, looking at Tyler: 'Eight o'clock it is, then, unless your mum is expecting you sooner?' Again I felt the discrepancy between the boy and the man, although Tyler seemed unfazed.

'She didn't set a time,' Tyler said.

'OK, so we'll say you leave here by eight o'clock and then Cathy can get on with what she has to do,' Rachel clarified. 'We'll just have a look around the house and then I'll be off.'

It's usual for the foster carer to show the social worker and the child around the house when a child first arrives, and I stood, ready to begin the tour. As I did, two sets of footsteps could be heard scampering downstairs and along the hall, and then Paula and Adrian appeared in the sitting room and stopped dead. Perhaps they thought that Jill and Rachel had gone, for they looked surprised to see all the adults.

'This is Adrian and Paula,' I said, introducing them to Rachel, Jade and Tyler. Jill knew my children from having been my support social worker for many years.

'This is Jade and her boyfriend, Tyler,' I said to Adrian and Paula. 'And this is Rachel, Jade's social worker.'

'Hi,' Rachel said. 'Good to meet you. Sorry to take up so much of your mother's time. I expect you're ready for dinner. I know I am.'

Adrian smiled politely and nodded while Paula, who was always a bit shy when first meeting people, came to stand beside me. I left Jill in the sitting room with Adrian – she was asking him how secondary school was going – and with Paula holding my hand, I began the tour of the house.

'This is the kitchen,' I said to Rachel, Jade and Tyler. 'We have our meals over there.' I pointed to the table and chairs in the dining area of the extension.

'Very nice,' Rachel said. Jade and Tyler stood side by side just inside the kitchen-cum-dining room, holding hands and looking very awkward, as teenagers often do.

'Cooker, fridge-freezer and washing machine,' I said, pointing them out. I then led the way out of the kitchen, down the hall and into the front room, which among other things contained a sofa, a small desk with the computer, a hi-fi system, and shelves of CDs, DVDs and books.

'I expect it's useful having more than one living room when you're fostering,' Rachel said.

'Yes,' I agreed. Then to Jade I said: 'You can use the computer in here. I'll show you how.'

Jade nodded but didn't say anything.

I then led the way upstairs and showed Jade her bedroom. 'I'm sure you'll be comfortable in here once you've got your belongings with you,' I said.

'Yes, it's a nice big room,' Rachel said, following Jade and Tyler in. 'There's lots of space for your things. And what a nice view – overlooking the garden.' She went over to the window.

Jade glanced towards the window but she didn't go over; nor did she say anything. She appeared lost and overwhelmed, and I felt sorry for her. As with any child coming into care, all that had been familiar to her had suddenly vanished and was possibly gone for good. Jade had spent last night at a teacher's house and now she was in another strange house with unfamiliar people and their unfamiliar routine.

'Don't worry,' I said, touching her arm reassuringly. 'You'll soon feel at home.'

'I'm not worried,' Jade said, putting on a brave face, but she obviously was. She appeared anxious and kept nervously pulling at a loose thread on the sleeve of her jumper.

We left Jade's room and as we went round the landing I pointed out Adrian's, Paula's and my bedrooms, and then we arrived at the bathroom.

'You can have a shower or a bath,' I said, showing Jade (and Tyler and Rachel) in.

'You like your baths, don't you?' Rachel said.

'Don't mind,' Jade said with a small shrug.

Having seen upstairs, we returned downstairs and into the sitting room, where Adrian was still making polite conversation with Jill. On my arrival he saw his release and immediately disappeared out of the room and upstairs, quickly followed by Paula.

'Thanks, Cathy,' Rachel said, picking up her briefcase. 'I'm going now.' Then, looking at Jade: 'I'll phone you tomorrow. Have a good evening.'

Jill said goodbye to Rachel and stayed in the sitting room with Jade and Tyler, while I went down the hall to see Rachel out. At the door Rachel said quietly: 'Meryl – the teacher at Jade's school – was planning on visiting you tonight, but I've told her to wait until Jade has settled in.'

'Thank you,' I said.

'I'm sure she just wants to be helpful but if it gets too much let me know. It could be unsettling for Jade if she keeps popping in.'

I thanked Rachel again, said goodbye and returned to the sitting room. Jade and Tyler were once more sitting side by side on the sofa, now listening to Jill, who was telling Jade that

I was a very experienced foster carer and a nice person who would look after her very well.

'Thank you, Jill,' I said with a small embarrassed laugh.

'Well, it's true,' she said. 'Now, if there's nothing you need I'll leave you good people to have your dinner.' Then to Jade and Tyler: 'Nice to meet you both. See you again soon.' As my support social worker Jill would visit me regularly to make sure Jade's needs were being met and I had everything I needed to look after her properly.

I saw Jill to the front door. 'I'll phone tomorrow to see how things are going,' she said. 'You may have to be firm when it comes to Tyler going. He's looking very settled and remember he's used to staying with Jade. Eight o'clock and he says goodbye.'

'All right, I will,' I said. Jill had a lot of experience working with teenagers and I appreciated her advice.

Having seen Jill out I returned to the sitting room. It was nearly seven o'clock and we needed to eat. 'Are you both OK?' I asked Jade and Tyler. 'I'll see where Adrian and Paula are and then I'll make dinner. It won't take long.'

Jade didn't say anything but Tyler nodded. I smiled positively and, leaving the sitting room, I went upstairs.

I appreciated Adrian and Paula might feel a bit awkward fostering a teenager, and might do so for a few days, but hiding in their bedrooms wouldn't help; they needed to come down and be sociable. I too felt a little awkward and clearly Jade and Tyler were struggling too. I found Paula in Adrian's bedroom, where they were both playing with the robotic crab he'd had for Christmas.

'I'm starving, Mum,' Adrian said as soon as I walked in. 'When will dinner be ready?'

'Ten minutes,' I said. 'And while I make dinner I want you two to go downstairs and talk to Jade and Tyler. We can't just leave them sitting there by themselves.'

'Do we have to?' Paula sighed.

'Yes. It's polite. If you feel awkward – in your own home – imagine how Jade must be feeling.'

'Is that boy staying?' Adrian asked.

'Tyler. Yes, just for dinner and then he'll be going home.'

'When?' Adrian asked, tersely.

'At eight o'clock.'

'I'll be in bed then,' Paula moaned.

'Exactly, so you can come down now and talk to them. They don't bite.'

Adrian and Paula made no move to do as I asked. 'Now, please,' I said more firmly.

Paula pulled a face but they both stood. Then, without their usual enthusiasm for spending time with new children, they followed me downstairs and into the sitting room. 'Adrian and Paula have come to join you,' I said brightly as we went in.

Tyler and Jade looked at them blankly and Adrian and Paula looked back equally blankly. Usually when we fostered younger children Adrian and Paula suggested games or activities to 'break the ice' and make the children feel welcome, but I realized that they now felt a bit intimated and shy.

'Perhaps you'd all like a game of Sunken Treasure?' I suggested. 'It's a game for all ages.'

'What's Sunken Treasure?' Tyler asked, reasonably enthusiastically.

Seeing Tyler's interest Adrian said: 'I'll get it from the cupboard.'

'Thank you,' I said.

27

Adrian went to the cupboard in the conservatory containing toys and games and returned with the large boxed game, which he set on the coffee table in front of Jade and Tyler.

'Cor, that looks good,' Tyler said, taking off the lid and peering in. 'We ain't got nothing like that at my house.'

Encouraged by Tyler's enthusiasm and easy manner, Adrian and Paula pulled up a stool each as Tyler began removing the contents from the box: the board on which the game was played, showing brightly coloured underwater scenes in 3-D, a dice, shaker, various galleon boats and little treasure chests containing gold, sliver and pearls.

Jade shuffled to the edge of the sofa so that she too could see.

'How do you play?' Tyler asked.

'You all choose a galleon,' I said, picking up one of the little boats. 'Then you take turns to shake the dice and move the galleon around the board, like this. If it stops over the treasure chest, the chest rises from the bottom of the ocean and attaches itself to your boat.'

'Wow! How does it do that?' Tyler asked, the little boy in him surfacing.

'There's a small magnet at the base of the boat,' I said, turning over one of the boats to show him. 'And another magnet in the treasure chest.' I opened one of the chests and pointed it out. 'Magnets attract.'

'That's cool,' Tyler said, impressed.

'The person who has the most treasure wins,' I said. 'But you have to watch out for the killer sharks and giant octopus; they eat you and your treasure.' I pointed to the little models of open-mouthed sharks with rows of vicious teeth and giant octopuses with long, thick tentacles. 'Adrian will explain the rules while I make dinner.'

Feeling the ice had been broken, I left the four of them grouped around the game while I went into the kitchen to cook the spaghetti and heat the bolognese sauce. Toscha, our cat, miaowed; her dinner was late too and I fed her before turning my attention to ours.

My first impression of Jade and Tyler was that, while pleasant, they were young and immature and would struggle to cope with a baby. I didn't know what involvement Tyler intended to have with his child but realistically – given that he was sixteen and still at school – he wouldn't be able to offer much in the way of support. Whether or not Jade could cope alone with a baby remained to be seen and that wasn't really any concern of mine. My role was to see Jade through the next month, after which she would go to a mother-and-baby placement.

I thought it wouldn't be long before Adrian and Paula felt more at ease around Jade (and Tyler) and vice versa. Excited voices soon rose from the sitting room as sunken treasure was found and then lost, which seemed to confirm my optimism for them all getting along. But as I lowered the spaghetti into the pan of boiling water, Tyler's voice rose above the others: 'Fuck no! It fell off. That's not fucking fair!'

Chapter Four

First Evening

Leaving the spaghetti boiling in the pan, I left the kitchen and met Paula who was coming out of the sitting room and on her way to me.

'Mum, that big boy swore,' she whispered, clearly worried.

'I know, I heard,' I said. 'Don't worry, I'll deal with it.'

While swearing might be acceptable in Tyler's house and with his friends, it wasn't acceptable in my house in front of Adrian and Paula. I knew from previous experience – with other children I'd fostered – that if I didn't stop the swearing now it would escalate. And although Tyler wasn't a child I was fostering I had a feeling we'd be seeing a lot of him, so I needed to put in place the ground rules straightaway.

As I entered the sitting room Adrian looked up at me anxiously, aware the words Tyler had used weren't acceptable, while Jade and Tyler were concentrating on and enjoying the game. Indeed, having got over whatever it was he thought was unfair, Tyler was happily telling Jade to hurry up, as it was her turn.

'Er … Tyler,' I said, taking a few steps into the room. 'Please don't swear. There are children present.'

'Yeah, sure,' he said amicably. 'Sorry.'

First Evening

I smiled reassuringly at Adrian and Paula who, relieved that the matter had been dealt with so easily, returned to the game.

I returned to the kitchen and ten minutes later called everyone to come, as dinner was ready. They must have been very hungry, for they didn't protest at having to break off from their game, which wasn't finished. I could see Paula was tired and 7.30 was late for her to be eating, so as soon as we'd eaten I would take her upstairs for her to wash and get ready for bed. Once everyone was at the table I served the meal. When Jade was seated at the dining table her bump was even more emphasized, as it stopped her from getting close to the table. I could see Adrian and Paula stealing surreptitious glances at her as we ate and I knew that certainly Paula would have questions later about bumps and babies.

The first few meals – and indeed the first few days after a new child arrives – are often a little strained, with everyone reserved and not saying much. However, this wasn't true of that evening, thanks to Tyler, who seemed very relaxed and at home and led the conversation. He began by saying how nice the spaghetti bolognese was, which immediately won him a place in my heart, and then between mouthfuls he talked easily to Adrian and Paula, so that after a while I asked him: 'Do you have brothers or sisters? You're good with children.'

'Yeah, two,' Tyler said, sucking a long piece of spaghetti into his mouth until it disappeared with a loud plop, making Adrian and Paula laugh. 'I've got a brother and sister, younger than me. They're great kids. I love them and me mum. She's made a lot of sacrifices to bring us up and I'm grateful.' Which I thought was a lovely thing to say, especially coming from a teenage boy. Tyler also said he didn't see much of his dad, as he only appeared a few times a year – when he wanted a loan from his mum. So he didn't really know him and he hadn't been a 'proper dad'.

'That's why I'm gonna make sure I'm there for my kid,' Tyler continued. 'I want my kid to have a proper dad. I'm gonna do all the things dads should do and see my kid behaves proper as well.' Highly commendable, I thought, although I did wonder how he was going to achieve this in practice, given that he was at school and didn't have a job or home of his own.

'Does your dad live with you?' Tyler then asked Adrian and Paula.

Adrian shook his head and looked embarrassed, while Paula looked at me to explain, as she usually did when her father was mentioned.

'Sadly he doesn't live with us any more,' I said. 'Although he does see Adrian and Paula regularly.'

'It ain't the same, though,' Tyler said. 'Dads should be there for their kids.'

Although I agreed with this I always tried to stay positive for Adrian's and Paula's sakes and not lament over what could or should have been.

'Absolutely,' I said. 'But sometimes we don't have control over events and we just have to make the best of what we have. That's what we do and from what you're saying that's what you do too.'

'Yeah, and I'm going to be there for my child. I promised Jade.'

Jade didn't say anything but concentrated on her food.

Tyler was the first to finish and thanked me for the meal. He was then eager to be away from the table to finish the game of Sunken Treasure, just like a big loveable kid. He encouraged the others to 'hurry up' so that they could finish the game. Adrian and Paula ate faster while Jade, who'd said little throughout the meal, finished her meal at her own pace. She was slow in this, as she was in her other movements, as many women are in the late stages of pregnancy – a result of weight gain, hormones and sheer exhaustion.

To give him his due, Tyler waited until Jade had finished before leaving the table, and then the four of them returned to the sitting room to finish their game while I cleared the table. Five minutes later I heard Tyler shout he'd won and I called them for pudding – apple crumble and ice cream, which again Tyler said was very nice and thanked me for. Once we'd all finished I said it was time for Paula to go to bed and told her to say goodnight, which she did without a fuss.

'Shall we play another game of Sunken Treasure?' Tyler asked Adrian.

I glanced at the wall clock: it was 7.50. 'One quick game and then we all say goodnight,' I said, mindful of Jill's advice.

'Sure,' Tyler said easily and dashed into the sitting room, closely followed by Adrian, who was clearly enjoying playing with Tyler. Jade followed more slowly and seemed happy to go along with whatever Tyler suggested. I thought that once Tyler had gone home and Adrian and Paula were in bed I'd have a chance to talk to Jade and get to know her better.

Paula and I went upstairs and once we were in the bathroom and couldn't be overheard Paula's questions began. 'Is Tyler the baby's daddy?' she asked.

'Yes.'

'How can he be? He's only a boy.'

'He's old enough to father a child,' I said.

'What does "to father a child" mean?'

'Make a baby.'

'Why did he want to do that?'

'Because he likes Jade a lot.'

'Does he still go to school?'

'Yes.'

'He can't go to school and be a daddy, can he?'

I appreciated how confusing all this was to an eight-year-old. 'Well, he finishes school soon,' I said. 'But you're right. He's too young really to be a father. Now wash your face, please.'

Paula picked up the face flannel but it didn't reach the water or her face. 'Why didn't he wait to make a baby?' she asked, looking at my reflection in the mirror above the basin.

'Well, sometimes people make a baby when they don't mean to,' I said. 'It's called an accident, although the parents still love the baby when it's born.'

'Was I an accident?'

'No. Absolutely not. I waited three years for you.'

'Why did you have to wait, Mummy?'

'Because sometimes it takes a long time to make a baby and sometimes it happens very quickly.'

'But Jade didn't have to wait, did she?' Paula said, trying to clarify it in her mind and finally dipping the flannel into the water and dabbing her cheek.

'No.'

'Jade's baby was an accident.'

'Yes.'

'But she'll still love the baby when it's born, won't she?'

'Yes.'

'Good. Because it's horrible if someone has a baby and doesn't love it. That would make me upset.'

I gave her a hug. 'I know, love. Now finish washing. It's well past your bedtime.'

By the time I'd seen Paula into bed and read her a story it was 8.15. I kissed her goodnight, came out and went downstairs, thinking it was asking a bit much to expect a lad of sixteen who was in the middle of enjoying a game to realize it was time to leave. Entering the sitting room, I saw the game was continuing; each player had a little pile of treasure chests that they had won. Toscha, as usual, had found a comfortable spot and was curled up on the sofa next to Jade, who was absently stroking her between turns.

'It's 8.15,' I said gently as I entered.

'Oh, Mum!' Adrian cried. 'Can't we just finish this game?'

'Oh, yeah, please let's finish the game,' Tyler said.

'Five minutes and then you must pack away,' I said. 'You, Adrian and Paula have school tomorrow and Jade needs her rest.'

'I'm OK,' Jade said, clearly not wanting to be responsible for ending the game. 'Can I have a packet of crisps?'

'Yes, if you're still hungry, although a piece of fruit would be better.'

Jade pulled a face. 'I don't do fruit,' she said.

'Nah, she don't do fruit,' Tyler agreed.

I thought Jade needed to 'do' some fruit, but didn't say so. It was only her first evening with us and there'd be other times when I could help her eat more healthily. So I left the sitting room, went into the kitchen and returned with a large bag of assorted crisps.

'We have these at home,' Jade said as I offered her the bag and she took a packet of cheese-and-onion-flavoured crisps.

'Yeah, so do we,' Tyler said, taking a beef-flavoured packet.

Adrian, aware he didn't normally have crisps just before bed, grinned sheepishly and quietly selected a packet of roast-chicken ones. The resulting aroma as the various flavours mingled set Toscha's nose twitching. Although Adrian wasn't normally allowed crisps just before bed it would have been unfair to leave him out, so I could see that one of the issues with fostering a child older than one's own was that it could lead to double standards – with something being acceptable for a teenager but not for a younger child.

The game finished a few minutes later and they counted their treasure chests. Adrian had the most and had therefore won.

'Well done,' I said. 'Let's pack away the game now.'

'I'll beat you next time,' Tyler said good-humouredly.

He helped Adrian pack the pieces into the box and closed the lid, but then sat back comfortably on the sofa and made no move to go. I now had to get Tyler off the sofa, to say goodnight and out the front door.

'Your mum will be wondering where you are,' I said, trying the subtle approach first.

'Nah, she's OK. She knows I'll be back later.'

'Good, but we did agree eight o'clock was the goodbye time and it's nearly half past eight now,' I said.

'Oh yeah,' Tyler said, clearly simply not realizing the time. He stood. 'Well, thanks, missus. Thanks for dinner. It's been very nice.'

I smiled. 'You're welcome, but call me Cathy. We'll see you again soon.' Then to Jade, I said: 'Would you like to see Tyler out?'

Jade shuffled to the front of the sofa so that she could stand. Tyler reached out his hand and she took it. Then, in what appeared a familiar routine and was quite touching, he hauled her off the sofa with an exaggerated groan. 'Ten-ton Tess!' he joked. Adrian laughed but I wasn't sure Jade appreciated Tyler's humour; she didn't laugh.

'I'm going up to my room now,' Adrian said. 'See ya, Ty.'

'Yeah, see ya soon,' Tyler said, raising his hand so that Adrian could give him a high five.

'I'll be up shortly,' I said to Adrian as he left the room. Then to Tyler, who was also on his way out: 'Goodnight.'

'Night,' he called.

I waited in the sitting room while Jade went with Tyler down the hall to the front door. It went quiet, so I guessed they were having a goodnight kiss. Then I heard the front door open and it went quiet again. I felt the cold night air seep down the hall and into the sitting room, quickly cooling the house. I waited a minute longer and when there was no sound of the front door closing I called: 'Could you shut the front door, please, while you're saying goodnight? It's making the house cold.'

'I'm going,' Tyler called easily.

There was another silence, during which the front door remained open; I assumed they were having a final goodnight kiss. Then I heard the door close and I went into the hall.

'All right, love?' I asked.

Jade was standing in the hall by the coat stand. She nodded. 'Where's my bag?'

'I took it up to your room earlier. Would you like to unpack now? You'll feel more at home with some of your belongings around you.'

'Don't mind,' Jade said with a small shrug. 'But I need me phone. It's in me bag.'

'Come on, I'll show you where it is.' I led the way upstairs and into Jade's room, where I'd put the holdall on the floor. 'Shall I help you unpack?' I asked. Although Jade didn't have many things with her – we were collecting more from her home the following day – I thought she might like some help, and it would also give me an opportunity to chat and get to know her.

'No, I can do it.' She squatted down, unzipped the holdall and took out her mobile.

'Sure?' I asked.

She nodded and concentrated on her phone.

'I'll leave you to it, then,' I said. 'Let me know if you need anything. Come down when you're ready.' I smiled and came out, leaving Jade sitting on the bed texting.

I knocked on Adrian's door. 'Are you getting ready for bed now?' I asked quietly so that I didn't disturb Paula in the next room. Adrian knew he had to be in bed by nine o'clock on a school night.

'Yes,' he replied.

'Good. I'll come up at nine to say goodnight.'

I checked Paula was asleep, closed her bedroom door and went downstairs to the kitchen, where I washed the dishes and cleared up while I waited for Jade to come down. She hadn't much to unpack, so I was expecting to see her very soon, although I appreciated that at her age she might want some time to herself. When she hadn't appeared by nine o'clock I went upstairs. Her bedroom door was ajar and the light was on, but I couldn't hear any movement inside.

I knocked lightly. 'Jade? Is everything all right?'

There was no response so I knocked again. 'Jade? It's Cathy. Can I come in?'

Still nothing, so I opened the door wider and went in. Jade was lying on the bed on her side, in her clothes and fast asleep with her mobile in her hand. Her bag was open on the floor but not unpacked. The poor kid must have been exhausted. I didn't want to just leave her there for the night. Although she'd taken off her shoes it would be uncomfortable for her to sleep in her clothes, and without the routine of changing and getting into bed if she woke in the night she might wonder where she was.

Leaning slightly over her bed, I said: 'Jade, it's Cathy. Shall I help you to get changed and into bed? Are your night things in your bag?' I guessed they would be but I didn't like to just start rummaging in her bag to find them. With a younger child I unpacked their bags when they first arrived, but at Jade's age I needed to respect her privacy. 'Jade, love,' I tried again, gently stroking a few strands of hair away from her face. 'It's Cathy. Would you like to get changed so you are more comfortable?'

Still nothing. She was clearly in a very deep sleep. I then decided it might be best to leave her for now to have a sleep. I'd cover her with the duvet, leave the light on low, and listen out for her. She'd probably wake before I went to bed. I reached to the foot of the bed and began drawing up the duvet. Suddenly I jumped with fright as a loud noise shot from the bed: a hundred decibels of rap, scaring me silly and blasting Jade awake.

'Oh my God, Ty!' she cried, waking, sitting and answering the phone with one movement. 'I was asleep. Oh my God, where am I? Help!'

Chapter Five
Jade's story

'You're safe,' I reassured Jade. 'You're with me – Cathy.'

'Oh yeah,' she said, now fully awake and realizing where she was.

'That's quite some ringtone,' I said. 'I nearly jumped out of my skin.'

'I usually put it on silent at night but I fell asleep.'

'I know you did, love. You must be exhausted. Let me help you unpack and then you can have an early night.'

Jade nodded and swung her legs off the bed. Tyler was still on the other end of the phone and Jade said to him: 'I'll phone you later, Ty. I've got to unpack.'

She closed the phone and put it on the pillow. She looked pale and tired, and my immediate concern was for her to have a good night's sleep. 'What time do you usually go to bed?' I asked as she yawned.

'Any time, really. It doesn't matter. It was difficult sleeping in a single bed with Ty.'

I'd have thought it would have been impossible given the size of Jade's bump, and contrary to what Jade said about bedtime not mattering, it did matter. I knew that in pregnancy it was just as important to have enough sleep as it was to have a good diet; otherwise the expectant mother could become run down.

Jade's story

'I think you could do with an early night,' I said. 'How about you go to the bathroom and have a wash and change while I unpack your bag?'

'Do I have to have a bath?' Jade asked, as a small child would.

'No, I think that can wait until the morning if you're very tired. Just have a good wash and do your teeth, then have your bath tomorrow. You're not in school, so there's no rush in the morning.'

Jade nodded and yawned again.

'Are your nightdress and wash bag in your bag?' I asked.

She nodded, but remained sitting on the bed and making no move towards the holdall.

'Shall I find them for you?'

'Yeah, please.'

I unzipped the holdall and her wash bag and towel immediately came into view. I took them out and passed them to her. 'Do you have a nightdress or pyjamas in here?'

'I use those pink leggings and that T-shirt,' she said, pointing to the items in the holdall.

I took out the wash-faded pink leggings and a very large pale pink T-shirt, on which was emblazoned a bright pink pig. I thought one of the first things I would buy Jade would be some maternity nightwear, which would be more comfortable and make her feel good.

'You know where the bathroom is?' I asked, passing her the leggings and T-shirt.

'Yeah. You showed me earlier.'

I smiled. 'There's toothpaste and soap in there. Call me if you need anything. I'll unpack the rest of your bag while you're in the bathroom.'

41

I gave Jade my hand and helped her off the bed, and she ambled out of the bedroom and to the bathroom while I set about her unpacking. Jade didn't appear to have any maternity wear at all but there were two more pairs of black stretch leggings and two big sloppy jumpers, which I supposed were just as good. They were clean, although bobbled from being worn and washed repeatedly. There was also a bra, some pants and six soft toys. Indeed most of the bag had been taken up with the cuddly toys: two teddy bears, a panda, a kangaroo, a monkey and a lion. They were clearly childhood favourites, for they were well worn and ear-chewed. I thought it said a lot about Jade that, being essentially a child herself, she'd packed these cuddly toys to the exclusion of practical items like more clothes. At the very bottom of the bag I found the antenatal appointment card that Rachel had mentioned. Opening it, I saw that Jade's next appointment was scheduled for Wednesday at one o'clock, which was a good time, as it meant it didn't clash with me collecting Paula from school.

I folded Jade's clothes into the chest of drawers, arranged the toys on the bed and then zipped shut the now empty hold-all. It would be useful to take with us tomorrow when we went to Jade's house to collect some more of her belongings. I noticed there'd been no photograph of her family in her bag and I'd suggest to Jade she bring one from home. I'd found before with children I'd looked after that in all but the severest cases of abuse from parents, a child usually finds it reassuring to have a photograph of their natural family with them and on show.

I heard the bathroom door open and then Jade's footsteps on the landing, and she reappeared. She was wearing the pink leggings and T-shirt that acted as her nightwear and, having had a wash and brushed her hair, she looked a little fresher, but she still looked tired.

'I've put my dirty clothes in the laundry basket in the bathroom,' she said.

'Thanks, love. I do the laundry each morning. I've put your clean clothes in this drawer,' I said, pointing. 'And your cuddly toys are on the bed. You've got quite a collection there.'

Jade looked at her toys and smiled. It was the first time she'd smiled properly all evening and her whole face lit up. I thought she should smile more often, but then she was probably very anxious and worried about the future.

'I love my cuddlies,' she said touchingly, sitting on the bed and stroking the panda. 'They've all got names. These are Bert and Betty Bear,' she said, touching the two bears. They're named after my aunt and uncle who died. The panda is called Chi Chi. I got her when I went to the zoo with the school. The kangaroo is Hoppity and the monkey is Melvin. My brother called him that. And the lion is Simba from *The Lion King*. I love that film.'

'So do I,' I said, smiling. 'We all like our cuddlies here too, even Adrian, although he wouldn't admit it.'

Jade nodded. 'I'm going to buy my baby lots of cuddly toys. I've already started a collection at home.'

'Have you started buying the other things you'll need for the baby too?' I asked. 'There's a lot to prepare for.'

'I have some nappies but that's all,' Jade said. 'I haven't had much money. But now I'm in foster care I get an allowance, don't I?' And it crossed my mind (somewhat unkindly) that maybe this was the reason Jade had come into foster care. She wouldn't be the first teenager to put herself in care, or whose parent(s) had purposely made her homeless, aware the state would find her somewhere to live, pay for her keep, and also give her an allowance. However, Jade quickly added: 'But that's not why I'm in care.'

'Good. Because the allowance isn't much. As soon as I receive it I'll pass it on to you. But it's only enough to cover essential items.'

'Rachel said I need to get essential items and not spend any more on baby toys.'

'Yes,' I agreed. 'There's a lot to buy. Usually the hospital gives you a list of what you need at one of the antenatal appointments.'

'They might have,' Jade said nonchalantly. 'But I've lost it.'

'No worries. We'll get you a copy when we go for your appointment next week. I was also thinking we could go shopping together one day – buy you some maternity clothes and also some baby things. You want to be prepared well ahead of time.'

'Yeah,' Jade said. 'Ty's not interested in shopping, and Mum's always busy.'

I felt that although Jade was tired she was in the mood to talk, so I sat on the bed next to her. 'Being a mother keeps you very busy,' I said. 'Your mum has your younger brothers and sisters to look after.'

'Yeah, I know,' Jade said.

'Do you know the sex of your baby?' I asked out of interest. 'Did they tell you at the hospital when you had your scan?'

Jade shook her head. 'It was too early when I had the first scan. Then I missed the second scan. Ty wants a boy so he can play football and take him to see the matches, but I want a girl so we can talk and be best friends.'

I thought that while this was a delightful view of parenting it was also worryingly naïve and didn't take into account the many years of hard work, patience and dedication that lay ahead for Jade (and Tyler). 'Do you know when your next scan is?' I asked.

Jade shook her head.

'We'll ask when we go to the clinic next week. Your appointment card is over there.' I pointed to the bookshelf where I'd put the card. 'I'll make a note of the time and date in my diary too.'

'I'm going to love my baby and give it lots of attention,' Jade suddenly said. 'I'll show my mum she's wrong.'

'Wrong about what?' I asked.

'She wants me to give up my baby for adoption. What does she know?'

I thought Jade's mother probably knew quite a lot about babies, considering she'd had five of her own, but I didn't say so. It was important I kept the line of communication open to establish a relationship with Jade, and agreeing that her mother might have a point wouldn't endear me to her.

'Your mum's probably worried how you're going to cope,' I said. 'I know I would be if you were my daughter.'

'I'll manage, and I'm going to be a better mum than she is,' Jade said. 'I'm gonna give my kid everything it wants.'

Where to begin on the subject of parenting? I thought. I took a breath and chose my words carefully. 'You know, Jade, part of being a good parent is that as well as giving your child love, attention and presents, you put in place boundaries and say no when you have to. That's what makes a child grow up to be a responsible adult who knows right from wrong. If a parent doesn't put in place boundaries, but gives in to the child all the time, the child grows up to be very self-centred and doesn't know how to share or behave.'

'Yeah, I know,' Jade said. 'But I'm going to be there for my kids.'

'Good. Weren't your parents there for you?'

Jade shook her head. 'Dad comes and sees us sometimes but he always brings his new girlfriend and I hate her. Mum works and then she sees her boyfriend most evenings. She ain't there much either.'

'So who looks after your brothers and sisters when your mum is out?' I asked, for I knew from the referral that Jade's siblings were all younger than she was.

'Me usually,' Jade said. 'Now she'll have to find someone else to be her skivvy, cos I've got me own life to lead.' Jade shifted position on the bed to try to get more comfortable.

'Did you have a lot of responsibility at home?' I asked her gently.

'Yeah, but I love my brothers and sisters. I didn't mind really. I miss them.'

'You can still see them,' I said. 'You can go home and visit, can't you?'

Jade looked down into her lap and began tugging anxiously at her sleeve. 'Mum's pissed off with me. She says I'm a bad influence on the kids and I should stay away. Since I told her I was pregnant we've argued non-stop. She told me I was a silly cow for putting myself in the club. She said I've made the same mistake she did and I should have known better. She got pregnant when she was my age, when she was drunk. Two nights ago we had our worst row ever and I called her a slag, so she chucked me out.'

'Oh dear,' I said. 'I think you were both angry with each other. When you've had time to calm down and cool off I'm sure things will be better. Have you spoken to your mum since you left and went to Meryl's?' I asked.

'No.'

'If your mum's there tomorrow when we collect your clothes, it might be a good opportunity to make up,' I suggested.

'No, I don't want to see her yet. We'll go in the morning. She doesn't get home from work until one o'clock.'

Which I had to accept. I couldn't force Jade to see her mother. 'What work does your mum do?' I asked.

'Cleaning. She cleans offices early morning – six to nine, and then rich people's houses until twelve. She has a sleep in the afternoon.'

'So who looked after your brothers and sisters in the morning and took them to school if your mum was at work?'

'Me. And I ain't doing it any more. Who takes your kids to school? Because it won't be me.'

I smiled. 'I wouldn't ask you to. Adrian goes by himself or with friends, and I take Paula.'

'Just asking,' Jade said. 'Cos I know some foster carers take liberties with their foster kids and use them as cheap labour.'

'Do they?' I asked, shocked. 'I don't know any foster carers who treat their children that way.' However, I did know that foster carers and social workers often got a bad press on the estate where Jade lived.

Jade didn't answer but pulled a face and stretched out her legs to try to get more comfortable. 'I'll be glad when I've had this baby,' she said. 'No one told me how uncomfortable it was going to be being pregnant. It keeps kicking me, the little sod.'

She shifted again and then took hold of my hand and placed it on her swollen stomach. 'Here, feel this,' she said.

I had the palm of my hand gently resting on the outside of her T-shirt and for a moment there was nothing. Then suddenly I felt the wall of her stomach bulge and tighten as a little fist or foot kicked out.

'Isn't that truly wonderful?' I smiled. 'Don't you think it's incredible the way new life has grown within you? It's a little miracle.'

But Jade wasn't impressed. 'I'll be glad when it's out,' she said. 'Then I can walk and sit proper again.'

We continued talking for a while longer, and Jade asked me about childbirth and if it hurt. I reassured her, saying that while the contractions would be uncomfortable she wouldn't suffer, as pain relief would always be available at the hospital. She said she wanted Tyler to be with her when she had the baby but he wasn't sure he wanted to be there and kept making excuses.

'He's the dad. He should be there,' Jade said adamantly.

'It would be nice if he could be there,' I said. 'Although I can understand that at his age he might not feel he could. Who will be with you as your birthing partner if Tyler can't do it?' I asked.

'Me mum was going to but we're not speaking now. So I guess I'll be by myself.'

'Jade, love,' I said, patting her arm, 'I'm sure you and your mum will have made it up long before your baby is born, but if by any chance you haven't, and Tyler decides he can't be there, I will be with you. If you'd like me to.' Although Jade would have left me by the time her baby was born, there was no way I wanted her contemplating having her baby without the support of a birthing partner.

'Yeah, OK,' she said easily as though she was agreeing to go to the cinema or shopping with me.

We chatted some more – about everyday things – and then Jade said she was 'knackered' and wanted to go to sleep. I saw her into bed, making sure she was comfortable and fetching the glass of water she asked for.

'If you need anything in the night call me,' I said. 'Don't go wandering around in a strange house by yourself – you may trip and fall. I'll leave you to get up in the morning in your own time. I'm usually back from taking Paula to school by 9.15. So I'll get you some breakfast then, and then we'll go to your mum's. Is that all right?'

'Yeah, sure.'

'Goodnight then, love. And not too long on that mobile. You need your sleep.' For as I was leaving her bedroom, despite being 'knackered' Jade had found the energy to start texting again.

'I'm just saying goodnight to Ty,' she said.

'All right, love. Five minutes. Goodnight.'

'Night,' she called.

I came out and closed her door.

An hour later when I went up to bed I heard talking coming from Jade's room. It didn't take great insight to realize she was on her mobile. I knocked lightly on her door and then put my head round it. Jade looked up from beneath the duvet, where she was very comfortably settled in bed, surrounded by her soft toys and with her phone pressed to her ear.

'I won't be long,' she said, anticipating what I was going to say.

I nodded and came out.

Half an hour later when I'd finished showering, it was all quiet in Jade's room. I went to bed, read for a while and was just dozing off when I heard Jade's voice – raised and angry, nearly shouting, and very likely to wake Adrian and Paula. Throwing on my dressing gown, I went round the landing, knocked on her door and went in. Jade was still in bed but was now propped up on one elbow and arguing on the phone.

'Sorry,' she said to me as I entered, taking the phone from her ear. 'He's being such a dickhead.'

I assumed she was talking to Tyler, although goodness knew what he had or hadn't done. 'It's very late,' I said. 'Finish the call now, please. I don't want Adrian and Paula woken and you need to get off to sleep.'

Jade nodded, but I had the feeling that the moment I was out of the room the call would resume. It was then I remembered some advice I'd heard at a support-group meeting for foster carers, from a couple who were experienced teenager carers. They said one of their house rules was that all mobile phones were left downstairs at night and collected at breakfast. This had the double result of ensuring the teenagers weren't on their phones all night and also that they got up in the morning.

'Jade,' I said, kindly but firmly, 'if you can't take responsibility for switching off your mobile for the night, then you will have to leave it downstairs.' The couple had also said that separating a teen from a mobile was a bit like severing a limb.

Jade scowled. 'You can't do that,' she said defiantly.

'I hope I won't have to, so please make the right decision.'

Jade scowled again; then, returning the phone to her ear, said, 'I gotta go now, Ty. Speak to you tomorrow.'

'Good decision,' I said. 'See you in the morning. Goodnight, love. God bless.'

Chapter Six

Jackie

The rest of the night was quiet, and indeed no sound came from Jade's room the following morning while Adrian, Paula and I got up, had breakfast and then left for school. I was pleased Jade had cooperated the night before, although I appreciated I might have to deal with the same issue again, as teenagers have notoriously short memories when it comes to requests they'd rather not comply with. I also knew teenagers liked their sleep and can sleep all day if they are allowed to, so I was anticipating having to wake Jade when I returned home from taking Paula to school.

To my amazement as I let myself into the hall I heard music coming from the radio in the kitchen and the sound of some-one cooking. I slipped off my coat and shoes and hooked them on the hall stand, and then went into the kitchen. Jade was washed and dressed and, having found the largest frying pan, was cooking herself a full English breakfast: fried eggs, bacon, sausages, fried bread and baked beans.

'Good morning,' I said brightly.

I could see she'd already had cereal because her bowl with residue milk, the spoon, the open canister of sugar, the open packet of cereal and the four-pint carton of milk were all still on the work surface, together with the butter, a loaf of bread, a carton of eggs, a packet of bacon, a can of baked beans, a bag of frozen sausages, a mug of tea and a carton of juice which clearly Jade had struggled to open, as it was standing in a large puddle of its contents.

'That smells good,' I said.

Jade had her back to me and was concentrating on the frying pan, and she didn't turn or answer. It was then I saw she was wearing earphones. I switched off the radio, which seemed superfluous to her needs, and going over lightly touched her arm.

She turned with a small start, removed one earphone and beamed. 'Hi! Aren't you proud of me? I got up without being told, had a bath and hair wash, and now I'm doing me own breakfast to save you the trouble.'

'Excellent,' I said. I wondered if Jade was also going to save me the trouble of clearing up after her, but I knew enough of teenagers to know that was doubtful. At least she was up and not lazing in bed. I was pleased with her. 'Would you like a hairdryer?' I asked, seeing her hair was damp.

'Nah, it'll go frizzy. I leave it to dry,' she said, turning the sausages in the pan.

'If you've finished with these I'll put them back in the fridge so we can use them again,' I said. I began gathering together the butter, milk, eggs, sausages, etc., which needed to be kept in the fridge. 'And Jade, love, can I suggest you turn down the gas a little? When the fat splatters that much and you see blue smoke coming from the pan it usually means the fat is a little too hot.'

'Oh, yeah, sure,' she said, jigging in time to the music coming through the one earpiece. I opened the small window to stop the smoke alarm going off.

Satisfied that the house wasn't going to burn down and Jade had everything she needed, I thought it best to leave her to finish cooking her breakfast. I didn't want her to feel I was watching or criticizing her. I knew teenagers hated being watched and can easily feel they are being 'picked on'. In fact I was surprised at just how much I did know about teenagers, even though it was some years since I'd fostered one – knowledge gained from foster-care training and friends' teenagers, I suppose.

'I'll fetch your empty holdall from your room so it's ready for us to take with us later,' I called to Jade as I left the kitchen and went upstairs.

'Sure,' she returned amicably.

Going into Jade's bedroom I picked up the duvet, pink leggings, T-shirt and soft toys from the floor and returned them to the bed, although I stopped short of making the bed – Jade could do that. I then picked up the holdall and, leaving it on the landing, went round to my bedroom to collect the empty suitcase that I kept on top of my wardrobe; we'd take both cases with us. As I did, I passed the open door of the bathroom. I knew teenagers weren't renowned for their tidiness or for clearing up after themselves but how one person could use so many towels and products I'd no idea. I also wondered how hot Jade had had the water, for the bathroom was like a sauna, with water running down the window, mirrors and wall tiles. I opened the bathroom window; I screwed the tops back on the shower gel, bubble bath, shampoo, conditioner, body lotion and toothpaste; and then I mopped up the puddle of water by the bath so that it didn't seep through to the ceiling below. It was Jade's first morning and I wouldn't start nagging her about clearing up, although I now appreciated some of the discussions that had taken place at the foster-carer support-group meetings between carers who fostered teenagers.

I took the case and holdall downstairs and left them ready in the hall. As I did, Jade's voice called from the kitchen: 'Cathy! I've made you a mug of tea.'

'That's kind of you, love,' I said, going into the kitchen.

Jade had finished cooking and was now seated at the table in the dining area and tucking into her cooked breakfast. She'd set a mug of tea for me in the place opposite her and I sat down. 'Thanks, love,' I said again.

'Would you like something to eat?' she asked, waving her fork at her plate of food, which did look appetizing, apart from the river of grease and tomato sauce. 'We can share it if you like.'

'It's all right, love. You enjoy it. I had my breakfast earlier with Paula and Adrian.'

'Have they gone to school now?' she asked, eating and making conversation.

'Yes.'

'They're nice kids,' she said. 'I hope my mum's got someone to take my brothers and sisters to school.'

'I'm sure she has,' I reassured her. 'We'll check with Rachel when we speak to her later.'

Jade nodded. She clearly loved her brothers and sisters very much and felt responsible for them. I thought she'd probably had too much responsibility, although I could see how that had happened, with her mother being a single parent and working unsociable hours. Clearly Jade's help would be missed and I wondered if her mother, Jackie, now regretted their argument and throwing Jade out.

Once Jade had finished eating, I suggested she got ready while I cleared up the kitchen. She didn't object.

It took Jade over an hour to get ready, slightly longer than it took me to clear up after her in the kitchen. I'm not sure why it took her so long, as she was already washed and dressed; perhaps she was texting. I didn't nag her to hurry up. During that time Jill phoned and asked if everything was all right, and I confirmed it was and gave her an update. She said I should call her if I needed anything; otherwise she'd phone me again later in the week. Once I had cleared up in the kitchen I went through to the sitting room and made a note of Jade's home address, which I then looked up on a map to make sure I knew where we were going. When Jade finally appeared I checked with her to make sure she had her front-door key, and she pulled it from her pocket, together with some loose change, her mobile phone, and some chewing gum and sweet wrappers.

'Can I have a key to this house?' she asked, as we picked up the case and I opened the front door.

'Will you need one?' I asked, uncertain if it was necessary.

'Yeah, I'll need one,' she said. 'Supposing we're both out and I come back first. I won't be able to get in.'

I nodded. I could see her point, although I couldn't imagine she'd be out very often while she was so heavily pregnant. It was as much as she could do to get out of an armchair or go upstairs.

'All right. I'll get a key cut the next time I'm in town,' I said.

'We could go after we've been home and got me things,' Jade said as we got into the car.

Perhaps I should have heard alarm bells ringing, telling me that Jade was a little too eager to obtain a front-door key, but I didn't. I agreed we'd get a key cut after we'd been to her house, and I reversed the car off the driveway with Jade taking a call from Tyler, which continued throughout the thirty-minute journey and only stopped when we arrived on her estate and I asked her where I should park.

Jade carried the holdall and I carried the suitcase, as I followed her down the series of short walkways that linked the estate. It was a modern estate of low-rise social housing with pedestrian-only access to the fronts of the houses and flats. Jade's house was in the middle of a terrace. There was a large communal green and the front door was like most of the others on the estate: the same style and painted a similar blue. I waited to one side as Jade unlocked the door and then I followed her into a small square hall, which was full of children's outdoor toys. This led into the living room, the one main room downstairs, and it contained more toys, a long low sofa, a glass-topped coffee table, some bean bags and a large plasma-screen television. Although the room was full of children's things, it was clean and as tidy as you were likely to make it with four young children. I felt a bit uncomfortable being in Jade's home when her mother was out, as though I was snooping.

'Come up with me,' Jade said, crossing the room to the open-plan carpeted staircase that led off the far side. 'You can help me get my things.'

I went over and began up the stairs behind her. We were about halfway up when Jade suddenly stopped and exclaimed: 'Mum! What are you doing here?'

I looked up at the woman now standing at the top of the stairs, who was fastening her dressing-gown cord.

'I could ask you the same,' she said, beginning down the stairs.

'I've come to get me things,' Jade said tersely.

The stairs weren't wide enough for us to pass, especially with the holdall and suitcase Jade and I were carrying, so I turned and went downstairs. Jade did the same and her mother followed us into the sitting room, where there was an awkward silence.

'I'm Cathy, Jade's foster carer,' I said after a moment, smiling at Jackie.

'Hello,' she said. 'Jackie. Jade's mother.'

I knew from the placement forms that Jackie was in her mid-thirties; she was about five feet six inches tall with high-lighted hair. She was an attractive woman even without make-up and I could see a strong family likeness to Jade.

'Why aren't you at work?' Jade asked, quite rudely.

'I had a migraine,' Jackie said, touching her forehead.

'Are you all right now?' I asked, concerned, for she looked pale.

'Not too bad,' she said; then she added pointedly, looking at Jade: 'Thanks for asking.'

'Who took the kids to school?' Jade asked, or rather demanded.

'Me. Who else?' Jackie retorted.

'Are you alone?' Jade said, glancing up the stairs. From which I assumed Jackie's boyfriend stayed sometimes and Jade didn't approve.

'I said I was ill, didn't I?' Jackie snapped back.

'It hasn't stopped you before,' Jade said, scathingly.

'You little cow!' Jackie flared. 'How dare you criticize me! Have you looked at yourself in the mirror lately? At least your father married me!'

Jade flinched at this remark, which seemed to have continued from a previous argument. I had the feeling that Jade and

Jackie viewed each other as equals rather than mother and daughter; there was an undercurrent of unhealthy rivalry in their exchange.

'I'm going to get me things,' Jade said. Grabbing both cases, she stormed off towards the stairs. 'You coming?' she demanded of me.

'You go ahead,' I said. 'And make a start with the packing while I speak to your mother.' Jade huffed and stomped off upstairs.

I wanted to try to establish a relationship with Jackie; and also going with Jade now could have appeared to Jackie I was siding with her daughter.

'Don't believe what she tells you about me!' Jade shouted from upstairs. 'She never wanted me! But don't worry, I'm not coming back!' We heard her bedroom door slam.

Jackie's eyes immediately filled.

'Are you all right?' I asked gently, touching her arm.

She nodded and, taking a tissue from her dressing-gown pocket, blew her nose. 'We've always clashed,' she said, sitting on the sofa. 'But it's unbearable now. I did my best for her and what do I get in return? She ends up pregnant and hating me. After all the warnings and talks I've given her and she's done exactly what I did.' She gave a long, heartfelt sigh.

I sat on the sofa next to her, for clearly she wanted to tell me more.

'I told Jade right at the start to have an abortion,' Jackie continued. 'But she wouldn't. She called me a cold-hearted bitch. She says she wants to keep the baby, but I've been a teen-age mum and it wasn't easy and I had a husband. I can't look after Jade and the baby. I barely cope as it is.' Jackie blew her nose again as fresh tears fell.

Jackie

'Of course you can't be expected to look after Jade and the baby,' I said. 'You've got enough bringing up your younger children. Now the social services are involved with Jade they'll help. Your children are lovely,' I said, glancing at the school photographs on the wall. 'You're doing a good job.'

'Thanks,' Jackie said, wiping her eyes. 'I love Jade as I love my other kids, although she doesn't think so now. I want to help her but I'm not in any position to. She can't stay with you, can she?'

'No. She'll be with me until the social services find her a mother-and-baby placement. Then she'll live there and be assessed to see if she can keep the baby.'

'Then what's she going to live on?' Jackie said. 'Babies are expensive and Ty's not going to be able to support her. What sort of life will they have?'

I fully appreciated what Jackie meant: Jade's life as a single parent – with no job and no support other than from state benefit – was going to be an existence rather than living. My first impression of Jackie – from the referral – had been that she was uncaring and irresponsible but that wasn't so. She loved Jade, wanted what was best for her, but couldn't offer much support as she was struggling to cope herself.

'I know this sounds awful but part of me hopes Jade fails the parenting assessment,' Jackie said, her brow furrowing. 'Then the baby can be adopted into a nice home, and Jade can get on with her life. She was supposed to be staying on at school and taking A-levels. Did you know that?'

'Yes.' But while I could see Jackie had her daughter's best interests at heart I knew that if she'd said any of this to Jade it would have caused an argument. 'I think it's best to take this a step at a time,' I said. 'At present I'm concentrating on making sure Jade has a good diet, enough sleep, and attends her ante-natal appointments.'

'Ty's not staying with you, is he?' Jackie asked. 'Rachel said he wasn't allowed to, but I know how persuasive Jade can be.'

'No. The placement is for Jade only,' I confirmed. 'Tyler can visit; he was with us yesterday evening. But we've agreed he has to leave at eight o'clock.'

Jackie nodded and looked thoughtful. 'I let him stay here,' she said. 'I thought that as they were going to do it anyway it might as well be here rather than in a park or down an alley-way. I told Jade to go to the clinic for contraceptive advice but she couldn't have done, could she? I won't be making the same mistake with my younger kids. They won't be having their boyfriends staying, but I've always given in to Jade. With her being the eldest, we've been more like sisters or friends than mother and daughter. I guess I liked that but it hasn't done her any good.'

'It's difficult being a parent,' I offered gently. 'We have to make all sorts of decisions, and we learn as we go along. It's only with hindsight that we know if we made the right decision.'

'You can say that again!' Jackie sighed. 'And I've learnt a lot from bringing up Jade.'

I felt for Jackie and I thought she and Jade should really make it up. They needed each other more than ever now. I also felt that I'd spent long enough with Jackie and I should now go upstairs and help Jade, who would doubtless be feeling neglected and that I was talking to her mother about her. 'Shall we both go up and give Jade a hand packing?' I suggested.

Jackie shrugged, just as Jade did sometimes. 'She won't want me,' she said despondently.

'Let's go and try,' I encouraged. 'She's had time to cool off and you don't want to part like this, with harsh words spoken.'

Jackie wasn't convinced but she got off the sofa and I threw her a reassuring smile. We crossed to the foot of the staircase and I followed her up. At the top we turned right and Jackie knocked on Jade's closed bedroom door. 'Can we come in?' she asked quietly.

There was no reply.

I nodded an encouragement to Jackie. She knocked again and we went in. Jade was standing by her bed, stuffing hand-fuls of clothes into the suitcase. She didn't look up but I had the feeling that some of her anger had gone. Jackie clearly felt so too, for going over she said: 'Here, let me help you with that or it'll all need ironing.'

Jade moved away to allow her mother to pack the clothes that were strewn all over the bed, and took some more of her belongings from a drawer. I saw she had a framed photograph of her family by her bedside and I suggested she might like to bring that. Jade nodded and Jackie packed it. Satisfied that mother and daughter could be left together and thinking they needed some time alone, I went downstairs. I sat on the sofa and after a while I could hear their hushed voices, not arguing but talking, although I couldn't hear what they were saying.

Fifteen minutes later they reappeared, Jade carrying the now bulging holdall and Jackie the suitcase. I stood as Jackie set the case by my side, and she turned to say goodbye to her daughter.

'I'll give you a ring, love,' she said.

Jade nodded. I could tell from Jade's expression that she'd partly forgiven her mother but wasn't ready to relinquish all her grievances yet.

'I've told her not to worry about the kids,' Jackie said, looking at me. 'Margaret, next door, is going to help me out for now. She's in her late sixties but the kids respect her. I'll see if I can get my hours at work changed.'

I smiled at Jackie and then looked at Jade, who wore a blank non-committal expression. Jackie slipped her arms around her daughter and hugged her, and while Jade allowed the hug she didn't return it. I threw Jackie a reassuring smile, we said goodbye and she saw us out. As we made our way back along the walkways to the car I thought that while Jade and Jackie's relationship wasn't completely healed, it was a lot better than when we'd arrived and I was pleased. I was also pleased I'd had the opportunity of meeting and talking to Jackie, and it had given me a better understanding of Jade and her life before coming into care.

'Well done,' I said to Jade as I opened the car boot to load the cases. 'You did well. Life's too short to be angry and you know your mother loves you a lot.'

Jade gave a small shrug just as her mother had; indeed they shared many characteristics and mannerisms, which seemed to emphasize how close they'd once been, and I hoped they would be again.

As soon as we were in the car Jade said: 'Are we going to town now?'

I looked at her, puzzled. 'Why?'

'To get the key cut for your house. You remember, you promised.'

'Oh, yes. It slipped my mind.'

And again I should have heard alarm bells ringing at the urgency in Jade's request, but I didn't.

Chapter Seven

Testing Boundaries

That afternoon, after we'd returned home from town and as soon as Jade had finished her lunch, she said she was going out.

'Oh, really?' I asked, surprised, thinking she'd want a rest after her busy morning. 'Where are you going?'

'To a friend's,' she said. She left the table and went into the hall.

'Does she live far away? How will you get home?' I called, mindful that Jade's friends were likely to live close to where she had – on the other side of the county.

'Not very far away,' Jade called evasively. Then I thought I heard the front door quietly open and close, so I left the table and went into the hall where, sure enough, I found Jade's shoes and coat were missing and she had gone.

I was a little hurt by Jade's abruptness. I'd only wanted to make sure she was safe and had enough money for the bus fare home. I would also have liked to confirm a coming-home time, as it was dark by 4.30 p.m. in winter. However, I was aware that teenagers don't like to be questioned, so I just assumed she'd be home in plenty of time for dinner, which she knew was at about six o'clock. I got on with some housework and also took the bag containing the maternity clothes I'd

63

bought for Jade that morning up to her room, where I found her bed still unmade and the cases unpacked. She was supposed to have been unpacking them while I'd been making lunch. I left them where they were for Jade to do later when she came home.

An hour passed and then Rachel phoned to ask how Jade was settling in. I told her Jade was fine; that we'd collected her belongings from home and I'd had a chance to talk to Jackie. I said that Jade and her mother were now on better terms, and that after we'd left we'd been into town to go shopping and I'd also had a key cut for her.

'So Jade's out now?' Rachel said.

'Yes, she's gone to see a friend.'

'Did she say who?'

'No.'

'OK. I'll phone later. What time is she due back?' It's usual for the child's social worker to speak to the child within a day or so of the child being placed with a foster carer.

'I'm assuming she'll be home by dinnertime, which is six o'clock.'

'All right, I'll phone later or tomorrow.'

We said goodbye and I replaced the phone, feeling I should have been able to give Rachel more positive answers as to where Jade was and what time she'd be back. I knew that the next time Jade went out I needed to make sure I knew exactly where she was going and what time she'd be back, although that would be difficult if she just slipped out as she had done today. There wasn't the same problem with younger children, as you always knew where they were and what they were doing. I knew I was on a sharp learning curve when it came to fostering a teenager.

When I collected Paula from school, the first thing she said was that she was looking forward to playing with Jade. I had to tell her that Jade wasn't in right now but I was sure she would be back very soon.

'Good,' Paula said. 'I want her to play with my dolls' house with me.'

I smiled and thought that Jade might even be home by the time Paula and I arrived, but she wasn't. And when Adrian came home half an hour later there was still no sign of her. Although it wasn't late it was soon dark and I began making dinner, while listening for the sound of Jade's key in the front door. I should have asked her for her mobile number before she'd gone out so that I could have at least phoned her and confirmed a coming-home time and that she was safe.

It was then I had a sudden flash of inspiration – a 'light-bulb' moment: I realized that Jade's mobile number might have been included on the essential information forms. Leaving the preparation of dinner, I went into the sitting room and checked the forms in my fostering folder, but Jade's mobile number wasn't included, only those of her mother and the social worker. I wondered if Rachel had Jade's mobile number; I would ask her when she phoned back later, but given she'd been trying to contact Jade on my landline I thought it wasn't likely.

But Rachel didn't phone back that evening, and as we sat down to dinner, without Jade, I was starting to feel really worried and also a little angry: with myself for not asking Jade for a coming-home time or her mobile number, and with Jade for just going out without telling me. I hid my anxiety from Adrian and Paula and said simply that Jade was at a friend's and would be home later.

'But she's missing dinner,' Paula said, worried.

'I'll save her some,' I said.

Halfway through dinner the doorbell rang. Clearly it wasn't Jade, as she had a key, so I thought it was probably a salesperson on another ill-timed visit. But as with any unexpected caller it crossed my mind it might be the police with bad news, so I left my dinner and answered the door.

'Oh, Meryl,' I said, surprised. 'Hello.'

'I hope it's not inconvenient,' she said. 'I just wanted to say hi to Jade and see how she's doing.'

'She's not here at present,' I said. 'Although she's fine. She's at a friend's house.' I didn't ask Meryl in, as there didn't seem any point. Jade wasn't here and we were in the middle of dinner.

'But she's doing all right?' Meryl asked.

'Yes. We've been home and collected some of her belongings, and I met her mother. Perhaps you'd like to call round another evening?'

'Yes, please. Some of the staff and Jade's friends at school have been asking after her. I don't want Jade to think we've forgotten her. I'll call round later in the week, if that's OK?'

'Yes. Sure.' Then I had another light-bulb moment. 'I don't suppose you have Jade's mobile number? It should have been included in the paperwork but it wasn't.'

Meryl nodded. 'Yes, I do,' she said, taking her mobile from her coat pocket.

'Great.' I wrote the number she read out on the notepad I kept by the phone in the hall. 'Thanks very much,' I said, relieved. 'I hope you don't mind if I don't ask you in tonight but we're just having dinner.'

Meryl smiled. 'I'm sorry. I seem to be making a habit of that. Shall I call round a little later next time?'

'Yes, please. After six thirty is usually good for us.'

'See you soon, then,' she said, and we said goodbye.

As soon as I'd closed the front door I keyed Jade's number into the phone. Disappointingly the call went straight through to her voicemail, so I left a message: 'Hi Jade, it's Cathy. I hope you're having a nice time with your friend. Could you give me a ring and let me know what time you'll be home? My number is –' For it occurred to me that she might not know my number; she hadn't asked for it and I hadn't thought to tell her.

I'd purposely kept my message short and light, as I didn't want to sound the heavy parent/carer. But an hour later when Jade still hadn't returned my call I was really worried and phoned her mobile again. It went straight through to her voicemail and this time my message was firmer: 'Jade, it's Cathy again. It's seven o'clock and I need to know where you are, and what time you'll be home. I thought you'd be back by now. Please phone straightaway. I'm worried.'

I returned to the sitting room, where Adrian and Paula were, and hid my anxiety. But they too were becoming worried. 'It's very dark,' Paula said. 'Where is Jade?' They both looked at me.

'She's a big girl,' I reassured them. 'She'll be home soon.'

When it was Paula's bedtime I helped her with her bath and then saw her into bed, but as I read her bedtime story my heart wasn't in it. It was now 7.30 and there'd been no word from Jade; I knew I needed to take further action. Although I would feel a complete fool and an incompetent foster carer reporting Jade missing when she had only been with me two days, I knew that's what I had to do. As soon as I'd finished reading and had kissed Paula goodnight I went downstairs and to the phone in the sitting room. Adrian was at the kitchen table finishing some homework. I dialled Homefinders' number and it was answered almost immediately by Michael, one of the agency's social workers, who was on duty and taking emergency calls. I quickly explained the situation.

'It's not your fault,' he said. 'Try not to worry. I'm sure Jade's OK. It's typical teenager behaviour. This is what you do: phone Jade's mobile one last time and if she doesn't answer, which I don't think she will, leave a message saying that if she doesn't phone you within five minutes you'll have to report her missing to the police. Say that you're worried and she's behaving irresponsibly, especially as she is pregnant and hoping for a positive parenting assessment. She should get the message.'

It seemed harsh but I knew that Michael, like Jill, was a highly experienced social worker whose advice I should follow.

'And if Jade does answer her phone I'll tell her to come home straightaway?' I confirmed.

'Yes, but put a time limit on it. Teenagers work on a different time scale to adults. Tell her she has to be back in half an hour or else you will have no alternative but to call the police and start a missing person.'

'Thanks for your help, Michael,' I said. 'I'm sorry to have troubled you.'

'No worries. That's what we're here for. Give me a ring back either way.'

Having ended the call to Homefinders I keyed in the number to Jade's mobile, but as before the call went straight through to her voicemail. I left the message Michael had suggested and then replaced the receiver, hoping that contacting the police wouldn't be necessary. I had just enough time to go through to the kitchen and check if Adrian needed any help with his homework when the phone rang. I returned to the sitting room, picked up the phone, and was relieved to hear Jade's voice.

'Hi, got your message,' she said casually. 'I'll be back soon.'

'Jade, I've been really worried about you,' I said. 'I phoned three times. Why didn't you return my calls?'

'I had me phone off. I've only just checked it.' Which may have been true, although it was a bit of a coincidence that she'd thought to check her phone a minute after I'd left my last message. But I gave her the benefit of the doubt.

'OK. Where are you, love?' I asked. 'It's dark now and getting late.'

I heard her sigh. 'I'm at Ty's,' she said, irritated by being questioned.

'How are you getting home?'

'Bus. Same as always.'

I didn't like the idea of a young girl riding a bus alone in the dark, but there wasn't much I could do – I couldn't collect her in the car, as Paula was asleep – and from what Jade had said she was used to using the buses alone at night. However, following Michael's advice, I said: 'Jade, I want you here in half an hour, love. No later. Do you understand? Otherwise I'll have no choice but to start a missing person.'

'Fine!' she snapped. And cut the call.

I replaced the receiver and sat for a moment, feeling a little hurt, but aware I was going to have to become 'thick-skinned' and be firm with Jade. Her mother had made the mistake of being a chum to her rather than a parent and I thought Jade now resented me stepping into the role of parent and telling her what to do, even if it was for her own good and ultimately for the good of her baby too.

Forty minutes later, as I sat in the sitting room with the television on low and when Adrian was in bed, I heard the key go in the front door. Relieved, I went into the hall as Jade let herself in and closed the door behind her.

'I'm pleased you're back, love,' I said. 'Isn't it cold out?'

Jade shrugged and was about to go straight up to her room. 'Jade, before you go to bed can we have a little chat, please?'

'Can't it wait?' she sighed, irritated. 'I'm tired.'

'It will only take five minutes. Have you eaten?'

'Yeah.'

'Let's go and sit down and have a chat,' I said, and I went down the hall.

With another sigh Jade reluctantly followed me into the sitting room and then sat in the chair furthest away from me. I knew I must make sure my approach was not threatening or accusatory. I smiled and in a calm, even voice I explained that I'd been worried about her, not knowing where she was, as I would have been about any young person I was looking after. I said that in future, for her own safety, I needed to know where she was going, how she was getting home and what time she would be back, which seemed reasonable to me.

'I'm not a kid,' Jade said huffily.

'I know you're not, love, but at seventeen you're still a minor and while you're with me I'm responsible for you. Apart from which I need to know you're safe or I'll worry about you. It's what parents and carers do.'

'Mum didn't worry,' she said moodily.

'I'm sure she did,' I said. 'In her own way.' Although of

course boundaries are a sign of caring and Jackie had admitted she hadn't put in place enough boundaries with Jade.

I looked at Jade, perched on the edge of the chair and eager to be away. I wasn't convinced she was receptive to what I was saying, so I upped it a little. 'Jade, when you didn't come home or return my calls I phoned my fostering agency for some advice. The social worker there said that soon the social services will be starting an assessment of you, to see if you are responsible enough to keep your baby. You need to make sure you behave responsibly or it won't look good.'

'Are you threatening me?' she said, her eyes blazing. 'I told you me phone was off.'

'I understand that and no, I'm not threatening you. I'm just trying to help you.'

'Well, don't,' she snapped. 'I don't need your help.' And hauling herself off the chair she stomped upstairs and to her bedroom.

Well done, Cathy, I thought, that was a successful chat, although in truth I wasn't sure how else I could have handled it. Jade clearly resented being asked to conform to boundaries and perhaps she resented me.

I gave her time to cool off and fifteen minutes later I went up to her room and knocked lightly on her bedroom door. There was no reply, so I knocked again and then slowly opened the door and went in.

She was changed and in bed, on her side and apparently fast asleep.

'Jade?' I whispered. But there was no reply, so I came out, and hoped that in the morning we could start afresh.

* * *

Before going to bed I remembered to phone Michael at Home-finders to tell him Jade had returned. He was pleased Jade had made the right decision and said she was just testing the boundaries. I told him I didn't think I'd handled the situation or our chat well and he said that I shouldn't worry, as he was sure it would all be forgotten in the morning.

I didn't sleep well; I tormented myself with what I should have said to Jade and what I could have said differently. I was realizing that dealing with teenagers is like walking on eggshells; I hoped I would do better and our relationship would improve.

The following day Jade stayed in bed, apparently asleep, until lunchtime. I checked on her a couple of times and then eventually I heard her get up and go straight to the bathroom, where she ran a bath. I was in the front room on the computer. Once she was washed and dressed, she came downstairs and on her way to the kitchen called a cheerful 'Hi, Cathy,' the previous evening apparently forgiven or forgotten. I heard her start cooking a fry-up, so I went in and checked she had everything she needed, and then I left her to it. She made me a cup of tea as she had the day before and we sat either side of the table and chatted amicably. She even washed up her breakfast things, so I didn't really mind clearing up the bathroom after her.

However, that afternoon while I was collecting Paula from school, without saying anything to me in advance, Jade went out. I returned home to find a hastily scribbled note: *Out with Ty. Back about 10. Jade.* While I was pleased Jade had taken notice of some of what I'd said the evening before and had acted responsibly by leaving the note, I was concerned that I didn't know where she was or how she would be getting home.

Testing Boundaries

Ten o'clock seemed far too late for her to be out alone, especially in her condition. It crossed my mind to phone her but I thought that might antagonize her, so I decided I'd talk to her face to face when she returned.

But when Jade arrived home, not at ten o'clock but at 10.45 and drunk, I was horrified. I knew I had to say something and I knew there would be a scene.

Chapter Eight
Silly, silly girl

'Jade, have you been drinking?' I asked, closing the front door behind her.

'Yeah, why not?' she said confrontationally. 'It was me friend's birthday.'

'What friend? I thought you were at Tyler's.'

'Nah. I was at me friend's birthday party,' Jade said, clearly having forgotten what she'd written on her note.

I looked at Jade, flushed from alcohol, with a stupid grin on her face and struggling to get out of her coat. Normally I would have asked a young person returning from a party if they'd had a nice time, but that wasn't appropriate here. Jade was pregnant and had clearly had a lot to drink; she smelt strongly of alcohol and was unsteady on her feet.

'Jade, don't you know the harm alcohol can do to an unborn baby?' I asked, deeply concerned. 'Do you know the damage it can cause?'

'Don't start!' Jade snapped, finally releasing one arm from her coat and swaying slightly. 'You sound like my mum!'

'But think about your baby,' I said. 'Alcohol can do permanent damage to an unborn baby, both physically and mentally. Surely you've seen all the warnings on television and in magazines about drinking while pregnant?' Jade shrugged as though she didn't care, but it was my duty to make her care and understand the harm she was doing. 'Meryl stopped by again this evening,' I said, hoping to shame her. 'I dread to think what she would say if she knew you'd been drinking, after all she's done to help you.' But of course you can't rationalize with someone who is under the influence of alcohol, especially a teenager who thinks she knows best.

'Don't know and don't care,' Jade said, finally getting out of her coat and throwing it on the hall stand. 'I'm going to bed.'

She went to the foot of the stairs and, grabbing the handrail with both hands, hauled herself onto the first step and then began unsteadily up the stairs. I followed just behind her to make sure she didn't fall. She was very unsteady, so I guessed she'd had a lot to drink.

At the top of the stairs she hesitated, as though she'd forgotten where she was going, and then turned right and, trailing her hand along the wall to steady herself, arrived outside her bedroom door. She pushed it open, went in, and then shut the door in my face. My first reaction was to go in after her and tell her not to be so rude, but I knew that wouldn't be the best course of action in her present state and would very likely lead to an argument. Sad and very worried, I walked away and checked on Adrian and Paula, who were both still asleep; then I returned to wait on the landing outside Jade's room. I could hear her clumsy movements as she staggered around her bedroom, presumably trying to get changed and ready for bed. Then it went quiet and I waited some more, half expecting her to come out to use the bathroom. When she didn't appear I knocked gently on the door. There was no reply, so I knocked again and went in.

Jade was on her side on the bed, fully clothed and fast asleep. The half-unpacked suitcases were open on the floor; also on the floor were a heap of clothes, her nightwear and the duvet. It was a real mess but that was the least of my concerns. I went to the bed, where I carefully eased off Jade's shoes so that she would be more comfortable; she didn't stir. Then I picked up the duvet and put it over her. She hadn't washed or cleaned her teeth but she was in no state to do that now; so she'd have to do it in the morning. I fetched a bucket from downstairs and, returning, placed it beside her bed; then I came out, leaving the door open so that I could hear her if she woke in the night or was sick.

For the second night in a row I didn't sleep well, as I was listening out for Jade and I was also very worried about her behaviour. Jade didn't wake in the night and the following morning as soon as I got up I checked on her. She was still asleep. I closed her bedroom door so that Adrian, Paula and I wouldn't disturb her, and we got ready and left for school.

When I returned shortly after 9.00 a.m. Jade was still asleep, so again I left her – to sleep off the drink from the night before. Rachel phoned fifteen minutes later, expecting to speak to Jade. I explained what had happened and finished by telling her that Jade was sleeping off the effects of her friend's birthday party.

'It was no one's birthday,' Rachel said bluntly. 'There's a group of them who drink together regularly. They've been friends since infant school and they all live close to each other on the same estate. It's a cheap evening: they put in a couple of pounds each and that buys them plenty of alcohol from the supermarket. It's a regular thing.'

'But Jade's pregnant,' I said, horrified. 'What about foetal alcohol syndrome? Aren't you worried that Jade's drinking could damage her baby?'

'Oh yes, I'm worried all right,' Rachel said. 'I've talked to Jade about the harmful effects of heavy drinking on an unborn baby. I've even given her leaflets on foetal alcohol syndrome, with gruesome pictures of damaged babies, but clearly she hasn't taken it on board. I hoped her pattern of behaviour would change once she was with you, but that doesn't seem to be happening.'

I now felt as though it was my fault Jade had been out drinking the night before and I was to blame. 'It's difficult,' I said lamely. 'I'm trying to put in place firmer boundaries but Jade likes to go out.'

'I know. And we've got the weekend coming up. Friday and Saturday nights are always worse. The kids' parents are often out, so there are plenty of empty homes to go to with supermarket booze. In summer they go to the park with their bottles and meet up with other under-age drinkers. Perhaps you could organize a family activity, maybe an outing, to keep her away from her drinking friends? There weren't many family outings at Jade's house; Jackie couldn't afford it. Jade might see it as fun.'

'Yes, I'll do that,' I said. 'We usually go out at the weekend. I'll think of somewhere to go that will appeal to Jade as well as Adrian and Paula. Pity it's not the summer – we could go to the coast for the day.'

'Oh yes, and while I think of it,' Rachel said, changing the subject, 'don't give Jade her pocket money all in one lot. It'll all go on booze. She'll want some for the weekend, so I suggest half on Saturday and the rest mid-week – on Wednesday.'

77

'Yes, all right,' I said, horrified that this precaution was necessary. At Jade's age she was entitled to £10 a week pocket money, which could buy three bottles of cheap wine or a bottle of spirits from a supermarket. I knew from my reading and the news on television that teenage binge drinking was a real problem, but I'd no idea it was so widespread. From the way Rachel was talking it seemed it was an issue she had to deal with on a regular basis.

'I'll talk to Jade again about her drinking when I see her,' Rachel said. 'I take it she's in no fit state at present?'

'No, she's still asleep,' I confirmed.

'All right, leave her to sleep it off. I'm due to visit you. Could I come on Monday at eleven o'clock?'

'Yes. That's fine with me. I'll make sure she's up.'

Rachel gave a small laugh. 'Well, at least you know where she is when she's in bed.'

'Yes,' I said, unable to raise a smile. 'See you on Monday, then. Have a good weekend.'

'And you.'

I put the phone down and sat, glum and deep in thought, for some moments. I was very worried. Apart from the damage Jade was doing to herself and her unborn baby by drinking alcohol, I knew her behaviour was stacking up against her and wouldn't look good when a parenting assessment was made. Although there were still some weeks to go before Jade had her baby, her behaviour would have to alter drastically if she stood any chance of being allowed to keep it. You can't be out drinking and looking after a baby, and not for the first time I wondered if Jade had a realistic idea of what parenting a baby truly involved.

* * *

When Jade finally woke – just before lunchtime – she came straight downstairs and into the kitchen for a glass of cold water. I was unpacking the dishwasher and looked up as she entered.

'Hello,' I said.

Jade nodded and concentrated on filling the glass. She looked dreadful: hung over, unwashed, with tangled hair and still in the clothes she'd slept in. Cleary dehydrated from the alcohol, she drank one glass of water, refilled the glass and drank another, before she said a quiet 'Hello, Cathy.' I knew this wasn't the time to give her a lecture, so for now I said simply that Rachel had phoned and she was coming to see us on Monday.

'I don't want breakfast yet,' Jade said quietly, and disappeared back upstairs.

Later, after Jade had had a bath and was dressed in clean clothes, she came down with the laundry bag stuffed full of her washing and I set the washing machine going for the second time that morning. Although she was looking brighter, she said she didn't want a fried breakfast and instead made herself a piece of toast.

Before she had a chance to disappear back up to her room I said, 'Jade, bring your toast and tea into the sitting room, please. I want to talk to you.'

'Do I have to?' she whined, as a small child would.

'Yes, please. It's important.'

Jade gave a small sigh and then followed me out of the kitchen and into the sitting room, where she sat in the chair furthest away from me. While she nibbled her toast and sipped her tea, in a non-confrontational manner I explained how worried I was for her health and safety and that of her unborn baby. I explained how binge drinking was bad for her body and the damage it was doing to her liver. 'Last night was not a "one off",' I said. 'Rachel told me you drink regularly with your friends and have been doing for some time. Jade, there are young people in their mid-twenties in hospital now who will die without a liver transplant because of their binge drinking as teenagers. And apart from the damage you're doing to your own body, you're doing even greater damage to your baby. Everything you eat, drink or breathe in crosses the placenta and goes into your baby. That includes alcohol and cigarette smoke.' For although Jade had told me she didn't smoke I thought I'd smelt smoke on her the evening before. 'Alcohol and smoking can badly damage your baby. You want a healthy baby, don't you?'

Jade gave a small nod. I thought she was a little more receptive to what I was saying now, although of course my warnings might all be forgotten once she left the house and met up with her friends. The more I managed to keep her at home with me, the safer she and her unborn baby would be. I continued talking to her by saying that Rachel was very concerned about her behaviour and that she needed to change it if she stood any chance of keeping her baby.

'Why did you have to tell her I'd been drinking?' Jade grumbled, as though I was responsible for Rachel's warning.

'Because as a foster carer I have a duty to keep your social worker informed,' I said. 'While you are in care she is legally responsible for you and I am responsible for your day-to-day care. Rachel phoned this morning while you were sleeping off the drink from last night. Of course I had to tell her – I had no choice – and she's worried about you, just as I am.'

Jade didn't answer, but at least she didn't shrug off or reject what I'd said as she had done before.

'Well, I've finished what I wanted to say, love,' I said. 'Please try to remember what I've told you, and make some changes to your lifestyle. You will be a mother soon and you want to give your baby the best start in life, don't you?'

Jade nodded and ate the last of her toast.

'Now,' I said, smiling at her, 'it's Friday and the end of the week, so I was thinking we'd have a takeaway this evening. We sometimes do on a Friday as a treat. What do you fancy? Chinese, Indian, Thai, pizza?'

'Chinese,' she said. 'Can Ty come?'

'Yes,' I said without hesitation. Anything to keep Jade happily at home with me. 'And tomorrow, Saturday,' I continued, 'I was thinking we'd go out for the day. If the weather is good we could go to the castle. It's got a new interactive section which is fun for all ages.'

'Can Ty come?' Jade asked again.

I hadn't anticipated taking Tyler but there would be enough room in the car. 'Yes, ask him if he'd like to join us.'

'I'll text him,' she said, finally brightening up.

And later, just to make sure Jade didn't disappear out that afternoon while I was collecting Paula from school, I told her I'd like her to come with me to collect Paula.

'Oh, do I have to?' she whined.

'Yes, please,' I said firmly. 'I'd like you to, and Paula will like it too.' I had begun to realize that despite Jade's age and the fact that she would soon be a mother she responded to the manner I would normally have used for a younger child, and I was gaining the confidence to do this.

Adrian and Paula were very excited when I told them we were having a takeaway that evening and then a day out on

Saturday. Paula was pleased at the prospect of Jade coming with us on Saturday, and Adrian was pleased that Tyler would be joining us, so everyone was happy.

Tyler arrived that evening just before six o'clock and we ordered from the Chinese takeaway menu. While we were waiting for the food to be delivered we all played Sunken Treasure, and then after we'd eaten we played some other board games. It was a lovely family atmosphere and I liked the way Tyler responded to Adrian: he made time for him and treated him with respect, despite Adrian's sometimes silly comments, which were typical of boys his age. Although Tyler was very young to be a father, I was forming the impression that he could be more responsible than Jade, so that I thought I might enlist his help in trying to alter Jade's behaviour.

When Jade went up to the toilet and Adrian and Paula were in bed, I confided to Tyler that I was worried about Jade's drinking and so too was her social worker.

'Me too,' he said. 'But she won't listen. I've told her lots of times she's got to stop drinking. Me mum's told her and so has Jackie. We've told her it's bad for her and the baby. Jade promises not to drink, but when she gets with her mates she forgets. We've had big bust-ups over it. I hope she changes when the baby is born.'

'So do I,' I said. And I hoped it wouldn't be too late and damage hadn't already been done to the baby. 'You're doing your best,' I said, for he looked very worried. 'I'm going to try and keep Jade at home with me as much as possible so there's less chance of her drinking with her mates.'

'Thanks,' Tyler said. 'I'll tell me mum. She'll be pleased.'

When it was time for Tyler to leave, Jade asked if he could stay the night – to save him the trouble of going home and then coming back first thing in the morning, she said. I knew if I said yes once it would set a precedent and be more difficult to say no next time. So I made the excuse that the fostering regulations stated that I was only allowed to have one person sleeping in her bedroom and that if anyone stayed the night (even if they slept downstairs on the sofa) they had to be police checked. Jade pulled a face but Tyler accepted this and, thanking me for the takeaway, said goodnight and, 'See you tomorrow.' What I'd said was mostly true – the room was only for one person and if anyone stayed *regularly* in the house they had to be vetted. Jade could be very insistent and liked having her own way, so it was better to avoid situations that could give rise to confrontation.

Although the weather was cold on Saturday morning it was dry and bright, so our outing to the castle went ahead as planned. Tyler arrived as arranged at 9.30 and was really looking forward to going; in fact, he and Jade were like overexcited children about to embark on a school outing. Rachel had said that neither of them had had much experience of family outings, so I was pleased I could treat them. Neither of them had been to the castle, although it was a much-publicized local attraction only a forty-five-minute drive away. We bundled into the car – Tyler in the passenger seat and Jade, Adrian and Paula in the rear – and as I drove, the four of them chatted excitedly about what they were going to see at the castle, like one big happy family.

We had an excellent day out, exploring the castle and the ruins and imagining what life was like in medieval times, especially in the dark dungeon with its macabre history. We had lunch in the castle café and when we got home Jade asked if Tyler could stay for dinner, and I said yes. They were all pretty tired from the walking, especially Jade, who nodded off on the sofa while Tyler, Adrian and Paula watched television and I cooked dinner. After we'd eaten we all watched some television together and then Tyler stayed with Jade in the sitting room while I saw Paula and then Adrian up to bed. Tyler finally left just before ten o'clock and although this was a lot later than the departure time Jill had suggested, it was the weekend, and I felt that if Tyler staying longer meant Jade was happily at home it was preferable to her wanting to be out with her mates. I liked Tyler and while he was naïve and had a lot of living to do he clearly thought the world of Jade and from what I'd seen so far he was a good influence on her.

By Sunday morning I was feeling very positive. The weekend was going well and I felt my relationship with Jade had improved considerably. I was looking forward to spending a relaxing day at home with Jade, Adrian and Paula after our busy one the day before.

Jade got up earlier than usual and was washed, dressed and downstairs in the kitchen cooking a fry-up before I came down at nine o'clock, having had a lie-in.

'I'm going out,' she announced as soon as I went into the kitchen. 'To see me mum.'

'Oh, OK. Have a nice time,' I said. 'Are you coming back for dinner?'

'Nah. I'm staying all day.'

'What time will you be back, then?' I asked.

'Nine o'clock.'

'All right, but no later if you are using the bus. And please say hello to your mum from me and give her my best wishes.'

'I will,' Jade said.

It would have been nice if Jade had stayed a little longer and had had the time to clear up after her cooked breakfast, or had picked up her wet towels from the bathroom floor and possibly even wiped the bath, but she didn't. She was too eager to go out and see her mum. I thought I'd give her a few more days to settle in before I gently mentioned the matter of clearing up after herself: nothing heavy, just a few carefully chosen non-accusatory words along the lines that it would help me if she could clear up when she'd been cooking or had had a bath. I didn't want Jade to think I was criticizing her, but Rachel had asked me to teach her some homemaking skills and clearing up was just as important as cooking and having a routine.

Adrian, Paula and I were mainly at home on Sunday. Adrian had some homework to do and when he'd finished we took the bikes out to the park for a while, but the wind was so cold we were soon back home again in the warm. Also on Sunday afternoon I telephoned my parents; we spoke at least once a week and usually saw each other every other weekend. My parents were very supportive of my fostering and they always welcomed, as family, the child or children I was looking after, and they were sad when the children left. My parents knew I was looking after Jade for a few weeks and they would meet her when we visited or when they visited us.

However, while Mum was quite liberal in her views my father was more traditional and had firm views about teenagers, especially when it came to teenagers and sex – they shouldn't. He'd had a loving but strict upbringing himself and believed that teenagers now had too much freedom. And while he would never have expressed his views to Jade – he was far too much the gentleman – I knew he would struggle when he met her, a heavily pregnant teenager who saw nothing wrong in her situation and would rely on the state to support her and her baby. I didn't blame him; he was of a different generation, and Adrian and Paula loved their grandparents deeply and since their father had left us a few years previously they had looked upon their grandpa as a father, a role my father happily embraced. We arranged for my parents to come to lunch the following Sunday. 'I'll have a chat with your dad before we come,' Mum said. 'Times are different now.'

Jade didn't arrive home at nine o'clock as she'd promised. I waited until 9.30 and then phoned her mobile, expecting the call to go though to her voicemail. It didn't. To my surprise she answered and was in very good humour. I could hear laughing in the background.

'Jade, it's Cathy, love,' I said, hoping she'd realize she was supposed to be home by now.

'Oh, yeah?' she said nonchalantly.

'Have you forgotten the time?' I asked gently. 'It's 9.30 now.'

'Oh, yeah,' she said again easily. 'I won't be long.'

I heard another burst of laughter. 'Where are you, Jade?'

'At me mum's. I told ya. I'll be back soon. Bye!' And amidst more laughter and shouting she hung up.

I sat for a moment with the phone in my hand and wondered. Possibly I'd heard something in her voice or in the laughter, something that didn't quite ring true. It could have been her brothers and sisters, but it sounded more like teenagers to me, and all girls. I sat for a moment longer and then reached for my fostering folder. I opened it at the essential information pages, as I knew Jackie's mobile number was listed there. I hesitated again, and then keyed in Jackie's number. If Jade was at home with her mother I'd simply say I wanted to confirm what time Jade would be back.

Jackie's phone rang a couple of times and then a female voice answered. 'Yes?'

'Is that Jackie?'

'Speaking.'

'Hello, it's Cathy, Jade's carer.'

'Oh yes. How are you?' she asked pleasantly.

'I'm all right, thanks. And you?'

'Not too bad.'

'I was just wondering if Jade was with you?'

'No. I haven't seen her.' My heart sank. 'I take it she's not with you, then?' Jackie asked.

'No. She left me this morning and said she was visiting you. I phoned her mobile just now and she said she was still with you.'

'No. She hasn't been here since she collected her things with you on Tuesday. She'll be with her mates.'

My heart sank further. 'Sorry to have troubled you.'

'No worries. I hope she hasn't been drinking again.'

'So do I.'

I replaced the receiver, closed my fostering folder and stayed where I was on the sofa. Jackie hadn't sounded anxious or worried at the news her daughter was missing and possibly drinking, but I could appreciate why. Jackie had had to deal with Jade's behaviour for months, probably years, as well as working and bringing up her younger children. Now Jade was in foster care she no longer had that responsibility. Jade was my responsibility and I was very worried and also angry.

'You silly, silly girl!' I said out loud. 'Whatever do you think you're doing?'

Chapter Nine
Hurt by Dishonesty

Taking a deep breath to calm myself, I keyed in Jade's mobile number. Her phone was answered, but amidst the laughing and shouting I couldn't be sure it was Jade.

'Is that you, Jade?' I asked.

'Yeah, who's that?' she shouted over the laughter. My number was permanently set to private so it hadn't appeared on her phone.

'Cathy,' I said evenly. 'I've just spoken to your mother. Where are you, Jade?'

'Who?' she shouted over the background noise.

'It's Cathy,' I said, louder.

It went quiet and when she spoke again there was no background noise or laughing: I guessed Jade had either covered the mic on her phone while she silenced her friends or gone outside, for it was very quiet.

'I'll be back soon,' she said, subdued.

'You'll come back now. Straightaway,' I said. 'If you're not here in thirty minutes I'll phone the social services, and then the police to report you missing. Do you understand?'

'Yeah, I'm coming,' she said. 'I don't feel so good.'

'I'm not surprised, drinking in your condition. How much have you had?'

'Dunno.'

'Are you able to come home by yourself?' I asked, concerned.

'Yeah.'

'Now then, please. Right away.'

The phone went dead and I replaced the receiver. I then spent an anxious half hour waiting for Jade to return. I was angry and also very worried. Jade had lied to me, which I wasn't happy about, but I was more concerned that she'd had a lot to drink again. Jade couldn't have listened to any of the warnings Tyler, his mother, Jackie, Rachel or I had been giving her. Bad enough if it was only her body she was destroying, but she was carrying a baby, a vulnerable little baby who didn't have a say in Jade's lifestyle or what she drank, and who deserved better treatment than this. I didn't know what else I could say to Jade to make her change; she seemed set on a path of self-destruction.

When I heard a key fumbling in the lock of the front door I went down the hall and let her in. She was very pale and her clothes and hair were dishevelled.

'I really don't feel so good,' she said, stumbling in and leaning against the wall.

'I'm not surprised,' I said, going to her. 'Drinking to excess makes you ill.'

'Ah, don't go on,' she said, rubbing her stomach.

Although I was annoyed with Jade, my immediate concern was for her health. She looked dreadful. 'Do you need a doctor?' I asked.

'Nah. I'll be OK,' she said, still leaning against the wall for support.

I wasn't convinced she'd be OK. 'When you say you don't feel so good, what exactly do you mean?'

'I feel sick,' she said, rubbing her stomach again. 'It was that cheap vodka from the corner shop. It doesn't agree with me any more.'

'Of course it won't agree with you!' I exclaimed. 'Alcohol in large amounts acts as a poison. You're carrying a baby, Jade. That baby eats and drinks everything you do. You shouldn't be drinking at all.'

'I know, I know,' she said, waving me away. 'I won't do it any more.'

I'd said it all only a few days before; there was nothing else I could say. I helped Jade out of her coat and then followed her upstairs, making sure she didn't trip or fall. We went into her bedroom, where I laid out her nightdress and told her to change while I fetched a bucket from downstairs.

When I returned Jade was changed and climbing into bed. 'Are you going to have a wash?' I asked.

'Nah. Tomorrow. I feel sick.'

I waited until she was in bed and then I placed the bucket within reach. 'I'll leave your door open. Call me if you're unwell in the night,' I said.

Jade nodded. She was on her side and under the duvet. 'Can you pass me Chi Chi?' she asked, referring to the panda, which sat with the other soft toys at the foot of her bed.

I handed her the panda and she tucked it in beside her on the pillow. She put one arm around its neck and then snuggled her face into its fur, as a young child would. It was a touching and poignant reminder of how young Jade really was. 'I love Chi Chi,' she said gently. 'And I'm going to love my baby.'

'Oh, Jade,' I sighed. 'I wish you'd listen to what people are telling you. You can't keep on like this. Please stop drinking.'

'I'll try,' she said sleepily.

A few strands of hair had fallen across her forehead and I lightly brushed them away. As I did, my fingers gently touched the skin of her forehead and Jade gave a little sigh. 'That feels nice,' she said. 'Can you do it again?'

I sat on the edge of her bed and began lightly stroking her forehead. Having your forehead stroked is very soothing and comforting, and I'd done this to Adrian, Paula and the younger children I'd fostered when they were worried or couldn't get off to sleep. After a couple of minutes Jade sighed with contentment, her eyes slowly closed and she fell asleep. I stayed where I was for a moment and looked at her. With her arm around her toy panda and her face relaxed in sleep she was a child again, as vulnerable and in need of looking after as the baby she carried.

That night I wrote up my fostering notes with a very heavy heart. Foster carer's notes should be objective and non-judgemental, and need to report what has happened during the day – good and bad. While I made today's account as positive as I could – including the fact that Jade had answered when I'd phoned and had come home when asked to – I also had to include that she'd lied to me about where she was going and that she'd been drinking heavily. I wondered what Jade would think of it all if she read my notes on her file at the social services when she was an adult, as she had a right to do.

I checked on Jade before I went to bed, again at 2.00 a.m., and then again in the morning when I got up at 6.00. The bucket was empty, so she hadn't been sick, and she'd hardly changed position all night, sleeping on her side cuddled up to Chi Chi. I closed her bedroom door and left her to sleep, while

Adrian, Paula and I got ready and went to school. Thankfully, Adrian and Paula were unaware of Jade's behaviour, as it had happened after they were in bed and asleep. As far as they were concerned, therefore, we'd all had a nice weekend with a takeaway on Friday and a day out on Saturday. Long may it stay that way, I thought.

When I returned from taking Paula to school there was no sign of Jade, so I went up to her room and gently woke her. She wasn't happy.

'Piss off,' she moaned, slowly coming round. 'Leave me alone.'

'You need to get up,' I said. 'Rachel is coming at eleven o'clock.'

'Not seeing her,' Jade said, pulling the duvet over her head. 'Tell her to come back later.'

'Of course I'm not telling her to come back later. She's a very busy social worker. Once you've had a wash you'll feel better. Now get up, please.'

I crossed to the window and opened the curtains. It was a bright clear day and the low winter sun shone onto Jade's bed.

'Close them bleeding curtains!' Jade cursed from beneath the duvet. 'I don't feel good. I've got a headache.'

'Of course you've got a headache!' I said, seizing the opportunity to reinforce my lecture. 'You had too much to drink. And if you're not feeling well, imagine how your poor little baby is feeling. You can't carry on like this, Jade. It's selfish. The social services have given you a chance to prove yourself to be someone responsible enough to care for a baby and you're throwing it away. Now get up, please, and come downstairs.'

I came out of her bedroom and closed the door behind me, hoping she'd think about what I'd said.

Jade hadn't come downstairs by the time Rachel arrived, although I'd checked she was up and had had a bath. 'She'll be down in a minute,' I confirmed to Rachel. Then I showed her through to the sitting room and made her a cup of coffee.

'Jade came home eventually last night?' Rachel said as I put her coffee on the table within reach.

'Yes,' I said, surprised she knew. 'You know what happened, then?'

Rachel gave a small nod. 'The couple who live in the flat below the one where Jade was drinking with her friends phoned the police and complained about the noise. The police went into the flat and recognized Jade, and also a runaway who's now been returned to her mother.'

'Has Jade been in trouble with the police before?' I asked, wondering how they'd recognized her.

'Not exactly. She's been with friends who have been in trouble. The police know the kids who hang around the estate by sight. And Jade always seems to be there – in the wrong place at the wrong time.'

'I'm sorry,' I said, feeling responsible. 'I didn't know she was going there. I'm very worried about Jade,' and I brought Rachel up to date as she drank her coffee and made a few notes.

'Meryl's very concerned about Jade's behaviour too,' Rachel said. 'Especially after all she's done to try to help her.'

I was puzzled. 'How does Meryl know? Jade was out when she called round. Has she seen Jade?'

Rachel nodded. 'One afternoon last week Jade was in a gang who were hanging around outside the school. It was only 5.30 but they all had cans of beer and bottles of wine. Jade ran off before Meryl could speak to her. Meryl tried phoning Jade's mobile but she didn't answer and she hasn't returned her voice-mail messages.'

'I'm so sorry,' I said again. 'Whatever must Meryl think? Jade's fine when she's at home with me but as soon as she's out with her friends something takes over.'

'Crowd culture,' Rachel offered. 'If it's any consolation, Jackie had the same problem with her.' It wasn't any consolation; in fact it made it worse. I felt I should have been doing a better job with Jade, not failing her as her mother had done. 'At her age you can't stop Jade going out if she has a mind to,' Rachel added. 'And at least you had a nice evening on Friday and day out on Saturday. I expect Jade enjoyed that.'

'Yes, she did,' I said. 'We all did. Pity it couldn't have continued.'

'Are you talking about me?' Jade said, suddenly appearing at the sitting-room door and making us start.

'Yes. Come on in,' Rachel said, taking Jade's sudden arrival in her stride.

'I'm gonna get a drink first,' Jade said.

'Would you like some breakfast?' I asked.

'Nah. Later.'

'Later, please,' Rachel corrected, raising her eyebrows slightly at Jade's lack of politeness.

Rachel and I waited until Jade had fetched herself a drink before continuing. Jade reappeared with a glass of orange juice and a handful of biscuits. When I foster younger children I regulate how many biscuits they eat, but at Jade's age she had free access to the kitchen (and therefore the biscuits), so all I could do was advise on a good diet – but not now: there were other, more pressing issues.

'You're not looking too bright,' Rachel said to Jade as she slumped in the armchair and took a sip of her juice. Although Jade looked fresher after her bath she still looked quite pale.

Jade shrugged and began eating the biscuits, her body craving sugar after all the alcohol of the night before.

'Are you taking your iron tablets?' Rachel asked Jade.

'Ain't got none,' Jade said.

'Didn't they give you any at the hospital?' Rachel asked. 'I thought all pregnant women were given an iron supplement.'

Jade shrugged. 'Dunno.'

'We've got Jade's antenatal appointment on Wednesday,' I said. 'I'll check then.'

'Thanks,' Rachel said, making a note. 'I know Jade has missed some of her antenatal appointments. I think she's overdue for a scan, aren't you, Jade?'

'Dunno,' Jade said.

'I'll check,' I said.

'It's important you look after yourself, as I've told you before,' Rachel said to Jade. Jade shrugged.

'I think we need to have another chat,' Rachel said.

It's usual when a social worker visits for them to spend some time alone with the child (or young person) so that they can raise issues which they may not like to raise in front of the foster carer. I thought I should offer to go. 'Shall I leave you two alone to have a chat?' I asked.

'Thank you, Cathy,' Rachel replied.

'Don't care,' Jade said.

'I'll be in the kitchen if I'm needed,' I said. I left the sitting room and closed the door behind me.

What Jade and her social worker talked about was in confidence and I would be told what I needed to know. Foster carers have to get used to facilitating meetings in their homes (between the child and their social worker) from which they are excluded and in which they may be discussed. Foster carers also have to get used to having their privacy invaded by spot checks on their homes as well as at their annual review when the whole house is inspected by their support social worker, including their own and their children's bedrooms. Some foster carers cannot get used to what they see as an unnecessary and intrusive invasion of their privacy and don't continue fostering. I feel that while some checks are necessary, for the well-being of the child, others have gone too far. For example, the contents of the carer's fridge and freezer are now examined to make sure there's enough food to feed the child. Surely if you trust a carer to look after a child you can trust them to feed them properly?

Rachel and Jade were together for about twenty minutes before I heard the sitting-room door open and Jade go upstairs. I left what I was doing in the kitchen and went round. 'Everything all right?' I asked, going into the sitting room.

Rachel looked up from writing in her notebook. 'Yes. Jade's gone upstairs to have a lie-down. She says she's still not feeling well. I expect she's still got a hangover but keep an eye on her.'

'I will,' I said.

I sat down and waited as Rachel wrote. 'Jade is eating and sleeping well?' she asked.

'Yes. She sleeps very well. She eats well but she likes fried foods and sweet things. I'm trying to get her to eat more fresh fruit and vegetables.'

'Good,' Rachel said, making another note. Then she put her pad and pen in her bag and looked at me. 'I've had a very serious chat with Jade and I've told her she's got to stop drinking.

She's promised to try. I've also explained that the only mother-and-baby placement free at present is outside the county and she doesn't want to move there – away from all her friends. I've told her I'm hoping a suitable placement will be free in the next few weeks, but if not then she'll have to move out of the county until one becomes free. She's not happy but it might be best in the long run: it would give her a fresh start, away from her mates.'

'Yes,' I agreed. 'It might be just what she needs. All her problems seem to stem from that group of friends.'

Rachel nodded and then stood, ready to leave. 'Well, thanks for all you're doing, Cathy. I know Jade's not the easiest child in the world but she's not the worst either.'

'No, indeed,' I said. 'I like her but I am concerned about her unsafe behaviour – both for her and for her baby.'

'I've told her she's got to stay in more and she's agreed.'

'Thank you,' I said. 'That's a relief. I've hardly seen her as she's been out so much.'

I went with Rachel to the front door, where she asked me to say goodbye to Jade for her and left.

A couple of minutes after Rachel had gone I heard Jade come downstairs. I was in the kitchen preparing us some lunch, but Jade didn't come in.

'I'm just going to the postbox,' Jade called from the hall. 'I've got a letter to post.'

'All right, love,' I said. 'You'll need your coat on, even though the postbox is just up the road. It's freezing out there.'

I heard the front door open and close and I continued making our lunch. A more savvy, experienced teen carer would probably have known that teenagers very rarely write letters; they text. But being naïve, and mindful of the thank-you letters Adrian and Paula sometimes wrote, I never thought to check if Jade was carrying a letter, which of course she wasn't.

The postbox was about a two-minute walk up our street and it normally takes the same amount of time to walk back again. Four minutes in total. So when fifteen minutes had passed and our lunch was ready, and there was no sign of Jade, realization slowly dawned. I went into the hall, put on my coat and, dropping my front-door keys in my pocket, went out. I walked far enough up the street to see the postbox. There was no sign of Jade. I turned and went home again, hurt by her dishonesty and now regretting that I'd ever agreed to look after her, for it seemed there was nothing I could do to help her.

Chapter Ten

'Like You See on the Telly'

I phoned Jade's mobile; she didn't answer. I hadn't really expected her to. I left a message on her voicemail: 'Jade, it's Cathy. I need to know where you are. Please phone me.'

Jade didn't return my call, so I phoned again at six o'clock and left another message: 'Jade, it's Cathy. I want you home by nine o'clock at the latest. Do you understand?'

I hid my concern from Adrian and Paula and continued with the evening as best I could. I told them only that Jade was out with her friends and would be home later – probably after they were in bed. They accepted this, although Paula said she would have liked Jade to be at home more often so that she could play with her; Adrian said she was probably with Ty. I hoped she was but I doubted it.

Then shortly before seven o'clock the doorbell rang and, leaving Adrian and Paula in the sitting room, I went down the hall and checked the security spyhole before answering the door. To my surprise I saw Jade standing in the porch.

'Hello, love,' I said, opening the door. 'Good to see you. Did you forget your key?'

'I'm ill,' she said, coming in and leaning against the wall for support.

My delight at her early return quickly disappeared. I assumed she'd been drinking again, as she heaved herself off the wall and without taking off her coat lumbered to the foot of the staircase. I went over, ready to help her up the stairs and into bed. I was anxious and annoyed that she was in this state again and this time Adrian and Paula would see her. However, instead of climbing the stairs Jade sat on the bottom step, bent forward, and with her arms looped around her knees, groaned loudly.

'I'm ill,' she said again.

'How much have you had to drink, Jade?' I asked.

'Nothing,' she said. 'Only water.'

I wasn't convinced, although I gave her the benefit of the doubt.

'Perhaps it's indigestion,' I suggested, patting her shoulder reassuringly. 'What have you had to eat?'

'Just chips for lunch,' she said, still bent forward.

'Where exactly is the pain?'

'Here,' she groaned, pointing to her bump.

'It could be Braxton Hicks contractions,' I said. 'Do you remember I talked to you about those?'

'Nah,' Jade said and groaned again.

'They are little contractions that go on throughout pregnancy. They're nothing to worry about and you can usually feel them if you put your hand on your stomach.'

'Yeah, I can feel them,' she said, clutching her stomach. 'Here, you feel.'

I gently placed the palm of my hand on the outside of her jumper. At first all I could feel was the warmth of her body coming through her taut jumper, but after a moment I felt her stomach wall tighten hard. Jade groaned with the pain.

'Is that a branston hiccup?' she asked, mispronouncing the word.

'I think so,' I said, although the only experience I'd had was when I was expecting Adrian and Paula. 'How long have you been having them?' I asked.

'It started this afternoon,' she groaned. 'Even before I ate the chips. Do you think I'm going to have my baby?'

'I don't think so,' I said, my calm manner belying my racing heart. 'You've still got quite a few weeks to go yet, but I think we'll get you checked by a doctor, just to be safe. I'll help you into my car and take you up to the hospital.'

'Nah. I want to go in an ambulance like you see on television,' Jade said.

'I don't think that's necessary,' I said. 'How did you get here?'

'On the bus, but the pain's worse now. Supposing I have my baby in your car?' And to prove her point Jade doubled over and groaned loudly.

It's very difficult to judge another person's pain; our thresholds are all different, and I didn't know if or how much Jade was exaggerating. If she'd been my daughter, whom I obviously knew very well, I would have helped her into the car and driven her to the hospital to be checked over, but I couldn't take the risk with a foster child, especially as Jade was asking for an ambulance. If I refused and something went wrong I'd be responsible and I'd never forgive myself.

'I'll phone for an ambulance,' I said.

Jade uncurled and stopped groaning.

As I went to the phone on the hall table Adrian and Paula appeared from the sitting room; they stood at the end of the hall, looking very worried.

'It's all right,' I said. 'Jade's not feeling so well so I am going to phone for an ambulance.'

I lifted the receiver and keyed in 999 for the emergency services. The control answered immediately and asked which emergency service I wanted. 'Ambulance,' I said.

'And the number you are calling from?'

I gave my landline number.

'I'm putting you through now.'

'I'm a foster carer,' I began as soon as I was connected to the ambulance service. 'I'm fostering a seventeen-year-old girl who is seven months pregnant. She appears to be having regular contractions.'

A calm male voice on the end of the phone asked for my name and address, which I gave.

'And you want the ambulance to this address?' he confirmed.

'Yes, please.'

'An ambulance is on its way,' he said. 'Stay on the line, please, while I take a few more details. What's the full name and date of birth of the young person?'

I told him.

'Have her waters broken?'

'I don't think so,' I said. 'I'll ask her.'

I looked at Jade, who had stopped moaning and seemed to be revelling in the drama.

'Jade, have your waters broken?' I asked her.

'Dunno,' she said. It should have been obvious to her if they had, and her leggings were dry.

'I'm sure they haven't,' I said to ambulance control.

'All right. Stay with her and reassure her. The ambulance will be with you soon.'

'Thank you.'

I replaced the receiver and smiled reassuringly at Jade, although she was pain free at present. 'It's OK,' I said to Adrian and Paula, who were looking serious and watching me intently from the other end of the hall. My thoughts were racing. I needed to phone Homefinders, who would notify the social services – they always had to be informed if a child or young person went into hospital as an emergency. I should also phone Jackie and tell her what was happening, and I would need someone to stay with Adrian and Paula while I went in the ambulance with Jade.

'I'm just going to phone Sue, next door, and ask her to look after you both,' I said to Adrian and Paula. 'Then I can go with Jade in the ambulance.'

'Nah. I want me mum to come,' Jade said, grasping her knees again and moaning loudly.

'Yes, I'm going to phone your mother,' I said. 'But there won't be enough time for her to come here before the ambulance arrives. I'll tell her to go straight to the hospital.' Clearly I didn't know if Jackie was available to go to the hospital with such little notice but I appreciated Jade wanted her mother with her and I dialled Jackie's mobile first.

Jackie answered after a couple of rings and when she heard my voice she immediately assumed Jade was missing again, as she had been the last time I'd phoned her. 'She's not here,' she said straightaway.

'No, I know. Jade's with me,' I said. 'Look, don't worry, Jackie, this might be a false alarm, but I've called an ambulance as Jade is experiencing some contractions.'

'I told her she needed to check her dates!' Jackie exclaimed. 'I always thought she was further gone than she said.'

This was news to me. I didn't know on what Jackie had based her assumption, but now wasn't the time to ask. 'She wants you to be with her,' I said, as Jade groaned loudly in the background so that her mother could hear. 'Are you able to go to the hospital?'

'Yes. I'll get Margaret from next door to sit with my kids,' Jackie said. 'Tell Jade I'll see her in A&E.'

'I will. Thank you.'

I relayed what Jackie had said to Jade, and throwing her, Adrian and Paula another reassuring smile, I telephoned Homefinders. To my delight Jill answered; it was her turn on out-of-hours duty. I explained what was happening: that Jade appeared to be having contractions and I wasn't taking any chances, so had called for an ambulance. I also said I'd phoned Jackie and that she was on her way to the hospital, where she'd meet us in the Accident and Emergency department.

'Good. Well done,' Jill said. 'I'll inform the duty social worker at the social services. Take your mobile with you and keep me updated; I'm on duty all night. If Jade has gone into labour and has her baby early, it will probably go into an incubator. But first thing in the morning I'll make sure Rachel has a mother-and-baby placement ready. I suppose it could be a false alarm?'

'Yes, it could be,' I agreed. 'But I didn't want to take any chances, and Jackie says Jade might have her dates wrong.'

'You've done right,' Jill said.

I ended the call to Jill and again reassured Jade: 'The ambulance won't be long.'

I saw Paula was now looking very anxious with all Jade's groaning and moaning, so I asked Adrian to take Paula into the sitting room, which he did while I keyed in the number for my neighbour. Sue was a good friend and neighbour and knew I fostered; we'd helped each other out before.

'Everything all right?' she asked as soon as she heard my voice, for I didn't normally phone her in the evening. I quickly explained what had happened and before I'd finished she'd said, 'You'll need someone to look after Adrian and Paula. I'll come round now.'

'Thank you so much,' I said. And I thought: thank goodness for good neighbours!

I replaced the receiver and as I did Jade cried: 'Phone Ty! He needs to come too.'

'I will, but I don't have his number.'

'It's in me phone,' Jade said. 'I'll do it.' Delving into her pocket, she took out her mobile and pressed Tyler's number. It took him a while to answer, so that Jade wasn't in the best mood when he did. 'You need to get your arse up to the hospital now!' she cried down the phone. 'I'm having our baby. Yes. Now!' she bellowed in response to something he'd said. I guessed Tyler had been playing pool with his friends, for Jade now exclaimed: 'If you finish that game and put pool before me, you've had it! Do you hear?' Poor Tyler, I thought.

I stayed with Jade in the hall, lightly rubbing her back and reassuring her while we waited for the ambulance. I suggested to her that she might be more comfortable in a chair rather than sitting on the bottom step but she didn't want to move. Adrian stayed with Paula in the sitting room until Sue arrived five minutes later.

'How are you doing, love?' Sue asked Jade as she came into the hall.

Jade groaned loudly.

Adrian and Paula, having heard Sue's voice, came out of the sitting room. 'Hi, kids,' she said. 'Don't look so worried.'

'Is Jade having her baby?' Paula asked, while Adrian smirked, embarrassed.

'I'm not sure,' I said.

Then we heard an ambulance siren come along the high road and turn into the top of the street. Sue went to stand with Adrian and Paula at the end of the hall while I waited with Jade. As soon as the ambulance pulled up outside the house I opened the front door, ready. Two paramedics – one male and one female – climbed out of the front of the ambulance.

'This is Jade,' I said to them as they came into the house. 'She's seventeen and I'm her foster carer.'

'Hi, I'm Dave and this is Lyn,' the male paramedic said.

They went over to where Jade was sitting on the bottom step and Dave knelt down so that he was at eye level.

'How are you doing, Jade?' he asked.

Jade groaned loudly in response. Dave asked Jade some questions: when was her baby due? When did the contractions start? How often were they coming? Lyn then checked her pulse and blood pressure while Sue, the children and I waited anxiously.

'Are you coming in the ambulance?' Dave asked me.

'Yes, please. Her mother is meeting us at the hospital.'

Dave then asked Jade if she could stand and they would help her walk to the ambulance.

'I want to go on a stretcher like you see on the telly,' Jade said.

Dave laughed but he went out to the ambulance and returned, not with a stretcher but with a collapsible wheelchair. 'I bet you've seen these on the telly too, Jade,' he said. 'Much better than a stretcher.'

Standing unaided, Jade sat in the wheelchair while I went down the hall to say a quick goodbye to Sue, Adrian and Paula. 'I've no idea what time I'll be back,' I said.

'Don't worry,' Sue said. 'I'll put the kids to bed if necessary.' Then to Adrian and Paula: 'We'll be fine, won't we?'

They nodded, and I knew they would be fine. They liked Sue and when she'd babysat for me before they had been allowed to stay up past their normal bedtime and play for longer.

I kissed Adrian and Paula goodbye, thanked Sue, and returned down the hall to where Dave was wheeling Jade over the doorstep. Remembering to take my handbag, I followed them out and closed the front door behind me. Lyn had gone ahead and was already in the back of the ambulance with the doors wide open. As we went down the front path Jade's mobile rang. It was Tyler and he must have told her he was on his way to the hospital, for Jade said: 'Good. See you soon, Ty. Hey! Guess what? I'm leaving Cathy's in a wheelchair, and there's an ambulance waiting with flashing lights, just like you see on the telly!'

Having got Jade settled onto the couch in the rear of the ambulance, Dave closed the back doors and went round to the driver's seat, while Lyn stayed with Jade and me in the rear of the ambulance. Lyn had a kind and gentle manner and seemed used to talking to teenage girls; she easily established a rapport with Jade. As she checked Jade's pulse and blood pressure she talked to her in a reassuring manner and told her that while her blood pressure was up a little that was quite normal. Then she asked Jade if she was looking forward to having her baby.

'Will it hurt?' Jade asked, as she had previously asked me.

'A bit,' Lyn said. 'But you'll be able to have an epidural if you want. And before you know it, it'll all be over and you'll have a bouncing baby. Do you know the sex of your baby?'

Jade shook her head.

'Jade was due to have a scan on Wednesday,' I explained as the ambulance turned a corner and the siren wailed. 'She missed an earlier appointment.'

From the way Lyn was talking it sounded as though she thought Jade was definitely in labour and about to have her baby, although neither she nor Dave had said so. 'Jade's not due for at least another month yet,' I said. 'Do you think she is in labour?'

'Could you be out on your dates?' Lyn asked Jade.

'Dunno,' Jade said.

Fifteen minutes later the ambulance pulled into the ambulance park at the side of the main A&E entrance. Dave got out and opened the rear doors, and then he took out and unfolded the wheelchair. Lyn helped Jade off the couch and down the steps while I followed with Jade's coat, which she'd taken off in the ambulance. Once seated in the wheelchair, Jade took out her phone and was about to use it. 'Not in the hospital, Jade,' I said. 'It affects the instruments.' She sighed but closed her phone.

Lyn called a goodbye and stayed with the ambulance while I followed Dave, pushing Jade in the wheelchair. We went into the hospital, down a short corridor and into a curtained cubicle. A nurse appeared and helped Jade out of the wheelchair and onto the couch. Dave collapsed the wheelchair and said goodbye. I thanked him as he left.

'Is me mum here?' Jade asked the nurse.

'I'll find out in a moment,' she said, setting up the monitor.

'Shall I have a look?' I asked, to save her the trouble.

'Yes, please, and can you register Jade at reception?'

I left the cubicle and went down the corridor that led into the main reception and waiting area. It was busy, with the rows of seats full of people waiting to be seen. As I appeared through the double doors Jackie rushed up to me.

'I've just arrived,' she said, breathless. 'How is she?'

'A nurse is with Jade now,' I said. 'I guess we'll know more when she's been seen by a doctor. I've been asked to register Jade. Can you come, as you know all her medical history?'

Jackie and I went to the reception desk, where Jackie gave the information that was requested, and then I showed her through the double doors, back down the corridor and to the cubicle where I'd left Jade.

'Oh, Mum!' Jade cried as soon as she saw her mother.

Jackie went over and hugged her daughter, all previous hostility between them now gone.

'The doctor will be in to see Jade soon,' the nurse said, and left the cubicle.

Jackie pulled the only chair in the cubicle closer to the bed head and sat beside her daughter while I hovered at the foot of the bed. Jade seemed to be more relaxed now she was in hospital and had stopped groaning; I suppose she felt reassured. While I was more than happy to stay for as long as necessary, as mother and daughter talked I began to feel I was intruding and that perhaps I should offer to leave Jackie alone with her daughter for a while. I was thinking of suggesting that I sat in the waiting area when Jade looked up from the bed and said, a little rudely: 'You can go home now. Me mum's staying with me.'

'I can stay,' Jackie confirmed, glancing at me. 'Margaret is looking after the kids. She can stay all night if necessary.'

Had Jade been a younger child in care I would have had to stay even if the child's mother had been present; as the foster carer the child was my responsibility, and to leave her alone with her mother would have been unsupervised contact. But at Jade's age she could decide who she wanted with her in hospital and she wanted her mother, not me.

'All right, if you're sure,' I said.

'Yeah. I'll see what the doctor says and take it from there,' Jackie said.

'I want you to stay, Mum!' Jade cried theatrically, grabbing her mother's hand.

'Yes, I'm staying, baby,' Jackie said. Then to me: 'Give me your number and I'll phone you when there's any news.'

'Thank you,' I said, and gave Jackie my mobile number. 'Do you want me to get you a coffee or anything from the machine before I leave?'

'No thanks, love. I had one earlier.'

I said goodbye to Jade and Jackie and came out of the cubicle, still not really knowing if Jade was in labour. It was now after 9.00 p.m. and I went through reception and outside, where I stood under the canopied entrance and phoned for a cab. While I waited for the cab to arrive I phoned Homefinders. Jill answered and I updated her.

'Thanks, Cathy,' she said. 'Jade will be in the hospital overnight whatever the outcome, so go home and get some sleep and I'll speak to you in the morning.'

The cab arrived ten minutes later and so did Tyler, although he didn't see me, as he was in too much of a hurry, and ran straight past.

'Like You See On The Telly'

It was 9.30 when I arrived home and Adrian and Paula were asleep in bed. Sue was watching television. I told Sue I'd left Jade with her mother, who would phone me when there was any news.

'Jade's very young to be having a baby,' Sue said.

'I know.' Sue, like most of my friends, appreciated I couldn't discuss the children I fostered and didn't press me for more details.

I thanked Sue again as I saw her out. 'You're welcome,' she said.

I was exhausted but I knew I wouldn't sleep; I was still high on adrenalin. I made a hot drink and with my mobile on the sofa beside me I watched television until eleven o'clock. Then, more relaxed, I settled Toscha in her basket in the kitchen and went upstairs. I was asleep within minutes and I slept soundly until 6.00 a.m.

As soon as I woke, my thoughts went to Jade and I took my mobile from the bedside cabinet. A text had come through at 3.21 from a number my phone didn't recognize. I opened it: *Jade had a baby girl at 3 a.m. Courtney. 6lb 8oz. They're both well. Jackie x*

111

Chapter Eleven

'Smelly Baby'

I thought 6.00 a.m. was probably too early to telephone Jackie, especially as she would have been at the hospital most of the night, so I texted: *Congratulations! Love Cathy x.* I texted the same message to Jade, who I guessed would have her mobile switched on at the hospital, I hoped on silent.

Before getting out of bed I telephoned Jill, who I assumed would just be finishing night duty. I was right.

She yawned as she spoke. 'Hi, Cathy. Any news?'

'Yes. Jade had a baby girl at three o'clock this morning. Courtney. Six pounds eight ounces. Jackie texted that they are both fine.'

'Fantastic,' Jill said, rallying from her tiredness. 'That is good news. Although at six pounds eight ounces she doesn't sound like a premature baby to me – more like full term. Do you know if she's in an incubator?'

'Jackie didn't say. But I think she would have mentioned it if she was, so I guess not.'

'So it's likely Jade had her dates wrong. Oh well, at least they are both well. Do you have any other details?'

'No. Just the text message.'

'OK. I'll phone Rachel later when I've had a sleep. In the meantime let the agency know if you hear any more news, please.'

'Smelly Baby'

'I will.'

The arrival of a baby – whatever the circumstances of its birth or the problems surrounding the mother – is, I feel, a miracle. A new life is truly a wondrous occasion and guaranteed to raise the spirits and put a smile on anyone's face. As I showered and dressed that morning my heart was light, lighter than it had been since Jade had arrived, for I hoped – no, believed – that now Jade was responsible for a baby she would turn her life around and get back on track. I therefore envisaged a happy ending to what could have been a very tragic story.

I was still very light-hearted when I woke first Paula and then Adrian and told them it was time to get up and ready for school. 'Jade had her baby last night,' I said to each of them, smiling. 'She's called Courtney and they are both well.'

Paula was more impressed than Adrian and, grinning broadly, she said, 'I'm telling all my friends at school that our big girl has a baby.' And with a little clap of her hands she leapt out of bed.

Adrian was more reserved, natural for a lad of twelve, and said: 'I hope she's not bringing it here. Babies cry a lot and smell disgusting!'

'Adrian,' I admonished lightly, opening his bedroom curtains. 'You were a baby once. Just as well I didn't think that about you. Babies smell lovely. But no, Jade won't be bringing her baby here. Her social worker will have found her a mother-and-baby placement by the time Jade leaves hospital.'

Just before I left the house that morning to take Paula to school I received a text from Jackie in response to the one I'd sent earlier, congratulating her: *Thanks. Tkng day off work 2 go 2 the hospital.* Which added to my feeling of well-being: now Jackie was reunited with her daughter and was supporting her, all would be well.

Let me know if there's anything I can do, I texted back.

Thnk u, came the reply.

For the same reason I hadn't stayed at the hospital the night before – that Jade had wanted her mother – I didn't go to the hospital that morning. After taking Paula to school I went home, got on with the housework and some foster-carer train- ing I had been asked to facilitate, and waited for news. I didn't really expect to hear anything for a couple of hours, as Jill would be sleeping after being on night duty and Rachel would be busy arranging Jade's transfer. At some point I'd have to pack up Jade's belongings and either they would be collected or I would take them to wherever Jade was being discharged to. If I was honest, in terms of a fostering placement Jade's stay with me hadn't really been very rewarding; I didn't feel I'd achieved much. Rachel had asked me to teach her home-care skills, but Jade had hardly been at home, so that other than advising her about her diet – fewer fry-ups and biscuits and more fresh fruit and vegetables – teaching her anything hadn't really been possible.

By one o'clock I was expecting news at any moment, so when the phone rang at 1.30 I sprang to answer it. As I thought it might be, it was Rachel, and from the quick way in which she spoke I could tell she was very busy and stressed.

'Sorry I haven't phoned sooner,' she began. 'I've been on the phone all morning trying to arrange Jade's transfer. I've left a message with Homefinders and Jill will phone you later. We've got a problem. There's still only one mother-and-baby place- ment free at present and that is out of the county. The carer is a lovely lady and an experienced carer but Jade is refusing to go. I've just spoken to Jackie again and she says Jade is adamant she won't move out of the area, even for a few weeks.'

'So there's no chance of Jade going home, then?' I asked. 'Now she is reunited with her mother?'

'No. There isn't the space. Also Jackie's at work for a large part of each day and has her other kids to look after. She can't give Jade the support and supervision she'll need; she struggled before. Now Jade has the baby she'll need someone with her to help and advise her.' Which I understood. 'I've spoken to the ward sister,' Rachel continued. 'And they're waiting to discharge Jade, but she's refusing to go if she has to live outside the county. She's really dug her heels in, little madam.' Rachel paused to take a breath and I thought she was going to ask me if I could go to the hospital and try to persuade Jade to go, but Rachel said: 'So I was wondering if Jade could come back to you? Just for the time being, until I can sort something out.'

'So the baby's staying in hospital?' I asked, misunderstanding what Rachel was saying.

'No. Courtney is healthy and nearly full term. There is no reason to keep her in hospital. They will both need to come to you.'

'Oh,' I said. 'Well, no. That's not possible. I don't have any baby equipment. And Jade's room isn't big enough for two. It's a single room.'

'Yes, I know, I've seen the room and it's big enough short term. There's enough space for a cot, and Jade is used to sharing. I could speak to Jill about helping you get the baby things you need.'

I felt my pulse start to race. 'When? Which day is she being discharged?'

'She's free to go now.'

'But Rachel, it's after one thirty! I'll be going to school in just over an hour to collect Paula. I've nothing here ready for a baby. Nothing. Sorry, I can't do it.'

It went quiet at the other end of the phone and I hoped Rachel appreciated that her request was totally impractical, although I understood why she'd asked me. There are never enough foster carers, particularly specialists who can take a mother and baby, and while I always tried to help the social services whenever I could this just wasn't possible.

'What if I asked the hospital to keep Jade and Courtney for another night?' Rachel now said, coming back on the line. 'Would that give you enough time to prepare?'

I was about to say no – it takes weeks to prepare for the arrival of a baby – but I stopped and thought. Then I made some funny umm and errr noises. I had a cot and pram packed away in the loft. They'd been Adrian's and Paula's, and I'd used them three years previously when I'd looked after Harrison (whose story I told in *A Baby's Cry*). At that time I'd bought a new mattress for the cot, and Rachel had just said she would speak to Jill about helping me with the other baby equipment I needed. I ummed and ahhed some more and then said: 'What time tomorrow? It can't be in the morning. I need time to prepare.'

'If I arranged their discharge for one o'clock, would that give you enough time?'

My thoughts raced. 'I'll need to know what Jade has and what I need to buy,' I said, thinking aloud. 'Then I could go shopping to get what I need first thing in the morning after I've taken Paula to school.'

'So is one o'clock all right with you, then?' Rachel asked, pressing me for a definite response.

'I guess so,' I said. 'Yes. All right.'

'Thank you. You're a star!' Rachel declared, sounding very relieved. 'I'll phone the hospital now and speak to the ward sister. Then I'll talk to Jade, Jackie, Jill, and get back to you.'

I didn't feel like a star; I felt panic-stricken. Whatever had I agreed to? I walked away from the phone trying to reassure myself that I liked a challenge and that I could rise to this one as I had risen to others. But fostering a teenage girl and her newborn baby was very different from the challenges I usually faced: children who were angry or withdrawn as a result of abuse or severe neglect. Was I up to it? Had I made the right decision? I sincerely hoped so.

Twenty minutes later I was releasing the loft ladders, ready to go into the loft to see what baby equipment was stored there, when the phone rang. Leaving the ladders in place, I went round the landing and answered the call in my bedroom. I was pleased to hear Jill – in her best organizing mood.

'I'm making a list,' she began. 'Rachel's phoned and I've asked her to find out what Jade has at home so that we know what we need to get you. I've printed out the list of essential items from the maternity page of the hospital's website.'

'Thank you, Jill,' I said. 'That's a big help.' One of the great advantages of working for an independent fostering agency as opposed to a local authority is that their level of support is fantastic and practical when necessary. 'I'm just about to go into the loft and check what's up there,' I said. 'I'm sure there's a cot and a pram. Can I get back to you when I've had a look – in about ten minutes?'

'Sure,' she said. 'Has Jade got any baby things with her at your place?'

'No. Nothing.'

'I had a feeling that might be so. OK. I'll let you get on and speak to you shortly.'

Returning round the landing I climbed the loft ladders, switched on the light and peered into the loft. Straight in front of me, wrapped in polythene to protect them from dust, were the dismantled cot and the three-in-one pram, which converted into a pushchair and a carry-car seat. I also spotted a bouncing cradle I'd forgotten I had, and the equipment I'd bought when I'd fostered Harrison: a new cot mattress, a baby bath, a changing mat and a sterilizing unit. All of which I'd packed away, intending to car-boot sale them at some point, never imagining I might need them again.

I carried them carefully down the loft ladders, one piece at a time, and stacked them on the landing. The cot would need assembling and I'd ask Adrian and Paula to help me later. It would be nice for them if they felt involved. Once I had all the baby equipment down I retracted the loft ladders and closed the hatch. Then I went round to my bedroom and phoned Jill. I went through the list of things I had, finishing with 'a cot but no bedding, and a sterilizer but no bottles'. For health and safety reasons – to minimize the risk of spreading infection – foster carers are advised to discard bottles and bedding once an infant has left them and not use them again for another baby, even though they will have been washed and sterilized.

'I've made a note,' Jill said. 'Rachel has spoken to Jackie and she says that apart from some baby toys and one packet of disposable nappies Jade hasn't bought anything. However, Jackie has. A few weeks ago she bought some first-size Baby-gros, vests, socks and a shawl.'

'Sensible lady,' I said.

'Yes. Courtney will also need a warm zip-up suit to come home in from the hospital. It's cold. I've put that on the list. Also Jade says she doesn't want to breastfeed, so we'll need to get some bottles and formula milk.'

I gave a little sigh. 'There's so much to do and so little time.'

Then Jill said: 'We're reasonably quiet in the office at present. Shall I pop out and get you what you need now?'

'Oh, yes please, Jill, would you?' I said, grateful. 'Thank you. That would be a big help.'

'Can you think of anything else?'

'Baby wipes and lotion?' I suggested.

'I've got those written down already.'

'I think that's all, then.'

I thanked Jill again and we said goodbye. I then went round the landing to Jade's bedroom, where I began preparing the room for Jade's return by first unpacking her case, which she'd never got around to doing. I stowed it out of the way on top of the wardrobe, made her bed, and folded away the clothes she'd left strewn across the furniture. I then pushed the bed to one side to make more space in the room for the cot. Rachel was right: now the room was tidy there was space for the cot.

On my way downstairs I took the sterilizing unit and bouncing cradle, and then returned for the pram, which I left in the hall. Seeing these items again sent my thoughts back to little Harrison and I remembered the apprehension I'd felt when I had first been asked to foster him – a tiny newborn baby. I had worried then that I wouldn't remember what to do, as my last experience of looking after a baby had been with my daughter Paula – five years previously. But of course I'd remembered what to do, just as I would remember when Courtney arrived, although this would be a little different, for it wouldn't be me who was looking after the baby but Jade. I would be on hand to advise Jade and keep an eye on the welfare of them both. And as I began to picture how I could help Jade look after Courtney my anxiety lessened and I found I was actually looking forward to their arrival. I just hoped Adrian and Paula agreed.

'Yippee!' Paula said when I told her that afternoon as I met her from school. 'I'm going to tell Sara and Maxine!' And she skipped across the playground to share her good news with her two closest friends.

Adrian's reaction when he returned home from school was predictably less enthusiastic: 'Not a smelly baby. Gross!' he said, rummaging in the kitchen cupboard for a snack. Then: 'Will Ty be visiting?'

'Yes, I would think so, although not necessarily this evening.' Which helped.

'Cool,' he said. 'Ty can play on the PlayStation while Jade plays with the baby.' And he disappeared up to his room, munching an apple while opening a bag of crisps.

Shortly before 5.30 p.m. the doorbell rang and it was Jill, loaded with bags and packages, having come straight from the shopping mall.

'Welcome, welcome,' I enthused, ushering her in. 'You're an angel!'

'You bet,' she joked. 'I think I've got everything. Shall I leave the bags here in the hall for now?'

'Yes, please. I'll sort them out later. Coffee?'

'Just a quick one. After I leave you I'm going to drop the coat I've bought for Courtney in to Rachel, so that she can get it to Jade this evening. She's visiting Jade at the hospital after work. Has Rachel been in touch about the arrangements for tomorrow?' Jill asked, following me into the kitchen.

'All I know is that Jade is being discharged at one o'clock,' I said, filling the kettle.

'OK. I'll tell you what's happening,' Jill said. 'You won't have to go to the hospital to collect Jade and the baby, as Jackie's going. Jackie wants to be involved and will go to the hospital straight from work. She'll take with her the baby things they have at home – first-size clothes and nappies. She should be there soon after one o'clock and then Jackie, Jade and the baby will come here in a cab. Jackie would like to see Jade settled in and I told Rachel I thought that would be fine with you.'

'Yes. So I guess they'll be here about 1.45?' I said.

'I would think so.'

'I'll have to leave just before three to collect Paula from school. I assume it's OK to leave them here alone?' I passed Jill her mug of coffee.

'Thanks. Yes. If you're comfortable with that?' I nodded. 'Although Jackie will be here with Jade tomorrow, there will be times – like when you do the school run – when Jade and Courtney will be left alone. That's fine. Jade needs supervision and support but you're not expected to be here with her the whole time.'

'I understand,' I said.

Jill took a sip of her coffee and her gaze fell on the sterilizing unit I'd put ready on the work surface. 'It's strange seeing that in here again, and the pram in the hall,' Jill said. 'How do you feel about it all now?'

'OK, I think.'

'You'll be fine,' Jill reassured me. 'And remember, if you have any concerns or problems don't hesitate to contact the agency.'

'I will. I'm sure I'll be fine once Jade and Courtney are here. As with any new child, it's the waiting that makes you nervous.'

Jill finished her coffee standing in the kitchen as she was in a rush and called goodbye to Adrian and Paula on her way out.

After we'd had dinner Adrian and Paula came with me upstairs to Jade's now tidy bedroom and helped me assemble the cot and then make it up with the new bedding Jill had brought. Paula then disappeared into her bedroom and returned with one of her small soft toys, which she placed in the cot.

'That's a present for Courtney,' she said. 'I hope she's happy here.'

'I'm sure she will be, love,' I said. 'That's very sweet of you.'

While Adrian remarked dryly: 'Jade's room is next to mine. I hope I don't hear her baby bawling all night.'

'I'm sure you won't,' I said, for Adrian had slept through thunderstorms that had woken Paula and me.

While Adrian played on his Nintendo, Paula, eager to see what Jill had brought, helped me to unpack the bags and put away their contents: the baby bath oil in the bathroom with the baby flannel and sponge; the lotion, nappies and wipes in Jade's bedroom; the bottles in the sterilizer; and the formula in the kitchen cupboard.

Later when the children were in bed I read the instructions on the packet of formula to remind myself how to make up a bottle of formula. I also placed the changing mat on the table in Jade's bedroom with the nappies, wipes and cream within reach. The table usually doubled as a desk for older children to study at but would now be a baby-changing station. By the time I'd finished I felt I was as prepared as I could be, and before I settled on the sofa to watch some television before bed I phoned my parents and brought them up to date with the news: that Jade had had her baby and I would be looking after both of them for a few weeks.

'How wonderful, a little baby!' Mum cried, delighted. 'And will we be able to see them both when we visit you on Sunday?'

'Yes, of course. They'll be here.'

'Fantastic. I'll tell your father.' And I knew that when my father saw the baby he would be just as enthusiastic as my mother was.

Chapter Twelve

Worth It

The following afternoon I had been looking expectantly from the front-room window on and off for about twenty minutes when I finally saw the mini-cab arrive. I was out the front door before the driver had switched off the cab's engine. Arriving on the pavement, through the window of the cab I could see Jade with Courtney on her lap; ideally she should have been in a car seat, but no one had thought to take one. Jackie was sitting on the seat beside her.

'Oh, isn't she beautiful!' I gasped, gazing at Courtney as Jade opened the cab door. 'Well done, love.' I kissed her cheek. 'Congratulations. You have a lovely baby. She's beautiful.'

'Hi, Cathy,' Jackie said.

'Congratulations, Jackie. You've got a lovely grand-daughter.'

'Thank you.'

I helped Jade out of the cab as Jackie paid the driver. Courtney was indeed a lovely baby, really cute, and without the redness that newborn babies often have. Her tiny features were relaxed in sleep and seemed even cuter under the little white hat she was wearing. She was dressed warmly in the zip-up suit Jill had bought, and a shawl Jackie had presumably brought from home.

'You go on in with Courtney,' Jackie said to Jade. 'I'll bring the bags.'

Jade took a couple of steps towards the garden gate and grimaced, so I guessed she was sore from the birth. 'Can you carry her in?' Jade asked, holding Courtney out to me.

'Yes, of course, love,' I said.

I carefully took the precious bundle in my arms and, holding her close, followed Jade slowly up the garden path. I could smell that lovely newborn-baby smell and I couldn't help but kiss Courtney's little cheek. Jade took off her coat and threw it over the hall stand, and then continued into the sitting room. I left the front door open for Jackie, and carried Courtney into the sitting room.

Once Jade was comfortably settled on the sofa I placed Courtney in her arms. Jade looked at her and then up and around the room; she seemed overwhelmed, which was hardly surprising with everything that had happened since she'd last been in this room.

'It's bound to seem strange at first,' I said. 'Your body has been through a lot and will need time to recover. I'm here to help you all I can. You know you're staying with me for now?' I asked, and she nodded. 'Would you like to take off Courtney's coat?' I suggested. 'It's warm indoors.'

Jade looked at me and then at Courtney but didn't move. 'Undo the zip and take out her arms first, and then her legs,' I said. 'It's easier to do it that way round.'

Jade began sliding down the zipper of the all-in-one coat and then awkwardly took Courtney's arms out of the sleeves, and then her legs. Courtney screwed up her face but didn't wake or cry. 'Well done,' I said to Jade, and helped her slide the suit from under Courtney. As with many procedures in caring for a baby, Jade would find it became easier with practice, so that before long she would have Courtney in and out of the suit in no time, and without disturbing her if she was asleep.

'Shall I take these baby things up to Jade's bedroom?' Jackie called from the hall.

'Yes, if you like,' I said, going to meet her. I thought Jackie would probably like to see Jade and Courtney's bedroom. 'I'll show you where it is.'

I led the way upstairs and to Jade's room. 'It's not very big,' I said apologetically as we entered. 'But Rachel said it would be fine short term.'

'It's nice,' Jackie said pleasantly, placing the carrier bags on the bed. 'You've got a lovely home.'

'Thank you.'

'It's a lot bigger than my place. Although now Jade's gone we've got a bit more space. Mikey and Danny are in her room now.'

I knew from the paperwork that Mikey and Danny were Jade's younger brothers. While I could see the practicality in utilizing Jade's bedroom straightaway I hoped Jackie hadn't told Jade, for it seemed a bit insensitive to move them in so quickly, as though Jackie couldn't wait to get rid of Jade. But Jackie continued: 'I've told Jade I'm boxing up her things and I'll store them until she has a place of her own.' By 'a place of her own' I assumed Jackie meant a council flat, but this too seemed a little premature, for when Jade left me it would be to go to a mother-and-baby foster home, where she could stay for a year or more while a parenting assessment was completed. Only if Jade demonstrated adequate parenting and was allowed to keep her baby would she be eligible for social housing – as a single mother.

We returned downstairs, where Jade was on the sofa with Courtney still asleep in her arms. 'Would either of you like a drink?' I asked Jade and Jackie.

'Orange, please,' Jade said.

'No thanks,' Jackie said. 'I'll need to be off soon.'

I went into the kitchen and poured Jade's drink, and then returned to the sitting room. Jackie and Jade hadn't spoken in my absence and although Jackie was sitting next to Jade on the sofa looking at Courtney I sensed an atmosphere.

Presently Jackie said to me: 'Ty phoned me. I think he might be coming over later.'

'That'll be nice,' I said to Jade. 'Was he with you during the birth? I saw him arrive as I was leaving the hospital.'

Jade shrugged. 'I guess so. Sort of. I was out of it with that gas and air.'

'He was in the room, some of the time,' Jackie said. 'Although he wasn't much use. Just as well you can rely on your mother,' she added, turning to Jade.

Jade didn't reply or look at her mother and again I sensed an atmosphere. There was a small silence as Jade drank her orange juice and then Jackie stood. 'Well, I'd best be off, then. The bus takes ages.'

'I'm sorry I can't offer you a lift,' I said, also standing. 'But I wouldn't be back in time to collect Paula.'

'No worries,' Jackie said. 'I'm used to the buses.' Then to Jade: 'See you soon. You know where I live.'

Jade frowned and looked annoyed. 'I can't go on the bus yet, can I?' Which was a fair comment.

'I could take you to see your mum in the car one afternoon,' I suggested.

'Or I'll get a cab,' Jade said.

'We'll sort something out,' I said to Jackie.

Jackie said goodbye, kissed Courtney's forehead but didn't hug or kiss her daughter. I saw Jackie out and then returned to the sitting room, where I sat on the sofa next to Jade. Courtney gave a little yawn and my heart melted.

'She's certainly a lovely baby,' I said. 'Do you think she looks like you or Tyler?'

'Dunno. Can't really tell,' Jade said.

'No,' I agreed, smiling. 'People often see a family likeness in a newborn baby but it's very difficult to tell. I couldn't see any likeness in Adrian or Paula until they were about three months old.' Courtney yawned again and then stretched as though she might be waking and I wondered if she was due for a feed. 'When did you last feed her?' I asked.

'Just before we left the hospital,' Jade said. 'I'm using bottles. I'm not breastfeeding.'

'I know.' I glanced at the clock. 'Courtney shouldn't need feeding again until after I've returned from collecting Paula from school,' I said. 'But if she does, everything you need is ready in the kitchen. If you come with me I'll show you. I've made up some bottles ready, and then later, when we have more time, I'll show you how to prepare the formula.'

'All right,' Jade said without moving, and then suddenly burst into tears.

'Oh, love,' I said. 'What's the matter?' I instinctively put my arm around her shoulders to comfort her.

'It's her!' Jade said, nodding towards the sitting-room door her mother had gone out of.

'Your mum?'

128

'Yes. D'you know what she's done? She's packed away all my things and given the boys my room. I'm homeless now.'

'You're not homeless, love,' I said, hugging her. 'Try not to upset yourself. Your mother mentioned to me your brothers were sleeping in your old room. I think she was desperate for the space.'

'I know but I haven't got anywhere to go now,' Jade cried. 'I bet they're all a lot happier without me. I always caused them problems.'

'That's not true,' I said, holding her close as she cried. 'Your mum loves you. And you have a home here with me for now.' But of course I could appreciate how Jade felt. I'd thought Jackie had acted prematurely and insensitively in packing up Jade's bedroom so quickly, and having just had a baby Jade would be more emotional than normal and would feel the rejection more deeply.

I comforted Jade and reassured her as best I could, while Courtney, bless her, slept on. I also told Jade that now she and her mother were living separately they would probably get along a lot better, and Jade agreed. After a while Jade wiped her eyes and blew her nose. Then, mindful that I needed to leave soon to collect Paula from school, I took Jade into the kitchen, where I showed her where the made-up bottles were in the fridge and explained how to heat one and test it was at the right temperature.

'If Courtney needs changing while I'm out, everything you need is ready in your bedroom,' I said. 'But she's fast asleep now, so hopefully she'll wait until I come home. I'll be as quick as I can.'

'Thanks, Cathy,' Jade said, and gave a small, sad smile. I felt sorry for her; she looked so lost and out of her depth. I knew she was going to need a lot of help and support during the first few weeks.

I was away from the house for only half an hour but as soon as Paula and I stepped into the hall we heard Courtney screaming upstairs, together with Jade crying. Then to my surprise Tyler suddenly appeared on the landing.

'I'm glad you're back!' he cried. 'Come and help, quick! We need your help.'

Without taking off my coat or shoes I ran upstairs and into Jade's room.

'She won't stop crying,' Tyler said anxiously. 'Jade's tried to feed and change her but she can't. We don't know what to do.'

Courtney was lying on her back on the changing mat with her little face screwed up and her mouth wide open in an almost continuous cry. Her nappy was off and Jade was standing at the foot of the changing mat with a nappy in one hand and a full bottle of milk in the other, also in tears.

'Dear me, what a noise,' I said gently, going over and stroking Courtney's cheek. 'What's the matter, little one?'

'She won't stop crying,' Jade blurted. 'She began just after you left and she hasn't stopped.'

'Don't worry. She's probably hungry,' I said calmly.

'I tried feeding her,' Jade said. 'But she wouldn't suck, so I thought she needed changing, but I can't do the nappy. She won't stop screaming.'

Clearly Jade (and Tyler) had panicked, which was understandable given the noise Courtney was making and that they were inexperienced parents. My instinct was to pick up Courtney but I didn't want to take over, as that could have undermined Jade's confidence even more. 'Let's get her nappy on first,' I said to Jade, as I stroked Courtney's forehead to soothe her. 'Open the nappy so it's completely flat and slide it under her bottom.'

I held up Courtney's legs to make it easier for Jade, and she slid the nappy into place and then secured it with the sticky fastening tabs, while Tyler stood watching.

'It'll be your turn to change a nappy next,' I said with a smile. Jade sniffed and managed a smile too.

'Now put her Babygro back on,' I said to Jade. 'Newborn babies often cry when you change their nappies or take off their clothes. It's nothing to worry about; they just don't like the feeling. They soon get used to the routine.'

Courtney whimpered a little but didn't cry as Jade finished dressing her.

'Excellent,' I said. 'Now let's wrap her in the shawl so she's nice and warm.' I placed the shawl in Jade's arms and then lifted Courtney off the changing mat and laid her in the shawl; then I helped Jade wrap the shawl around Courtney. 'Good,' I said. 'Well done. Now sit on the bed with Courtney in the crook of your arm so you are both comfortable and you can feed her.'

Jade did as I suggested and I picked up the bottle, checked the milk was still warm and that it was flowing through the teat by shaking a little onto the back of my hand, and then passed the bottle to Jade. She put the teat to Courtney's mouth but Courtney didn't take the teat – or latch on, as it's known – and, frustrated, screwed up her face as though she was about to cry again.

'See!' Jade said, immediately losing confidence. 'That's what she does!'

I sat beside Jade on the bed and placed my hand over hers and the bottle, as Courtney reddened with frustration at not being able to feed. 'Try this,' I said, and I guided the bottle so that the teat brushed against the side of Courtney's mouth rather than trying to push it between her lips. Feeling the teat Courtney instinctively opened her mouth, searched for the teat and latched on.

'Success,' I said as she suckled and Jade finally relaxed. 'A nurse showed me that trick when I had Adrian. Brushing the corner of the baby's mouth with the teat, or nipple if you are breastfeeding, seems to stimulate a reflex action.' I smiled at Jade. 'Now enjoy feeding her. Hold her close so she can feel the warmth of your body and you can feel hers. I'll be back in a minute to show you how to wind her. All right?'

Jade nodded and I left her feeding Courtney with Tyler looking on, while I went downstairs, took off my shoes and coat and went to find Paula. She was in the sitting room, kneeling on the floor and stroking Toscha. 'It's OK,' Paula was saying soothingly to our cat. 'Mummy knows what to do. Baby has stopped crying now.' I thought that Courtney's screaming, together with Jade's crying, Tyler's panicked shouting and me rushing upstairs, had frightened Paula.

'Jade and Courtney are all right now,' I confirmed. 'Would you like to come up and see Courtney?'

Paula nodded and, leaving Toscha, slipped her hand into mine and we went upstairs. Tyler was sitting on the bed next to Jade as she fed Courtney. They both looked up and smiled at Paula.

'Hi, Paula,' Tyler said. 'How are you?'

Paula nodded shyly.

'Would you like to see my baby?' Jade asked, far more relaxed and confident now Courtney was happily feeding.

Paula stood beside Jade and watched Courtney feeding, mesmerized. Indeed we all were, for there is something enthralling about a newborn baby feeding: completely engrossed, Courtney was the epitome of contentment, as all her needs were being met.

When the bottle was half empty I suggested to Jade that she wind Courtney. I showed her what to do: how to sit Courtney forward, support her chin and gently massage her back. I then moved aside so that Jade could do it; here was something else she would become more proficient at with practice. Tyler then had a little go at winding his daughter and laughed hilariously when Courtney burped. It crossed my mind that they were like children playing 'mummies and daddies', only of course this was no game – it was for real. I then told Jade she should give Courtney the rest of her bottle, which she did.

'What time did you get here?' I asked Tyler as we waited for Courtney to finish the bottle.

'About ten minutes before you arrived,' he said. 'I left school early.'

'Can he stay for dinner?' Jade asked.

'Yes, of course.'

'I'll text me mum and tell her I'll be back later,' Tyler said.

Once Courtney had finished the bottle and Jade had given her another little winding we all went downstairs. Jade, Courtney, Tyler and Paula went into the sitting room while I went into the kitchen, where I washed the empty bottle and put it in the sterilizing unit; then I began the preparations for dinner.

When Adrian arrived home from school five minutes later it was to a calm and quiet household. He was pleased to see

Tyler and the two of them played on the PlayStation while Paula sat next to Jade on the sofa and gazed at Courtney, who slept.

When it was time to eat I suggested to Jade that she put Courtney into her cot to sleep. I went with her and she laid Courtney on her side, as she'd been shown to do at the hospital. Courtney slept until just before eight o'clock, when she woke for another feed. Paula was in bed by that time and I was reading her a story; Adrian was downstairs with Jade and Tyler. I heard Courtney begin to cry and when Jade didn't come upstairs to see to Courtney I went down and into the sitting room, where Jade was still on the sofa.

'You'll need to warm up a bottle now, love,' I said. 'Courtney's ready for another feed.' I wasn't sure if Jade hadn't heard Courtney or had preferred to stay with Tyler and Adrian, perhaps hoping she'd go back to sleep.

Jade hauled herself off the sofa and we both went into the kitchen, where I waited while she warmed the bottle to the right temperature and tested it as I'd shown her. 'Will you come with me while I feed and change her?' Jade asked me a little anxiously. 'I don't like it when she cries.'

'Sure. But don't let it worry you. She's not crying because she's upset; babies cry because they are hungry or uncomfortable.' I smiled reassuringly and we went upstairs and into her room. Courtney was a bit red in the face from having to wait for her bottle but soon settled once she was feeding.

'She's going to be a very good baby,' I said encouragingly to Jade. 'And you're going to be an excellent mummy.' I knew I needed to take every opportunity to praise Jade to build her confidence in parenting Courtney.

* * *

It wasn't until Tyler had gone home and Jade was getting ready for bed, having said she was exhausted and was having an early night, that I thought to ask Adrian if he had any homework. The PlayStation was usually reserved for use at weekends and holidays, but Tyler and Adrian had been playing on it for most of the evening.

'Yes,' Adrian admitted a little sheepishly. Then he added quickly: 'But it doesn't have to be in until next week.'

I always preferred homework to be done on the day it was set so that it didn't build up and become unmanageable, which Adrian knew.

'Adrian,' I said, 'while Jade is living with us I think you are going to have to be very self-disciplined and go to your room and do your homework. I know you like Tyler's company but he could be here most evenings.'

'I know,' he said with an embarrassed shrug.

And I left it at that.

Jade was exhausted and was in bed and asleep by 9.30 p.m. I too was tired. I wrote up my log notes, let Toscha out for a run, made up some more bottles for the night and then went upstairs. Before I got into bed I went round the landing and stood outside Jade's and Courtney's room, listening. Jade had closed her bedroom door and I didn't want to risk waking them by opening it so that I could check on them. I couldn't hear anything so I assumed all was well and went to bed.

Just before midnight I heard Courtney crying for her next feed. I immediately slipped on my dressing gown and went round to Jade's room to help. Once Jade was in the routine of caring for her baby I wouldn't get up at night unless I was needed, but for now she needed my help; also I didn't want

Courtney to be left to cry in case she woke Adrian and Paula. I knocked lightly on Jade's bedroom door, went in and, switching on the light, turned the dimmer to low. Jade was slowly waking.

'You go and warm up Courtney's bottle,' I said quietly to Jade, 'while I soothe her.'

Heavy with sleep, Jade stumbled from her bed and went downstairs to the kitchen while I picked up Courtney. She stopped crying immediately on being held and I gently rocked her. 'There, there,' I soothed. 'Mummy's fetching your bottle now. She won't be long.'

I knew from feeding Adrian and Paula that breastfeeding was so much easier than bottle; you just fall out of bed and the milk is ready and at the right temperature. Why Jade had decided not to try to breastfeed I didn't know and clearly it was her decision. I soothed and gently rocked Courtney until Jade reappeared with the bottle – it took her a while – and once she was seated on the bed I put Courtney in her arms. Jade lightly rubbed the teat against the side of Courtney's mouth as I had shown her and she latched on. Once I was sure Courtney was sucking I reminded Jade to wind her and told her to call me if she needed me.

Leaving her bedroom door slightly open, I returned to my bed but I didn't go to sleep. I listened out for any noise that might have suggested that Jade needed some help, but I didn't hear anything. After about half an hour I went round the landing. Jade's bedroom door was still open and the light was on low. I crept in. They were both fast asleep, Courtney on her side in her cot facing Jade, and Jade mirroring her position in bed and surrounded by her cuddly soft toys. It was a touching scene – mother and daughter in the half light, relaxed in sleep and without a care in the world – and I hoped and prayed everything would work out well for them.

Just after 4.00 a.m Courtney woke for another feed and I went round to Jade's room. I held Courtney while Jade went downstairs and warmed the bottle; then as before I waited while Jade settled Courtney on her lap and she was feeding, before I said goodnight again. 'By my calculations her next feed will be about eight o'clock,' I whispered to Jade as I came out. 'She's doing very well. Night, love.'

I was right: at eight o'clock, just as Adrian and Paula were finishing breakfast, we heard Courtney cry. 'It's OK,' I said to them. 'Jade knows what to do. She'll be down soon for a bottle.'

A minute later Jade appeared in her nightwear and, rubbing her eyes and yawning, went to the fridge.

'Good morning, love,' I said.

'I'm tired,' she mumbled. 'I didn't get any sleep.'

'Welcome to the world of motherhood,' I said with a smile. 'But it's worth it.'

Chapter Thirteen

Assessment

The rest of the week passed in a blur of bottles, nappies, visitors, telephone calls, shopping and teaching Jade how to parent Courtney. What I needed to know about looking after babies came flooding back to me and in addition to showing Jade how to make up formula and wash and sterilize bottles, I showed her how to wash and bathe Courtney, clean and cream her bottom, and soothe her when she was fractious, as well as simply spending quality time with Courtney and enjoying her, all of which bonds a mother with her baby.

My parents visited as planned on Sunday and arrived with a present and a congratulatory card for Jade. Jade already had some cards, including one from her social worker, one from Tyler's mother and one from me and the children. I'd told her that when she felt up to it I would take her shopping and she could choose something she needed for Courtney as a present. Jade was like an excited child as she unwrapped the present from my parents, which was a beautiful little dress with matching leggings, jacket and bootees. Jade thanked my parents, although I had the feeling that she was a bit disappointed, perhaps assuming it was a personal present for her.

As I thought would happen, my father was as besotted with Courtney as my mother was, and they took turns holding

Courtney and chatted easily to Jade – both about her baby and her plans for the future. Jade told them she hoped to go back to college and continue her studies when Courtney was older. My father said he thought that was sensible and I could tell he was impressed. Then over dinner he kept us all amused with stories of when my brother and I were little and some of the silly things we got up to, which made Adrian and Paula laugh loudly and Jade giggle. It was a very pleasant day and, as when I'd taken Jade and Tyler on the day trip to the castle, we were like one big happy family. I was pleased Jade had relaxed and enjoyed herself.

After my parents had gone home Jade said to me: 'I wish I had a gran and grandpa like them. They're so nice.'

'Yes, we're very lucky,' I said. 'But I'm sure your mum will be a good gran to Courtney. Have you told your dad yet you've had your baby?' For I knew there was some estrangement in the family and that often the arrival of a baby can help to repair past differences.

'Mum said she'd tell him,' Jade said.

I took Jade to see her mother on Tuesday afternoon. In preparation for the outing I showed Jade how to pack a 'baby bag', which included nappies, wipes, disposable nappy bags, cream and a change of clothes for Courtney. Jade was amazed at the preparation needed for a few hours away from home, having previously simply put on her coat and gone. I also showed her how to fasten Courtney safely into the carry-car seat – not that Jade had a car or could drive, but it was all part of educating Jade and giving her as much parenting information as possible for now and the future. At Jade's house I said hello to Jackie but didn't go in, as she had just got in from work. I returned as arranged to collect Jade after I'd collected Paula from school. When Jade got into the car I asked her if she'd had a nice afternoon. She shrugged and said, 'I guess so. But Mum keeps telling me what to do with Courtney.'

'I'm sure she was just trying to help you,' I said. But I knew there was a fine line between offering helpful advice and giving the impression that you know best. No mother likes to be told how to raise her child (with the implicit criticism that she's not doing it right), especially when she's a teenager whose relationship with her mother is already fragile.

Rachel visited us on Wednesday and stayed for most of the morning. Courtney was awake to begin with and Rachel held her and made a fuss of her. Then she watched Jade feed and change her, and then settle her in the cot, while I waited in the sitting room. When they returned Rachel made some notes, which I assumed would go towards Jade's parenting assessment, and then asked us about Courtney's routine. Jade said it was 'fine' and I filled in the details and described the routine we were establishing for Courtney, emphasizing what a good job Jade was doing.

'Excellent,' Rachel said, making another note. 'Is Tyler still visiting?'

Jade nodded. 'Sometimes.'

'Most evenings,' I said. 'And he helps feed and change Courtney.'

'But not always,' Jade said a bit gruffly. 'He's not here during the day.'

'He's at school then,' Rachel pointed out.

'Yeah, I know. But it's not fair. He can come and go as he likes but I'm stuck here all the time.' Jade had said something similar to me the evening before, resenting that Courtney was more her responsibility than she was Tyler's. I'd said that even in two-parent families the mother often assumed the greater responsibility for the practical aspects of parenting. And of course as a single parent Jade was going to have even more responsibility – something she perhaps hadn't fully considered until now.

'Jade's quite tired,' I said to Rachel to excuse her negativity. 'I'm helping her all I can. I took her to see her mother yesterday.'

'How did that go?' Rachel asked Jade.

'OK, I guess,' Jade said with a shrug.

'I'll be visiting Jackie later this week,' Rachel said. 'I'll tell her how well you are doing.'

I was pleased Rachel was being so positive. She then asked Jade about her postnatal check-up and I confirmed she had an appointment at the hospital in a month and that the health visitor would be visiting us on Friday. I also said we would be going to the clinic every week to have Courtney weighed and measured.

'Excellent,' Rachel said, making another note and smiling at Jade.

Rachel then produced some forms from her bag and explained they were to enable Jade to claim benefit for her and her baby. She handed them to Jade but said they were lengthy and complicated, and suggested I help Jade fill them in, which of course I was happy to do. Rachel then said she'd like to have a chat with Jade alone and I left the two of them in the sitting room. They spoke for about ten minutes while I busied myself in the kitchen; then Rachel thanked me for all I was doing and I saw her to the door.

* * *

That evening Meryl, the teacher from Jade's school, visited, having heard that Jade had had her baby. She gave Jade a congratulatory card, which I stood on the mantelpiece in the sitting room with the others, and also a Mothercare gift voucher for £30, which was a collection from the staff at school.

'We didn't know what baby things you needed,' Meryl said. 'So you can choose something.'

Jade thanked her and I suggested she might like to take Meryl upstairs to see Courtney, who was asleep in her cot.

'Oh, yes, please,' Meryl said.

Jade hauled herself off the sofa and the two of them went up to Jade's room, where they stayed talking quietly for about fifteen minutes. Then only Meryl came down and into the sitting room, where I was reading to Paula.

'Jade says she's going to have a sleep, so I've said goodbye,' Meryl said. 'I'll be off now. Thank you.' Although it was only 7.30 I appreciated that Jade, still recovering from the birth and exhausted from having to get up at night, was tired. I too felt tired from a week of broken nights.

I went with Meryl to the front door. 'How's Jade doing?' Meryl asked.

'Yes. Very well,' I said. 'She needs help, obviously, but that's only to be expected.'

'No more binge drinking, then?' Meryl asked.

'No,' I confirmed.

Meryl nodded thoughtfully. 'Good. Don't repeat this,' she said, lowering her voice in confidentiality, 'but a lot of the staff at school think Jade hasn't got what it takes to look after her baby and that the sooner Courtney's adopted the better. I'm more optimistic. I think she can make it. I'll tell them she's doing well.'

'Yes, do,' I said. 'And please stop by again. I'm sure Jade would like to see you. She must be getting fed up with just looking at me.'

Meryl smiled, thanked me and we said goodbye.

Jade was still fast asleep at eight o'clock when Courtney woke for a feed, so I decided not to wake her, as the sleep would do her good. I quietly took Courtney out of her cot and went downstairs, where I warmed up a bottle and sat on the sofa in the sitting room and fed her. Paula was in bed but not asleep and soon appeared downstairs in her pyjamas. She sat with me and held Courtney's little hand while I fed her. Once the bottle was empty and I'd winded Courtney, Paula kissed her goodnight. I took Paula back to her bed, where she kissed Courtney again, and then I went into Jade's bedroom where, with the light on low so that I wouldn't disturb Jade, I changed Courtney and settled her in her cot. 'Night night,' I whispered and came out.

They were both still soundly asleep when I checked on them before I went to bed at eleven o'clock, although I noticed Jade had changed into her nightwear, so she must have woken at some point and gone back to sleep. Courtney was now in a pattern of four-hourly feeds and woke for her next feed just after midnight. I heard her cries and went round the landing and into their bedroom.

'Jade, love,' I said, picking up Courtney so that her crying didn't wake Adrian and Paula, 'Courtney needs her bottle.'

'Can't you do it?' she said, turning over. 'I'm knackered.'

I hesitated. 'All right. Go back to sleep, then.'

I wrapped the shawl around Courtney and carried her downstairs and through to the kitchen, where I warmed up a bottle, and then went into the sitting room and fed her. It was like old times, sitting on the sofa in the middle of the night and feeding a baby – first Adrian, then Paula, and Harrison. I held her close. Dear, sweet, little Courtney: she was such a beautiful baby and so easy to love. I hoped Jade appreciated just what a treasure she had in her. That Courtney hadn't been damaged by Jade's drinking was a miracle and I thanked God they'd both been given this second chance.

Once Courtney had finished feeding and I'd winded her, I returned to Jade's bedroom to change her and then I settled her in her cot. Jade was still fast asleep, now with one arm around her toy panda, Chi Chi. I went back to bed and four hours later I heard Courtney wake for her next feed. Slipping on my dressing gown I went round to Jade's room.

'Jade, love,' I said. 'Bottle time.'

'Can't you do it?' she mumbled from beneath the duvet. 'I'm still knackered.'

Again I hesitated. 'All right, but you have been in bed since seven thirty.'

There was no reply, so I wrapped Courtney in her shawl and went downstairs, where I warmed up the formula and then fed her in the sitting room. She was hungry and took the bottle quickly, so I was in my bed again at 4.30 a.m. At 6.00 I was woken by the alarm and I climbed out of bed, showered and fell into the weekday routine, exhausted, but at least Jade had benefited from twelve hours' sleep.

Adrian, Paula and I were finishing breakfast when Courtney woke for her next feed. We heard her cry and I expected Jade to appear to warm up the bottle but she didn't. After a few moments – when Courtney's cries were escalating – I left

Adrian and Paula to finish eating and I went upstairs and into Jade's room. Jade had turned over in bed, away from Courtney, and had pulled the duvet over her head to try to block out the noise.

'Jade, Courtney needs feeding,' I said, going over to the cot and picking up Courtney.

'I'm tired,' came Jade's muffled response from beneath the duvet. 'Can you feed her?'

'No, love,' I said. 'I have to take Paula to school soon.'

There was no reply and no sign of Jade getting up, so after a moment and a little more firmly I said: 'Jade, Courtney needs feeding. You have to warm a bottle now, love.'

A few moments more passed as I waited and soothed Courtney, who was now mouthing for a teat. Jade suddenly threw back the duvet and with a face like thunder got out of bed and stomped off downstairs. I gently rocked Courtney until Jade reappeared, and once they were settled on the bed and Courtney was feeding, I said, 'I'll see you soon, then, Jade. Bye, love.'

Jade managed a nod.

By the time I returned home Jade had forgiven me for making her get up. She was in her nightwear in the kitchen cooking herself a fried breakfast, so I guessed she was feeling better. She made me a cup of tea and I drank it at the table while she ate her breakfast and I took the opportunity to say again that she was doing well. I then suggested that once Jill had been to see us we could take Courtney out in the pram and go for a little walk.

'Why don't we take the bus?' Jade asked. 'I always use the bus.'

'That rather defeats the object of going for a walk,' I said. 'A breath of fresh air will do you and the baby good. I think you can manage it now. See how you feel later.'

Unconvinced, Jade finished her cooked breakfast and then made herself some toast and jam. She certainly had a good appetite, although I knew I should keep a watch on her diet, as she loved her fry-ups and sweet foods and had quite a few pounds to lose until she was a healthy weight.

Jill arrived as arranged at 11.00 for one of her supervisory visits and was naturally eager to see Courtney, who was asleep in her cot. Jade was in the sitting room, where she'd been most of the morning, watching *The Jeremy Kyle Show* on television. Jill went through, said hello to Jade and gave her a congratulatory card. Jade thanked her without taking her eyes from the television.

'I can't wait to see Courtney,' Jill said pointedly.

'Cathy will show you,' Jade said, still glued to the television and absently opening the card.

'She will,' I said, throwing Jill a knowing smile. 'Come on, this way.' Jill was a big fan of babies and could coochicoo over them for hours. 'But you'll have to be quiet,' I warned. 'Courtney's sleeping.'

'I will,' Jill promised as we went upstairs. 'How's everything?'

'All right,' I said. 'I'll update you after you've seen Courtney.'

I put my finger to my lips to remind Jill to be quiet as we crept into Jade's room and to the cot. Jill's face lit up the moment she saw Courtney, as I knew it would. 'Oh, my, what a lovely baby!' she breathed, clasping her hands together in delight. 'What a treasure! And Rachel tells me she's perfectly healthy. Thank goodness!'

Assessment

'Yes, she is, as far as we know,' I said, sounding a note of caution. For Jill (and Rachel) appreciated, just as I did, that although Courtney was thankfully not suffering from foetal alcohol syndrome, she could have suffered more minor damage as a result of Jade's drinking, which would only show up later – if she missed developmental milestones.

'She's a good size,' Jill said, as we gazed at Courtney. 'And she's feeding and sleeping well?'

'Yes. Very well. She's in a four-hourly routine.'

'Excellent.' Jill made a few restrained cooing noises with some oohs and aahs, and then we crept out. 'I need to speak to you before we go down,' Jill said once we were out of the room.

I stopped where we were on the landing and looked at Jill, slightly anxious.

'It's nothing to worry about,' Jill said. 'Rachel phoned and confirmed what I'd been thinking: that it could take months before a mother-and-baby placement is free in this area. Apparently, on her last visit Rachel explained this to Jade and Jade said she was happy to stay with you for now, but I need to know you're happy with that arrangement too. We said at the start it would just be for a few weeks and now it's looking more like months.'

'Yes, that's all right with me,' I said. 'I just worry that I am not doing everything I'm supposed to. I haven't had the training that the mother-and-baby carers have.'

'You're doing a good job,' Jill said. 'Rachel hasn't got any issues and the fact that Jade is happy to stay here says it all.'

'That's fine with me, then,' I said. 'I'm pleased I can help.'

'The other thing Rachel has asked me to check,' Jill continued, 'is that you are keeping detailed notes with a view to contributing to Jade's parenting assessment.'

'I'm keeping my log notes up to date,' I said, 'as I usually do.'

'Good, but make sure you include details of Jade's parenting skills and her ability to bond with Courtney. You know the sort of thing: how quickly Jade answers her baby's cries, if she is meeting her needs, and how she interacts with Courtney through play, etc. You're with her every day, so your report will form a crucial part of the social services' assessment – to decide if Jade is able to look after Courtney or if she should be adopted.' Which I really didn't want to hear.

Jill saw my face grow serious. 'Don't worry. The mother-and-baby carers are often asked to contribute to the assessment,' she added. 'Just write down objectively what you see.'

I nodded and we continued downstairs but my heart was heavy. Although the foster-carer's notes are often included by the social worker in assessments, this was different. Usually my contribution was in connection with the progress the child was making but now it seemed I would be contributing to the decision on whether Jade kept or lost her baby.

Later, after Jill had gone and Courtney had had her lunchtime feed, I persuaded Jade we should go for a walk and Jade suggested the local shops, as she wanted to buy a chocolate bar and also a new mascara. When we arrived at the small parade of shops she said she didn't have any money, so I gave her a £10 note and then waited outside the shops with Courtney in her pram while Jade went first to the newsagent and then to the chemist. As I waited it occurred to me that although I was giving Jade her allowance and I also bought nappies, formula and anything else she or Courtney needed as part of my weekly shop, Jade never seemed to have any money. Her mobile was included in her mother's account, so I wondered what she had been spending her money on and how she'd been spending it for since returning from hospital she hadn't been out until today. A couple of times she'd asked Adrian to buy her sweets on the way home from school and then didn't have the money to pay him, so I'd reimbursed him. I'd remarked casually to Jade, 'I don't know what you're doing with your money,' but she hadn't replied and I hadn't pursued it.

However, that evening the mystery was solved and I wasn't pleased by what I discovered. As usual Tyler was with us and had stayed for dinner; he'd fed and changed Courtney by himself and then I'd shown him how to settle her on her side in the cot. By 8.30 Jade and he were watching television in the sitting room, Adrian was in his bedroom finishing some homework and I'd just closed Paula's bedroom door, having checked she was asleep. I went downstairs to find Tyler watching television alone.

'Where's Jade?' I asked, for she hadn't come upstairs.

'Outside, having a fag,' Tyler said.

'What? I didn't know she was smoking. Where did she get the cigarettes from? You don't smoke, do you?'

'Nah. I don't smoke. It's a fool's game,' Tyler said, frowning. 'But I have to get the fags for Jade or she moans like hell. Tell her to stop smoking, will you, Cath? I've tried but she doesn't listen to me. It's bad for her and if the social worker finds her smoking around the baby she'll have a fit.'

'Jade certainly won't be smoking anywhere near the baby while she's with me,' I said forcefully. 'And I'm not having her smoking outside either. I suppose she's been popping outside for a fag whenever I've gone out. I'll speak to her. You're very sensible, Tyler. She should listen to you.'

Tyler beamed as though it was the first time he'd ever received a compliment and even looked a little embarrassed, but credit where credit's due – he was sensible.

I didn't wait for Jade to finish her fag and come in. I went through the kitchen and out of the back door, where I found her standing on the patio in the dark and cold, puffing on the last of a cigarette while talking on her mobile. Seeing me, she immediately dropped the cigarette and ground it out with her foot while finishing the call with a quick: 'Gotta go. Speak later.'

'I'm coming in now,' she said, going past me and towards the back door.

'Good. We need to talk.' I followed her in.

I heard her groan. I closed the back door as she marched through to the sitting room, where I heard her say: 'You'd better go, Ty. She's in a bad mood.'

I went into the sitting room. 'Don't be rude, Jade, please,' I said. 'And I think Tyler should stay while I talk to you.'

Tyler was holding the remote to the television and pressed the key to silence it. 'Listen to her,' he said, turning to Jade. 'She's only saying what I've said. You need to stop smoking and drinking. If the social services find out they'll take Courtney. And I've told you if you smoke around our baby it's bad for her. I've seen the warnings on the telly.'

'I don't smoke near our baby,' Jade said angrily. 'I always go outside.'

'And leave the baby in the house alone?' Tyler said, making a good point. 'Jade,' he continued, doing well without my input, 'I've started studying. I've decided I'm going to take my GCSEs in the summer. I want to get a job so I can support you and our baby. I'm doing this for us, so we stand a chance of being together, as a family, and you're not helping by smoking and drinking.' I was really touched by his sincerity.

'I'm not drinking!' Jade said, defiantly. Then she looked away and lowered her voice. 'But I need something,' she said plaintively. 'I've been stuck in this house for over two weeks and it's doing my head in. If I can't drink or smoke or go out what can I do? I have to enjoy myself sometimes.' She flopped onto the sofa next to Tyler. Jade had gone from being angry to upset and I could see she was close to tears.

'Jade, love,' I said, perching on the chair closest to the sofa. 'Don't upset yourself. Tyler and I only want what's best for you and Courtney. Smoking is taking all your money and is bad for your and Courtney's health. I appreciate you have been going outside to smoke here, but if you were in a flat on your own you couldn't leave her and go outside, could you? You'd open a window or smoke in the flat, and that's what your social worker will think.'

Jade shrugged.

'I understand being a mum has meant a lot of changes for you,' I continued. 'It's hard work, you're exhausted and your hormones are all over the place right now. I also appreciate you haven't been out much, so I have an idea: no more smoking and I'll babysit on Saturday afternoon so that you and Tyler can go out for a while – just the two of you.'

'I play football on a Saturday afternoon,' Tyler said.

I was about to suggest Sunday instead when Jade said quickly: 'It's OK. I can go out with me mates on Saturday.' I hesitated. 'Shopping or to the cinema,' she added.

While this wasn't what I'd intended – I'd thought it would be nice if Tyler and she went out together – I recognized Jade needed a break. I looked at Tyler.

'I guess that's only fair,' he said. 'I mean, I'm out with my mates, so she should go with hers.'

I thought if the outing were confined to the afternoon there would be less room for trouble. 'All right, then,' I said. 'Saturday afternoon. I suggest you go out after you've given Courtney her bottle and I'll expect you back by six o'clock. Is that all right?'

'Yeah,' Jade said, perking up. 'And I promise I won't go outside any more to smoke.'

'Good girl,' I said. 'And Tyler.' I now looked at him. 'I want you to promise you won't buy Jade any more cigarettes, even if she asks you to.'

'Sure,' he said. 'I never wanted to in the first place.'

'Excellent.' And I congratulated myself on handling the situation rather well.

Chapter Fourteen

Error of Judgement

That evening I tortured myself over what I should write in my log notes in respect of Jade's smoking. To make no reference to it at all would be a lie but to include it seemed like a betrayal and a minus point marked against her behaviour. I sat for some time with my pen hovering over the page and then closed my fostering folder and decided to finish the entry in the morning.

However, the following morning I was none the wiser, so once I'd taken Paula to school and Jade was occupied with Courtney I telephoned Jill, my trusted adviser, and explained my dilemma.

'Simply write objectively what happened,' Jill said. 'Put: "At 8.30 I found Jade smoking on the patio without my knowledge. Tyler, her partner, and I explained the dangers of smoking and she has promised to stop."'

'Thank you,' I said, feeling daft that I'd needed to ask a question that had such a simple solution, but then that's what support social workers are for – to help and advise when necessary.

'You're welcome,' Jill said. 'Let's hope Jade keeps her promise and stops smoking.'

'I'm sure she will.'

* * *

The health visitor came on Friday as arranged and, having weighed and measured Courtney, asked us about her feeding and sleeping routine. I let Jade do most of the talking and only added what Jade had forgotten to mention. The health visitor was pleased with Courtney's progress and told Jade she was doing a good job. She recorded Courtney's weight and length in the 'red book' which she gave to Jade, explaining she should keep this book safe and take it with her to the clinic each week when she had Courtney weighed and measured. These details, together with the dates of Courtney's vaccinations when she began the programme, and the results of developmental tests done at the clinic, would be recorded in the book.

After the health visitor had gone and we'd had lunch, and Courtney was fed and changed, I helped Jade fill in the forms Rachel had left that would allow her to claim the benefit to which she was entitled; it took over an hour. After that it was soon time to collect Paula from school. I suggested to Jade that she might like to come with me, as it would be a breath of fresh air for her and Courtney, but she didn't want to join me. It wasn't an issue, it was her decision, but I'm ashamed to say that when I returned I checked the patio for any sign of cigarette butts. Thankfully it was clear: Jade had kept her promise.

As it was Friday Tyler didn't visit us after school as he did most other evenings; he played pool with his mates on Friday evenings. It was strange not having him there; he'd become one of the family and nearly always stayed for dinner. Jade spent most of that Friday evening in the bathroom, having a long bath, washing and styling her hair, plucking her eyebrows, shaving her legs, squeezing a spot and then painting her nails, all in preparation for when she went out with her friends the following day.

'Because I won't have time to do it in the morning,' Jade explained to me. 'Now I'm a mum I have to plan in advance, so I'm getting ready now.'

'Yes,' I agreed, smiling. 'And you'll look very nice.'

That night when Courtney woke for a midnight feed I soothed her while Jade warmed her bottle and then I left Jade to feed her. When Courtney woke at 4.00 a.m. Jade was in a very deep sleep – probably exhausted from all the preparations for the following day – and couldn't easily be woken, so I took Courtney downstairs and fed her. I reasoned that if Jade had been married or living with a partner then he would have helped with the night feeds, so I didn't see anything wrong in me helping her a little. I hoped that in a few weeks, as had happened with Adrian, Paula and Harrison, the early-morning feed wouldn't be necessary and we would get a better night's sleep.

Jade and Courtney both slept until 8.30 on Saturday morning. Jade would have slept for longer but Courtney was more than ready for her next feed by that time and her cry wasn't something you could ignore; to use an expression, she had a good set of lungs on her. I was in the kitchen in my dressing gown, making myself a coffee, when Jade appeared in her nightwear, carrying Courtney. Jade passed Courtney to me to hold and I gently rocked her while Jade warmed the bottle of formula. It was one of those cosy scenes that has stayed with me: Jade and me, like mother and daughter, still in our nightwear with a more leisurely start to Saturday; Jade happy that she was going out later and, with a smile on her face, chatting easily while she warmed the bottle and I cuddled Courtney.

When the bottle was ready I showered and dressed while Jade fed Courtney in the sitting room. Then, when I was dressed and Courtney had finished her bottle, I suggested to Jade that she put Courtney in the bouncing cradle and I would watch her while she washed and dressed, which she did. Paula arrived downstairs and, sitting on the floor next to Courtney, talked to her quietly while lightly stroking her little hand. I knew Paula was bonding with Courtney and growing to love her, just as Adrian and I were, although Adrian would never have admitted it.

When Jade was dressed she put Courtney in her cot for a sleep – as part of the routine we had established. Then when Courtney woke for her lunchtime feed Jade fed and changed her and then I looked after her while Jade finished getting ready to go out – although what more there was to do I'd no idea, as preparations for going out had already stretched over two days.

When Jade appeared she was wearing new jeans, top and high-heeled shoes I hadn't seen before. She was also wearing some make-up.

'You look very nice,' I said. 'Have you decided where you're going yet?'

'To the mall, shopping,' Jade said. 'There's nothing on at the cinema.'

'All right, love, enjoy yourself. And you'll be home by six o'clock,' I reminded her.

'Yes. Thanks for looking after Courtney.'

'You're welcome, love. I'm happy to.'

* * *

Error of Judgement

And I was very happy to be looking after Courtney all afternoon. When Jade was there I played a secondary role and helped and advised Jade on how to look after Courtney rather than actually doing it. But now with Courtney all to myself I made the most of it: playing with her and talking to her. When she grew restless I cradled her in my arms and carried her around the house, pointing out all the different objects: 'That's a window, those are curtains; that's Toscha, our cat, she goes meow; that's her bed and that's her food bowl …' and so on, until eventually Adrian said: 'Excuse me, Mum, I'm not being rude but shall I start making the dinner? I'm starving.'

'You could certainly help me,' I said with a smile. 'I didn't realize the time.'

'No. You've been a bit preoccupied. Did you know Paula's smoking a joint?' he said with his dry humour.

I laughed, just. 'Don't joke about that.'

I settled Courtney in her cot and then Adrian helped me prepare the vegetables and meat for dinner. He liked helping and was a good cook. It was six o'clock when the three of us sat down to eat – the time at which Jade was supposed to have returned. I plated up her dinner and left it in the oven to keep warm, as I was expecting to hear her key in the front door at any moment. Six thirty came and went, still with no sign of Jade; I assumed the bus was late or one had been cancelled – which often happened – and that Jade would be home soon. We finished eating and cleared the table.

When seven o'clock approached and Jade hadn't returned, I was disappointed, and also starting to worry. However, I saw nothing sinister in her lateness. It was the first time she'd seen her friends in quite a few weeks, so I thought they'd probably had a lot to talk about and were having such a good time that she'd simply lost track of time. I was aware the shops in the mall stayed open until eight o'clock on Saturdays.

At 7.15 I telephoned Jade's mobile and it went through to her voicemail. I left a message: 'Jade, love, it's Cathy. It's after seven o'clock. I was expecting you home an hour ago. Can you phone, please?'

She didn't phone but five minutes later my mobile sounded with an incoming text. It was from Jade: *Sorry. I 4gt. I'm on d bus nw. GIV my luv 2 Courtney. X*.

Relieved, I continued with the board game I was playing with Paula. I knew the bus took half an hour to get from the mall to my house and Jade had said she was already on it, so I was expecting her soon.

When she hadn't arrived home by 7.40 I texted her: *R u nearly home? Cathy x*.

She texted back straightaway: *Yes x*.

Courtney woke for a feed at 8.00, just as I was running Paula's bath. I left the taps on, collected Courtney from her cot and returned to Paula in the bathroom, but Courtney wouldn't stop crying, so I switched off the taps, told Paula to get undressed but to wait for me before she got into the bath, and hurried downstairs for a bottle for Courtney. Even though Paula was eight years old I didn't leave her unattended in the bath in case she slipped or fell. With Courtney still crying in my arms I went into the kitchen, where I quickly heated the bottle of formula, tested it, and then put the teat to her lips; she latched on immediately and sucked ravenously. I carried her in my arms, still feeding, upstairs and into the bathroom, where I topped up Paula's bath with some more hot water and then sat on the floor and fed Courtney while Paula bathed and chatted.

Error of Judgement

It was 8.20 when Jade finally arrived home – over two hours after the time we'd agreed. Paula was in bed, waiting for me to read her a bedtime story, and Adrian was downstairs, watching a DVD. I was in Jade's room changing Courtney before settling her in her cot for the night. I heard the front door open and close and then Jade's voice call from the hall: 'Hi! I'm back, Cathy! Where's my lovely daughter?'

I knew straightaway, even before I saw Jade, that she had been drinking. Something in her voice told me she wasn't sober. 'We're up here,' I called back evenly.

Jade's footsteps sounded unsteadily on the stairs and then she came round the landing and into her bedroom. I didn't immediately look up but concentrated on fastening Courtney's nappy.

'How's my beautiful baby?' she said, slightly slurring her words.

'She's been fine,' I said coolly, glancing up. 'I've fed and changed her and now she's ready for bed.'

Jade tottered over on her high heels to the changing mat and, swaying slightly, leant over and kissed Courtney's cheek. As she did I smelt alcohol and also cigarette smoke. Straightening, she said to me: 'Sorry I'm late. I hope you're not angry with me?'

'Not angry, more disappointed,' I said.

'Why?'

'Because you didn't come back on time and you've been drinking and smoking.'

'No, I haven't,' she said belligerently.

I wasn't going to argue with her, and Courtney was ready to go to bed. I went to pick her up to put her into her cot and as I did Jade took a step forward.

'I'll do that,' she said a little aggressively. 'I want to give her a cuddle. I've missed her.'

She stooped to pick up Courtney and as she did she slipped off one of her high heels and stumbled heavily backwards, crashing into the cot before regaining her balance. I was thankful she hadn't been holding Courtney.

'I think it's best I put Courtney to bed,' I said. 'We don't want you dropping her.'

I picked up Courtney, held her out to Jade so that she could give her a kiss, and then laid her on her side in the cot.

'I don't know why you're angry with me,' Jade said, annoyed. 'I can have a drink with me mates on a Saturday if I want. It's not against the law.'

'It is at your age, and it's also against the law to be intoxicated while in charge of a minor,' I said firmly, tucking the blanket around Courtney. 'Supposing you'd tripped and fallen with Courtney in your arms? You could have done her real harm. It doesn't bear thinking about.'

'You worry too much,' she said dismissively. She hiccupped and then, giving Courtney a little wave, left to go to the toilet.

I kissed Courtney goodnight, raised the side of the cot and then went onto the landing, where I waited for Jade. I heard the toilet flush and then she came out, looking very pale.

'I'm going to bed,' she said. 'I'm tired and I feel sick.'

I stopped myself from telling her that given the amount of alcohol she'd probably drunk it was little wonder she felt sick; I'd save my lecture for the morning, when she would be in a better state of mind to hear it and understand.

'Go to bed and I'll fetch a bucket,' I said. Then I added: 'And leave Courtney in her cot.' For I had the horrific thought that in her inebriated state Jade might try to pick up Courtney for a cuddle. Had I known Jade was going to arrive home drunk, I would have taken the cot out of her room and placed it in my room for the night, so that there was no chance of her picking up Courtney during the night.

As I passed Paula's open bedroom door, where Paula was in bed still waiting for a story, I called: 'I won't be long.'

Downstairs I took the bucket from the cupboard and returned to Jade's room. She was in bed; she'd taken off her shoes and jeans and was lying in her top and underwear.

'I'll have a wash in the morning,' she moaned groggily, as I placed the bucket beside her bed. 'I'm too tired now. I don't feel so good.'

I checked Courtney, who was nearly asleep, and then came out, leaving the door wide open so that I could hear Jade if she got out of bed or was sick. I went into Paula's room. She was sitting up in bed, waiting patiently for her story.

'What's the matter with Jade?' she asked, worried.

'She's not feeling well,' I said, sitting on the bed next to her and resting my head on the headboard. 'It's nothing for you to worry about. Now, where were we up to in this book?' I was reading Paula *The BFG* by Roald Dahl – a chapter or two a night, for although Paula could read, like most children her age she still liked to be read to.

I had read two pages when I heard Jade begin to retch. Paula heard it too. 'Jade's being sick,' she said anxiously. 'She needs you!'

I left Paula in bed and hurried round the landing to Jade's room. She was hanging over the edge of the bed with her head in the bucket, vomiting, while Courtney slept in her cot a couple of feet away. I was about to go over to Jade and hold back her hair when the landline began to ring. Damn! I thought. Worried the ringing might wake Courtney, I left Jade and rushed round the landing to answer the extension in my bedroom.

'Hello,' I said, ready to tell the caller I'd phone back later. But a familiar female voice said: 'It's Jade's mum, Jackie. Is Jade home now?'

'Yes,' I said, surprised to hear her and that she knew Jade had been out. 'About ten minutes ago. She's being sick.'

'Well, I hope that teaches her a lesson,' Jackie said. 'The silly cow! You know the police were involved?'

'The police?' I said, shocked. 'Involved in what? Jade was supposed to have been shopping with her friends in the mall.'

'They were in the mall, not shopping but drinking, and making a lot of noise. Apparently they were there drinking most of the afternoon and then one of the shopkeepers called the police. The police gave the group a warning and told them to move on, but Chelsea – one of Jade's mates with a big mouth – swore at the copper and got herself arrested. Her mother's down at the police station now with her.'

'But Jade wasn't arrested?'

'No, not this time.'

'Thank goodness,' I said. 'I'm sorry. I'll speak to her.'

'No need to apologize,' Jackie said. 'I've been through it with her. You're doing your best but Jade needs to keep away from that lot now she's got the baby. The social services are bound to hear about this and it won't look good for her.'

'No,' I agreed. 'I'll talk to her. I'd better go and make sure she's all right.'

'OK. I'll phone again tomorrow and see how she is. I take it it's all right to use this number? Jade said it was.'

It was then I realized I'd never given Jackie my landline number, only my mobile. 'Yes. Did Jade give you the landline number?'

'Yes. She said you wouldn't mind. She calls me on it when you're collecting Paula from school if she's up to the credit limit on her mobile.'

'I see,' I said. 'Yes, phone tomorrow. I'd better go now and see to Jade.'

I said goodbye and returned to Jade's room, aware the use of the landline was something else I'd have to talk to Jade about the following day. While I had no objection to her making local calls to her mother, I hoped she hadn't been using the landline to call premium-rate numbers or chatting for a long time to her friends on their mobiles, which would be very expensive.

Jade had stopped vomiting and was now lying on her side in bed and groaning quietly, while Courtney slept. I was pleased Courtney wasn't old enough to witness her mother's behaviour.

'I'll get you a glass of water,' I said quietly to Jade.

She groaned: 'Please.'

On my way out I picked up the bucket, emptied it down the toilet, rinsed it out and returned it to beside Jade's bed. I then went downstairs for the glass of water. Adrian was still in the sitting room watching the DVD and oblivious to what had been going on upstairs. I filled a glass with cold water and returning upstairs placed it on Jade's bedside cabinet within her reach. I checked on Courtney again and came out, leaving the door open.

I went into Paula's room and, reassuring her Jade was all right now, I stretched out on the bed again and finished reading the chapter. As I kissed her goodnight she said thoughtfully: 'I suppose when you're a teenager it takes a long time to learn to be a good mummy?'

'Well, yes, I suppose it does,' I said, smiling at her. 'That was very wise. What made you say that?"

'Adrian told me. He said because you were old you knew how to be a good mummy, but Jade was young so she had to learn.' Which I took to be a compliment.

'Jade's doing fine looking after her baby,' I confirmed, giving her another kiss as I tucked her in. 'She just made an error of judgement while she was out with her friends. It won't happen again.'

Which was what I wrote in my log notes later.

Chapter Fifteen
Not an Ogre

That Saturday night I fed and changed Courtney when she woke at midnight and also at 4.00 a.m. I didn't try to wake Jade, which I thought would be nearly impossible, as she was in a very deep sleep from all the alcohol she'd had to drink. When Courtney woke for her 8.00 feed I woke Jade and she stumbled out of bed and downstairs to warm the bottle while I soothed Courtney. It took Jade longer than it normally did, presumably because she was badly hung over. When she returned I waited until she was seated on the bed with Courtney safely in her arms and feeding her before I left to have a shower.

However, fifteen minutes later as I stepped from the shower, before I was dressed, I heard Courtney crying. I thought this was odd, because she never cried during or after feeding, only when she was hungry. Wrapping the bath towel around me, I padded barefoot along the landing to Jade's room. It was obvious the moment I entered why Courtney was crying: Jade had fallen asleep and as her arms had relaxed the bottle had come out of Courtney's mouth. But what was more worrying was that Courtney had slipped to one side and was in danger of rolling off the bed.

'Jade!' I said, shaking her shoulder.

She came to with a start and, looking at Courtney, immediately realized what was wrong. 'Oh!' she said anxiously. 'I must have fallen asleep.'

She quickly resettled Courtney in her arms and returned the teat to her mouth.

'Now you see why you can't have a hangover when you're responsible for a baby,' I said sternly.

Jade didn't reply but I could tell from her expression as she gazed down at Courtney that she appreciated the danger in which she had placed her daughter. I returned to the bathroom, dressed, and then went back to Jade's room. Courtney had finished the bottle and Jade was winding her.

'Once she's in her cot I'm going back to bed for a while,' Jade said.

'All right. And then we need to have a chat.'

Jade came downstairs two hours later, bathed and dressed and looking a bit brighter. I waited until she'd poured herself a glass of juice before I approached her.

'Sit down, please, Jade,' I said, nodding to the chairs at the kitchen table.

She did as I asked and I sat opposite her. In a calm, even voice I warned Jade about her behaviour – drinking, smoking and being in trouble with the police. I didn't have to say much, for now she was sober Jade appreciated how irresponsible her behaviour had been.

She apologized and then said anxiously, 'I hope Rachel doesn't find out.'

'If she does you'll need to tell her what you've told me: that you're sorry and it won't happen again.' I then spoke to Jade about the use of the landline telephone – that I was happy for her to make local calls but not call premium-rate numbers or make long calls to mobiles, as they were very expensive.

'Oh,' she said. 'I didn't know that.' So I guessed there was a big bill on its way.

Just after lunch, when Jade, Courtney and I were in the sitting room and Adrian and Paula were playing in their rooms, Jackie phoned the landline. I answered the call and then passed the handset to Jade. I guessed from Jade's responses that Jackie was giving her a similar lecture to the one I'd given her about her behaviour in the mall. 'Yes, Mum. I know, Mum,' she said. 'No, I won't again. Cathy said. I promise.'

Then later that afternoon when I answered the front door it was to Tyler. Jade hadn't told me he was coming and I didn't think she knew, for she seemed surprised when I showed him into the sitting room. I could tell from his expression that he wasn't pleased about something and I guessed it might be the incident at the mall. News seemed to travel fast among teenagers on the estate where Jade and Tyler lived, for I doubted Jade would have told him.

Tyler's first words were: 'So what's been going on, Jade?'

'I don't know what you mean,' Jade said, feigning innocence.

'You. Drunk at the mall and giving it large to the police when you should be here looking after Courtney.'

I thought they probably needed time alone to talk, so I stepped out of the sitting room, but left the door slightly ajar so that I could keep a check on what was going on and intervene if necessary. I didn't think Tyler had a temper but I hadn't known him for very long, so I couldn't be sure and he was clearly annoyed. Adrian came downstairs, having heard Tyler come in, and I told him to play until Tyler and Jade had finished talking. A few minutes passed as I hovered in the hall and I caught snatches of Tyler's even but firm voice coming from the sitting room and telling Jade she was wrong and the social services were sure to find out. Then I heard Jade's raised voice cry: 'I've said I'm sorry! What more do you want?'

I knocked on the sitting-room door and went in. Jade was on the sofa, close to tears, and Tyler was sitting next to her. He looked pale and anxious, more worried than angry.

'All right?' I said gently to Tyler. 'I think Jade understands now. I've spoken to her and so has her mother. I'm sure it won't happen again.'

Tyler shrugged and glanced sideways at Jade. 'I've told her before that Chelsea is bad news. She's heading for the lock-up and Jade will be there too if she doesn't watch out.'

'Yeah. OK! You said!' Jade said, angry and upset.

'I'm sure she understands,' I said again, and I thought it was time to change the subject and move on. 'Courtney will be wanting her bottle soon and there are none ready,' I said to them both. 'I suggest you two go into the kitchen and make up some bottles. Then I'll make dinner. You'd like to stay for dinner, Tyler?'

'Yeah, thanks. I'll text me mum.'

Adrian reappeared with Paula, and Tyler said hi to them both. Then they all went into the kitchen, where Adrian and Paula watched while Jade and Tyler made up the bottles. The four of them then went upstairs to Jade's room; Courtney had just woken. Adrian and Paula waited by the door while Tyler changed Courtney's nappy, and then they came downstairs and into the sitting room, where Tyler fed Courtney. Adrian and Paula often shadowed Tyler and Jade; being that much older they looked up to them and were easily impressed by things they said or did. When Courtney had finished her bottle Tyler passed her to Jade and suggested to Adrian that they had a game on the PlayStation. Adrian didn't need to be asked twice and plugged in the PlayStation. He and Tyler played while Paula fetched her school project – on water – and showed it to Jade as she cradled Courtney in her arms.

When I called them for dinner Paula went with Jade to put Courtney in her cot and then after we'd eaten the four of us watched a Walt Disney film. Big as they were, Tyler and Jade loved these films and Tyler knew most of the songs, just as we did. When the film had finished Tyler helped Jade bath Courtney, give her a bottle and then settle her in the cot for the night, while I took Paula to bed. So all in all it was a pleasant afternoon and evening, when again I felt we were like one big happy family. Tyler eventually left at 9.00 p.m. and he and Jade were in the hall for some time, kissing and hugging goodnight. I felt very positive: the afternoon and evening had been a success, Jade appreciated the error of her ways, and she and Tyler had displayed very good parenting skills, which is what I later wrote in my log notes.

Rachel telephoned on Monday afternoon and was aware of the incident at the mall, but I quickly dismissed her concerns as an error of judgement Jade wouldn't make again and was very sorry about. I then concentrated on telling her how well she and Tyler were doing parenting their baby.

'Good,' Rachel said. 'I don't want to see another police report mentioning Jade's name.' So I assumed that the police report in respect of Chelsea had also mentioned Jade as one of those present, although she hadn't been arrested.

Rachel then asked to speak to Jade and I passed the phone to her. She went very quiet as Rachel talked to her. I guessed she was giving her a lecture. When Rachel had finished Jade said a subdued: 'Thank you. I will, I promise.' There was then some discussion about Jade's benefits before Jade returned the phone to me so that I could make an appointment for Rachel to visit us.

'Phew!' Jade said, smiling with relief when I'd finished and had hung up. 'Thanks for sticking up for me.'

'I only told the truth.' I said. 'You are doing well.'

Courtney grew and blossomed. She was a darling baby and we all loved her, including my parents, who always made a big fuss of her and gave her a present each time they saw her. We had also grown close to Jade and Tyler, whom we viewed as our extended family, as I believe they did us. Jade and Tyler were relaxed at home with us and sometimes asked for my opinion as one would a parent. They both played with Adrian and Paula as siblings and I was hoping that we'd all go on holiday together in the summer, although I hadn't mentioned this yet.

For the first month of Courtney's life I'd gone with Jade to the clinic each week to have Courtney weighed, measured and checked over, and then Jade had said she could manage alone. While I was happy to keep going with Jade, I recognized that she needed to take more and more responsibility for Courtney in preparation for when she was hopefully living independently and would have to do all these things herself.

Jade had a scheduled postnatal check-up at the hospital when Courtney was six weeks old and I was expecting to take them in the car, but Jade said she wanted her mother to go, which was understandable. I therefore offered to take Jade and Courtney in the car and collect Jackie on the way, but Jade said she could manage alone and was quick to point out that she needed to get used to the buses with Courtney and the pushchair, as she would be using them all the time eventually – after they left me.

Her appointment was at 11.00 a.m. and before Jade left I made sure she had a bottle of formula for the twelve o'clock feed, plus an extra bottle just in case, clean nappies, nappy bags, wipes, etc., all of which Jade put into the 'baby bag'. Satisfied that they had everything they needed and telling Jade to phone me if the bus didn't arrive, in which case I would give her a lift in the car, I waved them off at the door. Then I spent an anxious couple of hours hoping that every-thing was going to plan, as it was Jade's first outing on the bus with Courtney.

I was expecting them home by 1.00 p.m. and I had some lunch ready. When they hadn't returned by 2.00 I phoned Jade's mobile.

'Is everything all right?' I asked her.

'Yeah, sure. I've had me check-up and I've gone to me mum's. Don't worry. I'll be back later. Courtney's had a bottle and I've got the spare.'

'OK, love, enjoy yourself. And say hi to your mum from me.'

'I will,' Jade said.

I ate my lunch and threw Jade's away, did some housework and then collected Paula from school. I hoped Jade would return soon, as the afternoon was chilly for a young baby to be out. I then spent another anxious couple of hours clock-watching and hoping Jackie would have the good sense to tell Jade she needed to go before too long.

Jade finally returned a little after 6.00 p.m. with Courtney crying from hunger. I heard her cries before Jade opened the front door.

'I lost the other bottle,' Jade said, parking the pushchair in the hall and flying upstairs to the toilet.

I lifted Courtney out of the pushchair and carried her through to the kitchen, where I quickly warmed a bottle. Her little hands felt cold and I wondered why she wasn't wearing her mittens.

'You should have come home sooner,' I said to Jade as she reappeared. 'She's starving, poor little mite.'

'I know. She cried all the way on the bus. I lost the bottle and her mittens. I think I left them at the hospital.'

Accidents happen and there was no point in going on at Jade. I passed Courtney and the bottle to Jade, and she carried her into the sitting room, where she sat on the sofa and fed her. About twenty minutes later – when Jade was upstairs changing Courtney – the landline rang and it was Jackie.

'Is Jade home now?' she asked.

'Yes, about twenty minutes ago.'

'That's a relief. When she said she was going to the mall I was worried.'

'The mall?' I queried. 'What time did she go there?'

'About eleven thirty, I guess. Straight after we'd seen the doctor.'

My heart sank. 'So Jade didn't spend all day with you?' I asked quietly.

'No. Why? Is that what she told you?'

'Yes.'

Jackie gave a small laugh. 'I expect she thought you wouldn't approve of her going to the mall after the last time. Oh well, no harm done.'

'No,' I agreed. 'No harm done apart from Courtney being cold and hungry.'

Later when Jade and I were alone I asked her: 'Why didn't you tell me you'd been to the mall?' I was hurt that Jade had lied to me.

She shrugged. 'I thought you wouldn't let me go in case I got into trouble again.'

'And did you?'

'No.'

'Well, then.' I paused and looked at Jade, an adult in some respects but in many others still a child. 'Jade, love,' I said, 'I'm not an ogre. You know right from wrong. As long as you behave yourself, of course you can go shopping in the mall. Did you buy anything nice?'

'Nah. I was just window shopping.'

'Well, next time I hope you will feel you can tell me.'

'Yeah. I will.'

Courtney began her vaccination programme at two months of age. I went with Jade to the clinic for the first vaccination and then Jade took Courtney by herself for the follow-up appointments – at three and four months. Also at three months old we began to give Courtney a bottle at 11.00 p.m. and over the next week she started going through the night to 5.00 a.m. without waking. Then when Courtney was four months old the health visitor said we could introduce a little solid food into her diet, to go with the bottles of milk. I bought some baby rice and showed Jade how to make it up and feed Courtney with a spoon, which was lovely to watch. Now Courtney was on some solid food she began sleeping until 6.00 a.m., which was fantastic. Jade usually gave her the late-night bottle before she went to bed and I gave her the early-morning one, although sometimes if Jade was very tired and asleep early then I fed Courtney both times.

Rachel and Jill visited us regularly and Rachel made some unscheduled visits, which are known as 'unannounced visits'. This is normal social work practice when a client is being assessed, as Jade was. As usual I left Rachel alone with Jade and Courtney for some of the time and when Rachel had finished talking to and observing Jade, she asked me some questions in respect of Courtney's progress and Jade's (and Tyler's) parenting. I was always very positive, because as far as I was concerned they were doing well. Courtney was in a good routine of feeding and sleeping, and meeting the expected developmental milestones. Jade and Tyler were loving towards Courtney and learning how to be parents.

With exams approaching we saw less of Tyler – two evenings a week instead of nearly every night, which arrangement he said would continue until he'd sat his GCSE examinations in May and June. I respected him for this and persuaded Jade not to keep phoning him in the evenings when he was studying. She still felt it was unfair that she had more responsibility for Courtney than he did, although I think she appreciated that what Tyler was trying to achieve – examination passes so that he could find a job – would benefit them all. Jade took Courtney on the bus once or twice a week to see her mother and she also went out with her friends once a week – usually on a Friday, while I babysat Courtney. There was no repetition of Jade arriving home drunk, so as far as I was aware everything was fine.

It was therefore a huge shock when one Tuesday afternoon Jade arrived home in the back of a police car.

Chapter Sixteen

A Police Matter

It was a mild spring afternoon at the end of May; the air was warm and the days were growing longer. Adrian and Paula were in the garden on their bikes, making the most of the good weather. It had been Paula's birthday the month before and I'd given her a bike as a present, and she wanted to ride on it at every opportunity. Courtney was four and a half months old and Jade had taken her to see her mother for the day. I was expecting them home for dinner at about 6.00 p.m., which was the time they normally returned after visiting Jackie. It was five o'clock and I was in the kitchen beginning the preparations for dinner when I heard the front doorbell ring. I stopped what I was doing, wiped my hands on the towel and went to answer it. A policewoman in uniform stood on the doorstep and immediately my pulse soared with anxiety.

'Are you Cathy Glass?' she asked.

'Yes. What's the matter?'

'I understand Jade and Courtney live here?'

'That's right. I'm their foster carer. Whatever is it?' And for a moment I thought there'd been a dreadful accident and they were in hospital or worse, until the policewoman said:

'They're safe. They're in the car.'

I looked past her to the police car parked by the kerb outside my house, where I could make out a male police officer in the driver's seat and Jade and Courtney in the rear.

'I think it's best if we all come inside and I'll explain,' the WPC said.

I nodded, not knowing what to think. I stood by the front door and waited as the policewoman returned to the police car and opened the rear door. My mouth went dry and my heart began beating faster as I watched Jade step from the car and onto the pavement. Whatever the reason for the police bringing them home in a police car, I was sure it wasn't good. Jade reached into the back of the car and lifted Courtney out in the carry-car seat. The policewoman closed the rear door as the male officer went to the boot and took out the collapsible base for the car seat, which converted it into a pushchair.

Jade didn't look at me but kept her head down, her face expressionless, as she carried Courtney in the car seat up the path and past me into the hall. She threw her denim jacket over the hall stand, and then continued without speaking down the hall and into the sitting room. The policewoman came in and then the male officer, carrying the frame of the pushchair.

'Thank you,' I said, taking it from him and standing it in the hall.

I led the way into the sitting room, where Jade was sitting on the sofa with Courtney in the carry-car seat on the floor beside her. Courtney was yawning and gradually waking from being asleep in the car. Adrian and Paula were still in the garden and I closed the French windows in the hope that they wouldn't have to become involved in whatever I was about to.

'Please sit down,' I said to the police officers.

The policewoman sat on the sofa next to Jade while the male police officer and I took the armchairs.

'I'm WPC Wendy Banes and this is my colleague PC Clive Snowy,' the policewoman said, introducing them.

I nodded, and looked at her and waited, my gaze flickering to Jade and back.

There was a pause; then Wendy said to Jade: 'Do you want to tell your foster carer what happened or shall we?'

My eyes shifted to Jade, who was still staring at the floor. She shrugged and then in a low, almost inaudible voice said: 'You tell her.'

A cold chill ran down my spine as I braced myself for what I was about to hear. Speaking in an even, almost matter-of-fact voice, Wendy said: 'I'm afraid Jade was involved in a shoplifting incident this afternoon at the mall.'

'Oh, Jade!' I blurted. 'You were supposed to be at your mother's!'

Jade didn't look up or say anything, so Wendy continued: 'Jade and another girl were stopped by the store's security guard on suspicion of shoplifting when they tried to leave the store. They were taken to the manager's office where a number of items they hadn't paid for were found in their possession. Some had the security tags cut off while others were still intact. The store has a policy of prosecuting all offenders, so Jade and the other girl will be charged.'

'Jade! Whatever have you done?' I said, for immediately I could see the consequences of her actions.

Wendy looked at Jade, who was still staring at the floor, from shame or just trying to pretend this wasn't happening – I didn't know. Returning her gaze to me, Wendy continued: 'The security guard has also stated that he had seen Jade and her friend in the store before today shoplifting. He has given us a list of the items she's accused of stealing, so we'll need to search Jade's room.'

I stared at Wendy, shocked and horrified. Then Jade said antagonistically, 'You'll need a search warrant first.'

'We won't need a search warrant if we have Cathy's permission,' PC Clive Snowy said to Jade, clearly irritated by her manner. Then to me he said: 'Jade's social worker has been informed of what's happening.'

I nodded and looked at Jade, who still couldn't meet my gaze and had guilt written all over her face. I felt completely out of my depth. How much I would have appreciated a husband or partner by my side to help and support me now. I could have phoned Jill but I doubted she would be free at such short notice, and even if she was, Homefinders' office was twenty minutes away and I could hardly keep the police officers waiting. I looked from the WPC to her colleague and then down the garden to where Adrian and Paula were playing, blissfully unaware of what was unfolding inside.

'Jade,' I said quietly, 'I don't have any objection to the police searching your room, do you?' For there seemed nothing to be gained by prolonging the agony and insisting on a warrant; indeed it seemed to compound Jade's guilt.

Jade didn't reply, so looking at the police officers I said: 'You have my permission to search her room.'

'I'm afraid we'll have to search the whole house,' Wendy said awkwardly, 'in case she's hidden stolen goods anywhere else.'

My stomach churned and I felt like a common thief. I looked down the garden again to where Adrian and Paula were cycling. Just stay in the garden, I silently pleaded.

'There's no need,' Jade said, suddenly jumping up from the sofa. 'Everything you want is in my room. You don't need to search Cathy's house.'

Jade stormed out of the sitting room and down the hall. PC Clive Snowy followed her while Wendy said to me: 'Would you come too, please? As Jade is a minor we need you present.'

I nodded. I felt I was playing a part in some dreadful television crime drama; it just didn't seem real. I stood and then reached down and lifted Courtney out of her seat. She was wide awake – not crying for food but smiling and looking around her, as she often did now. My eyes filled with tears as I drew her to me and held her close, I couldn't help it. So innocent and beautiful, and mercifully unaware of what her mother had been doing. I kissed her forehead.

'She's a cute baby,' Wendy said, stroking the back of Courtney's hand. 'She was so good at the store. They were in the manager's office for ages. Then she fell asleep in the car on the way here.'

'What time did all this happen?' I asked, as we crossed the sitting room to the door.

'Jade and her friend were apprehended shortly after two o'clock, although the security guard said they'd been in and out of the store all morning.'

I felt gutted as I realized Jade hadn't been to her mother's at all but had gone straight from me to the mall.

'Do you know Jade's friend, Chelsea?' Wendy asked as we began up the stairs.

'I haven't met her but I've heard her spoken of. I understand she's been in trouble before.'

Wendy didn't comment – I suppose confidentiality forbade it – but she did say: 'As her foster carer you were presumably told that Jade had been warned about her behaviour by the police in the past?'

'Yes, but I thought all that was behind her,' I said sadly. 'She has been doing quite well since she had the baby.'

At the top of the stairs we continued round the landing to Jade's room. I waited at her bedroom door with Courtney in my arms while Wendy went inside. There wasn't enough space for the four of us with the cot up, but also I really didn't want to see Jade's disgrace. From where I stood I could hear her taking out various bags and items from the drawers and wardrobe – presumably the stolen goods the police were looking for.

Eventually after another drawer had opened and closed I heard Jade say: 'That's everything.'

Then I heard PC Clive Snowy ask: 'Are you sure?'

'Yes,' Jade replied. And I hoped she was telling the truth.

The police officers came out carrying about six store bags. Jade followed, head down and in silence. I began towards the top of the stairs to go down, but Wendy called: 'Could you wait there a minute, please, Cathy, while we quickly check the other rooms up here?'

'I've given you everything,' Jade said rudely.

'Good. But we still have to take a look,' Clive Snowy said.

I supposed, as the owner of the house, they needed me present and I stayed where I was on the landing near the top of the stairs while the officers went in and out of each of the rooms, with enough time just to give each room a cursory glance. Possibly they didn't make a thorough search because Jade had cooperated and given them the stolen items.

'That's fine. Thank you,' Clive Snowy said, coming out of the last room – Adrian's bedroom. I closed his bedroom door and we went downstairs.

I waited in the hall with Courtney in my arms while the officers checked the front room, and then we went through to the kitchen and annexe. Jade had returned to the sitting room and Courtney began agitating to be with her. Leaving the officers in the kitchen I went into the sitting room, where Jade was sitting on the sofa.

'When was she last fed?' I asked Jade, as I passed Courtney to her.

'About two o'clock,' she said.

It was now nearly six o'clock. 'She'll need some dinner and a bottle soon,' I said.

'Shall I get it now?' Jade asked.

'No, wait until the officers have finished in the kitchen. They won't be long.'

A minute later the officers came into the sitting room. At the same time Adrian and Paula ran up the garden and pressed their faces against the French windows. I opened one of the doors and they stared in and past me to the officers, their faces a mixture of shock and awe.

'Everything is OK,' I reassured them. 'There is nothing for you to worry about, but could you play in the garden for a while longer, please.'

'Hello,' Wendy and Clive said with a smile.

Adrian said hi while Paula stared at the officers and then at Jade. Adrian gave her a nudge and they turned and ran down the garden. What I'd tell them later I'd no idea.

'Nice kids,' Clive Snowy said.

'Thank you.'

'We're all done here,' Clive said to me. 'So we'll be off.' Then to Jade: 'We'll need to take a statement from you. We'll be in touch with your social worker to arrange an appointment.'

Before we left the sitting room Wendy said to Jade: 'You've got a nice home here and a lovely baby. Don't throw it all away, Jade. You've hurt Cathy, and your mother will be furious when she finds out what's happened. As if she didn't have enough to worry about already.'

Jade didn't say anything but she looked close to tears.

'Goodbye, then,' Wendy said to Jade as we left the sitting room.

I went with the officers down the hall to see them out.

'Thank you for your cooperation,' Clive Snowy said, opening the front door. 'We'll speak to Jade's social worker and then make arrangements to take Jade's statement.'

'She'll definitely be prosecuted, then?' I asked, clutching at a tiny hope that she might not.

'Yes, I'm afraid so. It's the store's policy.'

'I dread to think what effect this will have on her parenting assessment,' I said, voicing my worst fears. 'And whether she'll be able to keep her baby.'

'Perhaps they'll overlook it this once,' Wendy offered.

'Perhaps,' I said, but I doubted it.

The officers thanked me again for my cooperation, said goodbye and left. I closed the door and the tears I'd been holding back now fell. I hurried into the kitchen, pulled a tissue from the box and wiped my eyes. Just in time, for seconds later the back door burst open and Adrian and Paula appeared.

'Have those policemen gone?' Adrian asked excitedly.

'Yes. I'll explain later,' I said. 'You go and play and I'll call you when dinner is ready.' I needed to clear my thoughts before I talked to them.

They turned and ran off down the garden just as Jade appeared in the kitchen. 'Shall I make Courtney's tea now?' she asked, subdued.

'Yes. But don't leave her in the sitting room unattended. I've told you about that before. Bring the bouncing cradle in here.' I was sharp with her but my nerves were on edge.

Jade fetched Courtney while I surveyed the dinner I'd been preparing before the police officers had arrived. Mechanically, I picked up the peeler and continued peeling the potatoes, more as a displacement for my anxiety than from any real desire to eat. I wasn't hungry but Adrian and Paula would be. Jade settled Courtney in the bouncing cradle at the far end of the kitchen, where we usually put her so that we could keep an eye on her but she was away from the dangers of cooking. In silence Jade began preparing Courtney's baby food while I continued making our dinner. We worked around each other, my thoughts racing as I tried to think what to say to Jade.

I'd just put the casserole in the oven when the phone rang. I answered the call in the kitchen but when I heard it was Jill, I said: 'Hold on a moment, I'm going into the sitting room.'

I took the handset through to the sitting room and pushed the door to before I spoke. 'Have you heard what's happened to Jade?' I asked, guessing that was the reason for her phoning after office hours.

'Yes. Rachel's just telephoned me. Is Jade home with you now?'

'Yes. The police brought her home and they've taken away bags of things she's stolen. Why, Jill? Why did she do it? I give her her allowance each week, and I buy whatever she and Courtney need. Jade also has her benefit money now. She shouldn't have had to steal!'

'I know, Cathy, I know. She's acted very irresponsibly. She knew what was at stake. Look, I need to come and see you as soon as possible. What time will you be back from school in the morning?'

'Nine fifteen.'

'I'll be there then. Where's Jade now?'

'In the kitchen, feeding Courtney.'

'Make sure she stays in tonight.'

'I will.' Then I steeled myself to ask the question I probably didn't want to hear the answer to. 'Jill, how will this affect Jade's parenting assessment? The police officer thought it might be overlooked as it's her first prosecution.'

Jill went quiet before she said, 'I don't know. Rachel is calling an emergency case conference for the professionals as soon as possible. She has other concerns as well.'

'Has she? What concerns? Rachel hasn't said anything to me.'

'I'll explain when I see you tomorrow. But don't blame yourself, Cathy. You've done your best.' Which held an unsettling ring of finality, as though Jade's fate had been sealed.

Chapter Seventeen

Shaken to the core

The following morning Jill was sitting in her car outside my house when I returned home from taking Paula to school. She was early. As soon as she saw me she got out and said what seemed to me a stiff and reserved, 'Good morning, Cathy.'

'Good morning,' I said.

We went up the garden path and I opened the front door. 'Would you like a coffee?' I asked in the hall.

'Yes, please. And I should like to look at your log notes while you're making coffee.'

I was slightly taken aback by both the formality of Jill's request and the fact that she wanted to see my notes straightaway. Usually she read and then signed them at the end of her visit – after I'd updated her on the child I was fostering and we'd discussed any other business in relation to the child. But I fetched the folder as she'd asked and handed it to her. Then I went into the kitchen to make coffee while she went into the sitting room.

In the kitchen I could hear Jade moving around above me, as her room was directly overhead, and I was expecting her to come downstairs at any moment. I hadn't had a chance to talk to her the evening before, as she'd gone straight to bed after dinner, and this morning I'd only had time to wake her and tell her Jill was coming before I'd left to take Paula to school.

When Jade hadn't come down by the time I'd finished making the coffee I took the mugs into the sitting room, where Jill was still poring over my notes, and then went up to Jade's room and knocked on her bedroom door.

'What is it?' she asked a little grumpily.

'Are you ready? Jill's here.'

'Courtney is but I'm not. Can you take her?'

The door opened and Jade, still in her nightwear and looking tired and drawn, passed Courtney to me. Courtney grinned as usual and snuggled against me.

'I didn't sleep,' Jade said, rubbing her forehead.

'I'm not surprised. Neither did I. Come down as soon as you're ready. I'm sure Jill will have some suggestions that will help us.' Although Jade had acted stupidly I knew she loved Courtney and I hoped that this would count so much in her favour that her behaviour in the mall and the likely prosecution could be worked through.

Jade nodded and closed her door.

With Courtney chuckling and babbling in my arms, I went downstairs and into the sitting room, where Jill was still reading my log notes. I sat on the sofa and placed Courtney in her bouncing cradle so that she could see us. At eighteen weeks of age she was awake and playful for most of the morning and she continued babbling and chuckling as Jill turned the pages of my log notes and absently sipped her coffee. A couple of times – when Courtney made an especially loud noise – Jill glanced up and smiled. But her smile, usually full of warmth and enthusiasm, now seemed perfunctory and almost indifferent, as though her thoughts were a long way from darling little Courtney.

When Jill had been reading my notes for about fifteen minutes – scanning them from start to finish – and we'd both finished our coffee, she flipped through the last couple of pages and then closed the folder and placed it on the coffee table.

'Where's Jade now?' she asked sombrely.

'Getting ready. She'll be down soon.'

Jill paused. 'You do a lot for the baby, don't you?' she said thoughtfully, looking at Courtney.

'Well, yes, I help Jade. I'm happy to.'

Jill held my gaze. 'Cathy, there's no easy way to say this but it's not looking good for Jade. I don't think the assessment will come out in her favour. I don't think she will be allowed to keep her baby.'

I felt as though an ice spear had just pierced my heart. 'Why not?' I gasped. 'Jade made one silly mistake and she's sorry. It won't happen again. Surely that's not sufficient to take Courtney away?' I looked at Courtney and a lump rose in my throat.

Jill chose her words carefully before she spoke. 'Stealing from the mall isn't the only reason,' she said. 'Rachel has other concerns, about Jade's ability to parent her baby, some of which are confirmed by your log notes.'

'What? I haven't written anything detrimental about Jade looking after Courtney. Far from it. I've praised the way she looks after her.'

'I know,' Jill said with a small sad smile. 'I can see how positive you've tried to be, but I don't think you realize just how much parenting of Courtney you're doing. You've shown Jade what to do many, many times but you're still having to do it.

You're doing far too much because Jade hasn't taken responsibility. She's not meeting Courtney's needs.'

I felt hot and flustered. I went to interrupt but Jill continued. 'Courtney would never be fed at night if you didn't wake Jade and tell her to warm the bottle. In fact there would never be any bottles sterilized and made up ready if you didn't repeatedly remind Jade to do it or do it yourself. And how many times have you looked after Courtney in the evening and then put her to bed because Jade said she was too tired? Or given Courtney her late-night and early-morning bottle because Jade couldn't or wouldn't be woken? To be honest, Cathy, you, and Tyler when he's here, do more for Courtney than Jade ever does. At the professionals meeting Rachel and the others present from children's services will have to ask themselves if Jade could parent Courtney alone, and to be honest I don't think she could and neither does Rachel.'

Shaken to the core, I stared at Jill. My mouth was dry and my stomach churned. Apart from the shock of what Jill had told me, I felt responsible; clearly I'd been doing too much for Courtney when Jade should have been doing it. It was my fault.

'I'll stop doing what I do and make Jade do it,' I said, desperation creeping into my voice. 'She's only been here a few months. There's still plenty of time for Jade to take more responsibility. I'll make sure she does.'

'It's not your fault,' Jill said quickly. 'A mother-and-baby assessment placement – which is what this has become – usually only lasts for twelve weeks. That is normally considered sufficient time for an assessment to be made of whether a parent can meet the needs of their child or baby. Courtney is eighteen weeks old now. Rachel has already extended the placement because of Jade's age to give her more time. It can't continue indefinitely. And there are other issues as well.'

'Like what?' I asked, my voice rising and shaking slightly.

'I take it you didn't know Courtney missed her last vaccination?'

'What?' I stared at Jill, horrified. 'She didn't?'

Jill nodded.

'I went with Jade to the clinic for Courtney's first vaccination, but then Jade said she was all right to go alone for the second and third. She told me she'd been.'

'It'll be recorded in the red book. Where's that?'

'Jade has it.'

'Have you seen it?'

'Not since Jade started going to the clinic alone, no.'

'Courtney's second vaccination was two weeks late, and she hasn't had the third one yet,' Jill said. 'And Cathy, all those times Jade told you she was spending the day at her mother's, she wasn't. The last time Jackie saw Jade was over a month ago and then it was only for ten minutes to borrow some money, although Jade did text her last week.'

I was shocked and numb. I felt hurt that Jade had lied to me and foolish for being taken in.

'So where has Jade been going when she was supposed to be at her mother's?' I asked quietly after a moment.

'Various places,' Jill said. 'The mall, friends' houses, and she's been seen hanging around the leisure centre. A couple of times she went to the cinema with Chelsea. She left Courtney in the care of Chelsea's younger sister, who is eleven years of age.'

I gasped in dismay. 'Oh no, eleven? Anything could have happened.'

'Exactly. Fortunately Courtney came to no harm, but it was highly irresponsible of Jade to leave her baby with such a young child. Sadly, it's another indication that Jade can't put the needs and safety of her baby before her own wishes. Rachel wants to see Jade as soon as possible and she's asked if she can come here tomorrow at twelve o'clock. Is that all right with you?'

I nodded absently. 'I'll be here,' I said.

'And make sure Jade is here too, please. Rachel will go through all her concerns with Jade then, but I thought I should tell you first so it didn't come as such a shock.'

'Thank you,' I said numbly. I didn't know what to say. 'Jade loves Courtney but I can see that after all this ...' My words fell away. 'Shall I prepare Jade for what Rachel is going to tell her?'

'No, leave it to Rachel. There are other issues that Rachel will talk to Jade about – mainly about money. I haven't got the details but Rachel will explain it to Jade tomorrow.'

I nodded again, overwhelmed by the enormity of everything I'd heard and deeply saddened by Jade's behaviour.

Jill stayed a while longer and tried to reassure me that I'd done my best with Jade, while we waited for her to come down. Without any realistic hope of Jade being allowed to keep Courtney, Jill's words sounded hollow and were of no comfort to me. Jill asked if I wanted her to be present when Rachel visited tomorrow, but it would have meant her cancelling an important meeting so I said there was no need and I'd manage, for I knew how busy Jill was. She said she'd phone me tomorrow afternoon to find out how Rachel's visit had gone and that she'd also speak to Rachel.

Five minutes later Jill said she'd have to go. Jade still hadn't come downstairs so, leaving Jill in charge of Courtney, I went up to Jade's room. I was disappointed Jade hadn't come down as she was supposed to and I knew Jill would see this as another indication of Jade's unreliability.

'Jill's going soon,' I said, knocking on Jade's door. 'Come down, please, and at least say hello.'

'Do I have to?' Jade moaned from inside.

'Yes, please.' I opened the door so that I could see into the room. Jade was dressed and sitting on her bed, looking glum. 'Now, please,' I said.

With a sigh she reluctantly hauled herself off the bed and then came with me downstairs and into the sitting room, where Jill was cuddling Courtney. Jill looked up and smiled at Jade as we entered. 'How are you?' she asked her kindly.

Jade shrugged, but Courtney, seeing her mother, immediately reached out her arms and wanted to be held by her. Jill passed her up to Jade. I was pleased Jill had seen this, for it reinforced what I'd been saying about the strong bond that existed between Jade and her baby.

'I'm going to get a drink,' Jade said, holding Courtney and eager to be away.

'All right,' Jill said. 'Take care. I'll see you soon. Rachel's coming tomorrow.'

Jade didn't say anything but disappeared into the kitchen. 'It's OK,' Jill said to me. 'I've seen her. That's enough for now for my records. She's got a lot on her mind.'

I saw Jill to the front door and before she left she called goodbye to Jade, but Jade didn't answer. 'I know it's difficult,' Jill said compassionately to me. 'But you really have done your best and I know Rachel thinks so too.'

I shrugged despondently.

'I'll phone tomorrow,' Jill said and, giving my arm a reassuring pat, left.

As soon as I closed the front door Jade came out of the kitchen carrying Courtney. 'She needs changing,' she said, going past me and upstairs.

I went into the sitting room, picked up the empty coffee mugs and took them through to the kitchen, where I dumped them in the sink. The front doorbell rang and I thought it must be Jill, having forgotten something. I went down the hall and opened the front door. It wasn't Jill but Tyler, and I could see he was annoyed.

'I don't believe her!' he thundered, coming into the hall. 'What the fuck does she think she's playing at?'

'Tyler –' I began.

'She can screw up her life if she wants, but she's not screwing up my baby's.' So I guessed he'd been told about Jade's arrest.

'Calm down,' I said, closing the front door. He was breathing fast and his breath sounded heavy and laboured. 'Are you all right?'

He shook his head. 'Nah. I get asthma when I'm upset.'

'Come through to the kitchen and sit down and I'll pour you a cold drink.'

He followed me down the hall and into the kitchen, where I ran a glass of cold water. I could see he was finding breathing difficult and I knew from other children with asthma I'd fostered that he needed to calm down to avoid a full asthma attack.

'Do you have an asthma pump with you?' I asked, guiding him to a chair at the kitchen table, where I placed the glass of water.

'I left it at home,' he said, his breath rasping. 'I don't need it often. I was fine until I got on the bus.'

'All right, don't worry,' I said in a calm, even voice, taking control. 'I want you to sit quietly, relax and breathe slowly. It often helps if you lean forward slightly and rest your elbows on the table.' He did as I suggested and I placed a reassuring hand on his shoulder. I knew from experience and training that much of managing asthma was staying calm and reassuring the sufferer. 'Now breathe in and out very slowly,' I said, my voice slowing to the breathing pace I wanted. 'Very slowly: in and out. In and out.' Tyler did as I said and gradually over the next few minutes his breathing grew easier and eventually lost its rasp as the attack passed.

'Well done,' I said as he sat back and reached for the glass of water. 'Feeling better?'

He nodded, but as soon as he spoke he became anxious again. 'I can't believe Jade would do something so daft!' he said, his brow furrowing. 'The police are involved, thanks to her!'

'I know,' I said. 'But try not to upset yourself. It won't help. Jade knows she's done wrong. She's hardly said a word since she came home yesterday.'

'Where is she now?' he asked, his breath catching slightly. 'I've been phoning and texting all morning but she's not answering.'

'She's upstairs, changing Courtney,' I said. 'Jill, my support social worker, has just left, and Rachel is coming to talk to us tomorrow.'

Tyler took a slow breath to calm himself before he spoke again. 'Rachel phoned me yesterday evening and told me what had happened. She's coming to see me tomorrow after school.'

It was then I realized that Tyler should have been in school. 'Didn't you go to school today?' I asked.

'Nah. I couldn't concentrate.'

'Tyler,' I said gently, sitting on the chair next to him, 'I know how worried you must be, we all are, but try not to let this interfere with your studies. You've got important exams starting in a week. You've been working so hard. It would be a shame to throw it all away.'

'It all seems pointless now,' he said, rubbing his forehead. 'I was only doing the studying for Jade and Courtney, so I could get a job and we could all be together.' He paused and looked at me, pain in his eyes. I felt so sorry for him. 'Cathy,' he said, 'you've fostered lots of kids. Do you think Jade and me will be allowed to keep Courtney?'

I love fostering but sometimes it breaks my heart. I looked at Tyler and saw the desperation in his face. 'I honestly don't know, love,' I said. 'I've fostered many children but never a mother and baby before. We'll have to wait and see what Rachel says tomorrow.'

Tyler gave a small nod. 'Can I see Jade and Courtney now, please?'

'Yes, of course. You go in the sitting room and I'll bring them down.' I thought it was better that they were downstairs rather than Tyler going up to Jade's room, as I could keep an eye on them and intervene if necessary.

Tyler drank the last of the water and went through to the sitting room while I went upstairs to fetch Jade. I was anxious. I knew this was going to be a difficult and upsetting meeting for them both but nothing could have prepared me for just how upsetting.

Chapter Eighteen

Too Late

'Tyler's here,' I said, knocking on Jade's bedroom door and going in. She had finished changing Courtney and was standing in the middle of the room, holding her.

'I know, I heard,' Jade said in a flat voice, looking at Courtney. 'Is he angry with me?'

'More upset than angry, I think. You need to come and talk to him.'

Jade didn't make any move to come with me, so I reached out and lightly touched her arm. 'Come on, love,' I said. 'I'll be in the room with you. Tyler is your baby's father. You owe him something.'

I touched her arm again and then with a sad and apprehensive expression she came with me out of the room. Jade was silent going downstairs; so too was Courtney, as if she sensed the upset going on around her. Jade followed me into the sitting room, where Tyler was sitting on the sofa, looking sad and deep in thought. He glanced up as Jade entered but before either of them spoke Jade burst into tears. I was about to go to her and comfort her but Tyler stood and, crossing the room, enfolded Jade and Courtney in his arms.

'Oh, Jade, what have you done?' he said quietly, not demanding but upset. 'My mum says they're sure to take

Courtney off us now.' I saw his face crumple and then he too began to cry – silent tears that seemed even worse than Jade's loud emotional sobs.

I felt uncomfortable standing there watching their grief and unable to offer any consolation, but I didn't want to leave them alone and they needed to express their emotion. After a minute or so I saw Courtney grow anxious because of her parents' crying and that she was being held awkwardly between them.

I stepped forwards. 'Shall I take Courtney, love?' I said to Jade.

Pulling slightly away from Tyler and without speaking, she turned and, with a tear-stained face, passed Courtney to me. I sat in the chair with Courtney on my lap while Tyler led Jade to the sofa, where he put his arm around her and drew her close. She rested her head on his shoulder and they were both crying. Courtney looked at them from where she sat on my lap, her little face, usually so happy, now serious and concerned. After some moments Tyler reached forward and, taking a handful of tissues from the box on the coffee table, wiped his eyes and then passed some to Jade. With her head still resting on his shoulder she wiped her eyes and gave a little sniff.

'Maybe it's not as bad as Mum thinks,' Tyler said eventually, searching for hope. 'Maybe she's overreacted and has got it wrong.'

'No, she's right,' Jade said quietly. 'The last time Rachel was here she told me I was doing things wrong. She said I had to put them right, but I didn't listen to her. Now I've made it worse. I'm sorry, Ty. I'm so sorry. It's all my fault.'

Rachel must have issued her warnings when she and Jade had been alone together. I thought it would have been useful if Rachel (or Jade) had mentioned the concerns to me, as I might have been able to help before it was too late. Although of course from what Jill had told me it appeared I'd done too much helping already.

'The social services are sure to take her,' Jade now said, her sobs growing. 'They'll take my baby and have her adopted. Then she'll have a new mummy and daddy and we'll never see her again.'

Tyler's face creased with pain. It was pitiful to watch. 'We don't know that for certain,' he said, still grasping at any hope.

'I do,' Jade said decisively. 'Rachel said if things didn't improve adoption would be the only alternative. And they haven't improved. I've made them worse.'

I didn't know if Tyler was aware of all Rachel's concerns but she would tell him what he needed to know when she saw him the following evening. As they clung to each other in sorrow they were like two small children in some dreadful danger, waiting for a parent to come and rescue them. Only of course they were the parents now and no one was going to appear to save them.

After some moments Jade lifted her head from Tyler's shoulder and looked at him. 'Perhaps we could run away together?' she said, her voice rising slightly at the possibility.

'Yeah,' Tyler agreed, also brightening a little. 'We could go abroad. We could stowaway on a big liner and get off wherever it stopped. I could find work and the three of us could live together happily.'

'Yes. Let's do it,' Jade said. 'When shall we go? Which country?'

My heart ached for them, and while it was unlikely their plans would ever reach fruition I knew that some parents did flee abroad with their children when they were faced with them being taken into care. I thought it was wise to stop this plan before it went any further.

'You would get caught very quickly,' I said seriously. 'The social services would alert the police and Interpol and you'd be arrested and brought back. Then you'd definitely lose Courtney for good. She'd be in care and you two would be in prison.'

Their faces fell but Jade hadn't given up the idea of running away. 'What if we stayed in this country?' she suggested. 'We could live in a squat. We wouldn't need much money. Ty could get a job and I'd look after Courtney. They wouldn't find us.'

It was sad and pathetic, but I was aware that desperate parents made desperate decisions so I dealt with her suggestions seriously. 'And what sort of life would that be for Courtney?' I asked. 'Living in a squat? Filthy dirty with rats, and no running water, heating or lighting. I thought you wanted the best for your baby. Isn't that why Tyler's been studying?'

Jade shrugged. 'But at least we'd have her with us,' she said, still not completely giving up the idea.

However, I could see Tyler was starting to realize the impracticality of the plan. They were both silent for some time, holding each other and occasionally glancing over at Courtney, who was on my lap and gurgling quietly. Then Tyler took his arm from Jade's shoulder and, leaning forward slightly, looked at me in earnest.

'Cathy, I have an idea,' he said, his expression lightening. 'If we're not allowed to keep Courtney, will you have her? I mean for good. You could adopt her and then we could visit and see her whenever we wanted. You like kids and you're a good mother. Please say yes.'

I felt my eyes mist. Tyler was so sincere but naïve in his request, I could have wept.

'It's not that simple, love,' I said gently. 'I will certainly look after Courtney for as long as the social services want me to. But where she will live permanently won't be my decision. It will be up to the court to decide. Adoptive families are usually younger than me and have two parents.'

'We don't mind if it's just you,' Tyler said. 'Do we, Jade?'

Jade shook her head in agreement.

'It's not my decision, love,' I said again. 'I'm the foster carer and the social services will have lots of prospective adoptive families to choose from if Courtney doesn't stay with you.'

Painful though it was to talk about the possibility of adoption, as Tyler had raised the subject they deserved an honest response. They both fell quiet again and I dearly wished I could give them some encouragement, but based on what Jill had told me earlier I wasn't hopeful any more than she had been.

'We need to wait and hear what Rachel has to say,' I said, which was the best I could offer.

Tyler stayed for about another hour. He and Jade looked after Courtney and gave her lunch while I made our lunch, for we still had to eat despite the unhappiness that we all felt. Once Courtney had finished her lunch and bottle, Jade and Tyler changed her nappy and then settled her in her cot for a nap while we ate. They were both understandably subdued over lunch, but I managed to persuade Tyler to return to school for the afternoon revision session. After we'd eaten Jade saw him to the front door while I cleared the table.

When she returned she said: 'I'm going to have a lie-down, Cathy, I don't feel so good. Can you wake me when Courtney wakes, so I can look after her like Rachel told me to? I know I need to take more responsibility.'

My heart went out to her, for I knew that taking responsibility now had come far too late. 'All right,' I said quietly. 'Have a lie-down and I'll wake you. And Jade, love, you know I've always been positive in what I've said about you looking after Courtney, don't you?'

'Yes, I know. Don't worry. I know I've been stupid. It's not your fault.'

So why did I feel it was my fault, I wondered?

Later, when I heard Courtney wake from her nap, I went upstairs and woke Jade. She got out of bed straightaway and changed Courtney; then she brought her downstairs, where she looked after her all afternoon and evening. She was trying so hard to improve her parenting; I just wished she'd done it sooner. Dinner that night was sombre and not enjoyable. Adrian and Paula talked a little but there were big silences in between that were heavy with a sense of loss and foreboding. We all felt it, though no one said.

When Jade left the table to bath Courtney, Paula asked, 'What's wrong with Jade? Is it about the police coming?'

'Sort of,' I said. While I didn't want to burden Paula or Adrian with all the details, I did need to prepare them. 'Rachel is having to make some very difficult decisions about Jade and Courtney,' I said to them both. 'It's possible that they may be leaving us soon.'

'I don't want Jade and Courtney to leave,' Paula said passionately.

'I know. But they were always going to leave us some time, weren't they? Like all the other children we've fostered, who left us for new homes. It's just that it might be sooner than we expected.'

'I don't like fostering,' Paula said, pulling a face.

'Yes you do,' Adrian said. 'It's saying goodbye you don't like. It's horrible.'

And not for the first time I wondered about the impact – positive and negative – fostering had on my family.

That night Jade stayed up so that she could give Courtney her late-night bottle, and in the morning she woke when Courtney did. She fed and changed her and then kept her amused in her room while I showered and dressed. For the first time in a long while Jade had breakfast with us and then when I returned from taking Paula to school she said quietly to me: 'Cathy, you will remember to tell Rachel how well I've been looking after Courtney, won't you?'

'Of course, love. I always do,' I said and my heart clenched. I feared it was far too late for Jade's model parenting to have any effect on the outcome.

Rachel was due to arrive at twelve noon, which was the time Courtney usually had her lunch. I thought this was no bad thing, as it would give Rachel a chance to see first hand Jade feeding Courtney, which would I hoped remind her that Jade was doing some things right.

Before Rachel came I made sure the house was spotless; I vacuumed and dusted every corner. Jade helped me, which was a first, although I wouldn't be telling Rachel that. We also tidied Jade's bedroom, which like many teenagers' bedrooms was as usual a tip. We then dressed Courtney in her best clothes and brushed the little hair she had. There was a conspiratorial nature to our work, for we had a common aim:

to try to show Rachel (and the social services) that Jade could look after her baby and deserved another chance to prove herself.

Just before Rachel was due to arrive I quickly popped upstairs for a final check and it was just as well I did, for I found that Jade had left Courtney's last dirty nappy unbagged and on her bed. Had Rachel looked into her room, which she usually did during her visits, she would not have been impressed. I quickly picked it up and stuffed it into a nappy bag, which I knotted and took downstairs.

'You must remember to put Courtney's nappies in the bin,' I said curtly to Jade, as I returned from disposing of it outside in the wheelie bin. 'I've shown you what to do many times. It's unhygienic to leave them lying around and they'll smell now the warmer weather is here.'

The poor girl looked as though she was about to burst into tears, so anxious was she. 'I'm sorry, Cathy,' she said. 'How could I have been so stupid?'

'It's not the end of the world,' I said with a reassuring smile. 'I'm on edge too. Just try to remember what I've told you for next time.'

It was something of a relief when at 12.10 the doorbell rang. Jade was spoon-feeding Courtney creamy chicken and vegetable baby food.

'You carry on,' I said. 'I'll answer it.'

Going down the hall I took a deep breath to calm my nerves before I opened the front door. Rachel was dressed smartly in black trousers and a white shirt – too smartly: her outfit seemed to emphasize the formality of her visit rather than the casual dress of a friendly social worker.

'Hello, come in,' I said with forced lightness. 'Jade is just giving Courtney her lunch.'

'Hello, Cathy,' Rachel said a little stiffly. I sensed the distance she was placing between us.

'They're through here,' I said, leading the way down the hall and maintaining my bright, positive attitude. 'Can I get you something to drink? It's a warm day.'

'Just a glass of water, please.'

Rachel followed me into the annexe to the kitchen, where Jade was sitting at the dining table feeding Courtney. She glanced anxiously at Rachel as she came in.

'Hello, Jade,' Rachel said. 'How are you and Courtney today?' She didn't go over and make a fuss of Courtney as she usually did.

'We're doing well, aren't we, Cathy?' Jade said, looking to me for support.

'Yes, very well,' I said.

I ran the glass of water Rachel wanted and passed it to her.

'Thank you,' she said, taking a sip.

I noticed she was carrying a smart leather briefcase. Possibly she'd had it with her before but I couldn't remember seeing it. Now it seemed to emphasize the formal nature of her visit.

'I'll wait in the sitting room until you've finished feeding Courtney,' Rachel said.

This wasn't what I'd planned, not at all. Rachel was supposed to watch Jade feed Courtney and see the love between mother and daughter. Then, making matters worse, Rachel said: 'Cathy, if Jade's all right in here alone with Courtney can you come in the sitting room too so we can have a chat?'

I glanced at Jade, who looked betrayed, for it seemed that by going with Rachel I was conspiring against her, but I could hardly refuse. 'Come through and join us as soon as you've finished, love,' I said to Jade with a reassuring smile.

I went with Rachel into the sitting room, where she pushed the door shut. We sat in the armchairs and Rachel tucked her briefcase on the floor beside her feet.

'I understand Jill has explained to you the main reason for my visit today?' Rachel said, and I nodded. 'I'll talk to Jade when she's finished with Courtney and go through all my concerns then. It's obviously going to be very upsetting for Jade and I would like you to be present.'

'Of course,' I said.

'I've arranged an emergency professionals meeting for Monday, when a decision on Courtney's future will be made,' Rachel continued. 'Based on the information we have, I think that decision is likely to be that Courtney should be removed from Jade's care immediately. I have a baby carer on standby ready to take Courtney on Tuesday. Jade will also need to leave this placement on the same day and I shall be talking to Jackie to see if she can return home.'

I stared at Rachel as I struggled with what she'd said. Rachel looked back, serious and concerned. I knew she was finding this difficult.

'Is there really no alternative?' I asked after a moment. 'Jade knows she's been silly. I'm sure she's learnt her lesson now. She loves Courtney and she's trying really hard to be a good mum. Is there no way she can be given another chance?'

Rachel shook her head sadly. 'Jade's already been given many chances to prove herself. Now we have to think of the long-term future of her baby and what's best for her.'

Chapter Nineteen

'Please Don't Take My Baby'

Five minutes later when Jade had finished feeding Courtney she came into the sitting room with Courtney in her arms. She was already in tears – not loud sobs but the pitiful silent crying reminiscent of the newly bereaved. She sat on the sofa and held Courtney very close, while dabbing at her eyes with the tissue she clenched in one hand. Courtney looked at her mother inquisitively, not understanding her tears, and then touched her face. Rachel, I noticed, had her eyes down and concentrated on the floor, as though she couldn't bear to look at Jade or Courtney.

Finally Rachel looked up and across the room to Jade. 'I know how difficult all this has been for you,' she began in a low gentle voice. 'Having a baby is life changing, and for a girl your age the responsibility can be overwhelming. I want you to know that no one is blaming you, Jade, but we're having to make some important and very difficult decisions in respect of you and Courtney.' Rachel paused to allow Jade the opportunity to say something but Jade stayed silent, head lowered and fiddling with the pattern on Courtney's little jumper.

'When I've visited you here before,' Rachel continued, 'we talked about how you needed to take full responsibility for Courtney, just as you would if you were living independently. I know you've made some changes, which is good, but I'm afraid those are not sufficient to convince me that you could parent Courtney without a lot of support. And I'm afraid support of the type you would need isn't available long term.'

I looked at Jade and wondered if she was following what Rachel was saying: that she was leading her, as kindly as possible, down the path towards the inevitable conclusion that she was taking Courtney from her.

'Jade,' Rachel said in the same kind and patient manner, 'it's important you understand the reasons for the decisions that we are having to make in respect of you and Courtney's future.'

Jade gave a small nod.

'You remember the issues we discussed in relation to parenting Courtney?' Rachel asked.

'Yes, and I'm doing what you said,' Jade blurted, desperation in her voice. 'Ask Cathy if you don't believe me. She'll tell you.'

'I do believe you,' Rachel said.

'Jade understands what is required,' I said. 'She's making the necessary changes. I am doing less and less in respect of parenting Courtney.'

Rachel smiled weakly. 'Good, but there are other issues,' she said, returning her attention to Jade. 'Jade, you were late taking Courtney for her second vaccination and she hasn't had her third at all yet. In order for an infant to be fully protected the vaccines must be given within a set time – otherwise the child can contract diseases and even die.'

Jade didn't respond and kept her head down.

'When was the last time you went to the clinic to have Courtney weighed and checked?' Rachel asked. 'You're supposed to take her every week.'

I stopped myself from saying 'I thought she was.' For Jade had been telling me she'd been going to the clinic every Monday afternoon. When she'd returned and I'd asked her how much weight Courtney had gained, she'd given a figure, which I now realized must have been made up.

Jade couldn't look at either of us but carried on fiddling with Courtney's jumper.

'I'd like to see Courtney's red book, please,' Rachel said.

'I haven't got it,' Jade said.

'Can you arrange to get it for me, please?' Rachel asked.

'No. I lost it ages ago,' Jade said, which added to the deceit. Jade had been telling me that the nurse at the clinic had been recording Courtney's weight and measurements in the red book. I'd trusted Jade and had never thought to ask to see the book.

'We'll need to get another red book,' Rachel said, and taking a sheet of paper from her briefcase she made a note. There was then a short silence as though Rachel was summoning her thoughts and courage to continue. 'Jade, you and I have spoken previously about your behaviour when you are away from Cathy and outside this house. I understand you've been telling Cathy that you've been going to your mum's regularly – sometimes twice a week. But Jackie says she hasn't seen you for at least a month. However, you have been seen in a gang hanging around the mall, the bowling alley and on the forecourt of the Queen's Head pub. Those are not suitable places to take a young baby. Do you know a member of the public was so concerned to see a little baby in the care of a group of teenagers who were smoking and drinking that she called the social services? I'm sorry, Jade, but you need to see your behaviour as others see it.'

Rachel paused and Jade's face crumpled. Without raising her head, Jade wiped away the fresh tears that now fell.

'I'm sure you didn't intentionally mean to cause Courtney harm,' Rachel continued. 'But some of your behaviour has put Courtney in danger. My job is to protect your baby as well as looking after you. At least twice to my knowledge you have left Courtney in the care of Chelsea's little sister, who is eleven years old. Do you think that was responsible behaviour, Jade?'

Jade didn't look up or say anything, but I could tell from her anguished expression she understood what Rachel was saying and bitterly regretted her actions.

'There are other issues too,' Rachel said. 'Managing a budget is as important a part of parenting as making sure your baby is fed and warm. Jade, in addition to the money Cathy gives you from the fostering allowance, you are in receipt of benefit. You were also given a maternity grant of 400 pounds, which was supposed to buy essential items for Courtney like a pram and cot. But I understand you are still using Cathy's baby equipment. Where is that money, Jade?'

There was a silence before Jade said: 'I haven't got it.'

'Where is it?' Rachel asked.

'I've spent it.'

'On what?'

There was another pause before Jade said quietly: 'A new phone and other stuff.'

'Oh, Jade,' I sighed, as Rachel wrote.

'And Courtney was supposed to sleep in a new phone, was she?' Rachel asked without any trace of humour.

Jade shook her head and more tears silently fell.

'You're in receipt of benefit now,' Rachel continued. 'That money is to buy food and clothing for you and Courtney, as well as nappies, creams and so on. But I understand Cathy still buys these things in her weekly supermarket shop.' Rachel looked at Jade for a response but she kept her head down and shrugged.

'What are you doing with all that money?' Rachel asked.

'I don't know,' Jade said gloomily. 'It just goes.'

'On cigarettes and drink?' Rachel asked.

Jade shrugged.

It was now obvious to Jade, as it was to me, that her behaviour had fallen a long way short of what was required to take care of and protect her baby. I knew Jade loved Courtney but I was having to accept, painful though it was, that her love alone was not enough for Jade to be allowed to keep Courtney. I'd fostered children before whose parents loved them but for various reasons couldn't look after them. It's always dreadfully sad when a child cannot live with their natural parents, but sometimes there is no alternative and adoption is in the best long-term interest of the child. Whether the parents ever recovered from losing their child I didn't know, but I doubted it.

As Rachel finished talking the room had fallen silent except for Courtney's occasional chuntering. I braced myself for what Rachel was going to say next. Jade must have anticipated it too, for, hugging Courtney protectively to her, she looked up at Rachel and begged: 'I'll do anything, but please don't take my baby.'

I saw Rachel's bottom lip tremble and she paused to compose herself before replying. 'I'm not taking your baby now, Jade. There is a professionals meeting on Monday and they will make a decision on what is best for Courtney then.'

'Please Don't Take My Baby'

Jade's brow creased in pain and I swallowed hard. 'Will you tell the professionals that I've changed?' Jade pleaded. 'Tell them I know what I've done wrong and I'm very sorry. I promise it won't happen again. Tell them I love Courtney. Please tell them. If they give me another chance I'll be the best mother ever. But don't let them take my baby. Please.'

I felt my eyes brim. Rachel was struggling to contain her emotion too. 'I'll tell them,' she said quietly, her voice unsteady. 'I promise I will.'

Looking down, Rachel slipped the paper she'd been writing on into her briefcase, and it was a moment before she could look up again. I looked at Jade, who was holding Courtney very close and gently rocking her back and forth, as much for her own comfort as for her baby's.

'Do you have any questions?' Rachel asked after a moment.

Jade shook her head. 'Just tell them I love my baby, and I'll look after her.'

Rachel nodded and then stood. 'Goodbye then, Jade,' she said. 'I'll see you again on Tuesday.' Then to me: 'Is ten o'clock on Tuesday all right?'

'Yes,' I said.

I saw Rachel to the front door. She paused with her hand on the door before going out. 'Look after them both,' she said. 'Sometimes I hate my job.'

I had little doubt that once in her car she would cry, for what could be worse for a social worker than to have to permanently separate a mother from her baby?

I returned down the hall. I really didn't want to go into the sitting room and face Jade. My usual optimism had gone and I couldn't think of a single word that would offer her some comfort or support. There was nothing I could say that would ease her pain and I was acutely aware that we had five agonizing days until Tuesday, when Rachel would return to take Courtney.

In the sitting room I looked at Jade. She was on the sofa, still holding Courtney very close and gently rocking her. 'Do you want a drink of water or anything?' I asked quietly.

'No,' she said, and fresh tears fell.

I went over and sat beside her. I put my arms around her shoulders and gently hugged her. Courtney was now growing restless and I thought we needed to continue with her usual routine.

'Courtney usually has a nap now,' I said to Jade. 'Do you want to settle her in her cot?'

Jade nodded and without saying anything stood and carried Courtney out of the room. I heard her footsteps on the stairs and then go round the landing and into her bedroom. When she hadn't returned downstairs fifteen minutes later I went up to her room. Her bedroom door was closed and I knocked lightly. There was no reply. I knocked again and then opened the door.

Courtney was asleep in her cot and Jade was lying on her bed, watching her. 'Are you all right?' I asked quietly, taking a couple of steps into the room.

Jade gave a small nod.

'Are you coming downstairs now?'

'No. I want to stay with Courtney.'

'All right, love. I'll be downstairs if you need me.'

I came out and quietly closed the door. I didn't know if I was doing the right thing in leaving Jade lying there, watching Courtney, but I didn't have any other suggestions, and I could appreciate why she wanted to be with Courtney and make the most of every minute she had left with her.

Jill phoned as promised during the afternoon. 'How are you?' she asked. 'Rachel said it was a difficult meeting.'

'Yes, it was,' I agreed. 'Very difficult.'

'Where's Jade now?'

'In her bedroom, watching Courtney sleep.'

'Keep an eye on her. Make sure she doesn't do anything silly.' From which I assumed Jill meant running away or trying to harm herself.

'I will,' I said.

'And Cathy, Rachel forgot to tell Jade that she'll need to make a statement to the police about the shoplifting incident. Could you tell her, please? And that Rachel will arrange to go with her to the police station later next week or the following week.'

'All right,' I said, feeling that Jade really didn't need this on top of everything else right now. 'Did Rachel say anything else to you that she didn't tell us?'

'No. Just about having to make a statement.'

'So am I right in thinking that Rachel will definitely take Courtney on Tuesday?' I asked. 'She told me she had baby carers on standby.'

Jill paused before she replied: 'Yes, that's the plan. Cathy, I know how much this is hurting you, but some of Jade's behaviour has been so unsafe it has put Courtney at risk of harm. Many social workers would have made the decision to remove Courtney before this. Rachel has given Jade extra chances.'

'I know, I understand,' I said. 'Tyler asked me if I could adopt Courtney, but that isn't a possibility, is it?'

'No,' Jill said kindly. 'But the social services will find Courtney a family as loving as yours is to adopt her.' Which was supposed to cheer me up but didn't.

Jill finished by reminding me to call the agency if I needed any help or advice tomorrow or over the weekend.

'I will,' I said. We said goodbye and I replaced the handset.

The weekend loomed and I was dreading it.

Jade stayed in her room until Courtney woke and then she changed her and brought her downstairs. She sat on the sofa for most of the afternoon, deep in thought and holding her baby close. A couple of times I asked her if she was all right, which was a daft question, but I didn't know what else to say. She said she was, but clearly she wasn't, and we both concentrated on Courtney. But being with Courtney was bittersweet now we were aware it would be short-lived. All her charming little ways, which previously had been so endearing and made you love her even more, now seemed a torturous reminder of what we would be missing in the future. In some ways it would have been better if Rachel had taken Courtney with her that morning, to get it over and done with.

When it was time for me to collect Paula from school I asked Jade if she would like to come but she didn't want to. I was reluctant to leave Jade alone with Courtney in case she did something desperate like snatching her, but I couldn't force Jade to come with me. I waited until the last possible minute to leave the house and I took the car to school instead of walking. I was home again fifteen minutes later and to my relief Jade was where I'd left her: in the sitting room with Courtney on her lap.

Paula was pleased to see Jade, as in the past she'd often been out when Paula had arrived home from school, and Thursday had been one of the days Jade had supposedly visited her mother. However, Paula soon realized that Jade wasn't her usual chatty self and left her alone and went off to amuse herself. Indeed Jade hardly said a word to anyone. Dinner was another gloomy meal as it had been the evening before and I was pleased when we'd finished and I could clear away the dishes. I then helped Adrian with his homework and Paula with her reading, which redirected my attention, for a while at least, away from Jade and Courtney and the huge dark cloud that hung over us and seemed to be growing denser by the hour.

I encouraged Jade to continue with Courtney's normal routine and Jade gave her a bath at 7.00 p.m. and then settled her in her cot for the night. Jade then stayed in her bedroom watching Courtney sleep despite my suggestion that she should come down and watch television to take her mind off things. I knew that Rachel was visiting Tyler during the evening, and later I asked Jade if she'd heard from him, but she said she hadn't. I checked on Jade and Courtney a couple of times during the evening and then again after Adrian and Paula had gone to bed. Jade had changed into her nightwear and was in bed, propped on her side watching Courtney sleep. I asked her again if she was all right and she nodded, so I told her to call me if she needed anything and I came out. There was nothing I could say or do to help her.

Before I went to bed I wrote up my log notes, stating that Rachel had visited, what she'd told Jade and how she'd been during the evening. It was only a few lines because Rachel would write a lengthier report for the social services file, and to be honest I was fed up with writing my log. Indeed I was fed up generally. I felt a failure as a foster carer and had begun to torment myself with the thought that Jade's situation was my fault and that if I'd done things differently she wouldn't have got herself into trouble and might have been able to keep her baby. But what I could or should have done differently, other than not help Jade as much as I had, escaped me. I'd acted in good faith and had done my best for Jade and Courtney just as I did for all the children I fostered.

I was having a shower at 10.30 before going to bed when I heard Jade go downstairs for Courtney's night bottle. When I finished showering I went into her room to check she and Courtney were all right. Courtney had finished her bottle and was in her cot, going off to sleep; Jade was lying on her side in bed and watching her.

'I've had a text from Ty,' she said, glancing up at me and looking a little brighter. 'He's not going to play pool with his mates tomorrow – Friday. He's coming to see me.'

'Good,' I said. 'That'll be nice.'

'And, Cathy,' Jade continued, now almost smiling, 'guess what? Ty's asking his mum if she can adopt Courtney. So we'll still be able to see her whenever we want.'

I didn't want to dampen Jade's spirits but I had to be realistic. 'Jade, you understand that if Tyler's mother feels she can adopt Courtney her application will have to be considered by the social services? She'll be assessed to see if she is suitable, just as other applicants are.'

'But she hasn't got a police record,' Jade said defensively.

'I know, but there are other factors the social services will want to consider.'

'Like what?' Jade said, disgruntled by my realism.

'Her age, for example, and her home. How she will support the baby. Who will look after the baby while she is at work. It's a long process to adopt, love, and it takes time. Has she seen Courtney yet?'

'Yeah. Once.'

'All right. Let's wait and see what she says,' I said. For while I thought the social services would consider Tyler's mother's application, I'd no idea if her situation would meet the strict criteria for adoption, or even if she wanted to adopt and take on the life-changing responsibility a new baby would bring.

'I feel a bit happier,' Jade said.

'Good.'

I didn't sleep well that night and I was awake when Jade got up at 6.00 a.m. to give Courtney her early-morning bottle. I would normally have been relieved it was Friday and nearly the weekend, but not this Friday. The weekend seemed a huge hurdle to overcome before the professionals meeting on Monday, when a decision would be made on Courtney's future. Jade joined us for breakfast and made a big effort to talk to Adrian and Paula. When I returned from taking Paula to school she had a cup of coffee waiting for me, and for the rest of the day she was a model parent and foster daughter: tending to Courtney's every need, and even clearing up after herself in the bathroom and the kitchen. She was also a lot brighter and I knew that was because of the good news she hoped Tyler would bring with him that evening in respect of his mother wanting to adopt Courtney.

However, shortly after 6.30 p.m. Jade shouted distraughtly from the landing:

'She won't have her! Her own granddaughter and she won't help us!'

I stopped what I was doing and rushed upstairs.

Chapter Twenty

Prolonging the Agony

Jade was face down on her bed, her phone in her hand, and sobbing loudly. 'I hate her!' she cried, referring to Tyler's mother. 'She's never liked me. I bet she's pleased I'm losing Courtney.'

I sat on the bed beside Jade and rested my hand reassuringly on her shoulder. Courtney was in her cot watching her mother, her eyes rounded with apprehension at Jade's crying.

'I'm sure Tyler's mother does like you,' I said. 'But adopting a baby is a huge commitment, especially when your own children are grown up. Not everyone wants to start all over again with sleepless nights, nappies and bottles.'

'You do!' Jade sobbed.

'Yes, but I'm odd,' I said.

My small stab at humour helped a little. Jade stopped sobbing and raised her tear-stained face. 'Oh, Cathy, what am I going to do? I don't want to lose Courtney. I love her.'

'I know you do, love.'

She sat up in bed and slipped her arms around my waist and hugged me tightly. It was the first proper cuddle we'd had. I felt sad that it had taken this tragedy to finally bring us together. I held her close and stroked her hair until her tears subsided.

Then I gently asked: 'Jade, do you think I could have helped you more – for example, by being firmer? I did what I thought was right but now I'm not sure.'

Jade gave a small shrug, and without raising her head from my shoulder or moving her arms away from hugging me, she said: 'Nah. I didn't listen to me mum, so I wasn't going to listen to you.' Which, while easing my conscience a little, did nothing to help Jade's situation.

After a moment she raised her head and looked into my eyes, child-like and imploring. 'What am I going to do, Cathy?'

I shook my head and held her close. I didn't have any suggestions; I didn't know how you prepared a mother for losing her baby.

We held each other for a while longer – in silent desperation – and then Jade moved away. Taking a tissue from the box, she blew her nose and wiped her eyes. 'Ty will be here soon,' she said. 'He's on the bus now.'

I smiled sadly. 'Try to make the most of your time together,' I said. 'He'll be feeling as bad as you, so don't mention his mother's decision unless he does. Just try and enjoy your time with Courtney. I'll take more photographs and mount them in a special album for you.' I stopped as a lump rose to my throat and my eyes filled.

Tyler arrived ten minutes later and Jade let him in. Having said a brief hello in the hall they came through to the sitting room, where the children and I were watching a DVD. Courtney was in her bouncing cradle, also 'watching' the television. Tyler said hi to us and then scooped up his daughter and sat with her on his lap, kissing and cuddling her, and telling her how beautiful she was, which he continued to do for most of the evening, while Jade sat next to him and watched. It was touching and upsetting to see, but it wasn't until Adrian and Paula had gone to bed that Tyler spoke of the social services' plans for his daughter.

'Rachel visited me and Mum last night,' he said. 'She said we'll be able to have contact with Courtney when she leaves here and goes to the "baby" foster carers. She said it will be supervised contact at a family centre, but we'll be able to see Courtney right up until when she goes to her adoptive parents.'

I nodded. I realized Tyler was trying to be positive (just as Rachel must have been when she'd told him), but prolonging contact seemed to me an additional torture. What was the point in Tyler and Jade continuing to see their daughter and bond with her if in a few months she was going to be adopted, after which they would never see her again?

'Mum says she's sorry she can't have Courtney,' Tyler added, glancing at Jade. 'She said to tell you she feels bad and she's sorry things haven't worked out, but she can't bring up a baby and work full time.'

Jade didn't say anything but I could see Tyler was hoping for her understanding. 'Your mum mustn't feel bad,' I said. 'Jade's mum is in the same position.' For everyone had assumed, correctly, that Jackie couldn't look after Courtney, as she had enough to cope with bringing up her own family and working part time.

Tyler looked at me gratefully. 'Rachel says there are hundreds of couples who will want to adopt Courtney,' he said, trying to stay positive. 'So Courtney will have a lovely home, and her new family will love her as much as we do.'

I felt so sorry for Tyler, who was making such a big effort to be positive and was clearly struggling to keep his emotions under control.

'I don't want to talk about it any more,' Jade said quietly.

So we didn't.

Tyler continued to cuddle Courtney and I changed the subject by asking him how his studying was going.

I thought we might see a lot of Tyler over the weekend, as it would be the last weekend the three of them would be together. But later, as Tyler stood to leave, he told Jade he planned to revise over the weekend, as his exams started the following week, but he'd phone her. I could see Jade was disappointed and was about to say something, but perhaps remembering my previous advice about supporting Tyler's studies, she stopped. However, I did wonder how much of Tyler not seeing Jade and Courtney was studying and how much was Tyler's way of coping; perhaps he was starting to distance himself from Courtney in preparation for their inevitable separation.

We had ignored Courtney's usual routine that Friday evening and had kept her up so that Tyler could spend time with her, but once he'd gone – just before 10.00 p.m. – Jade said to me: 'I'm so tired, Cathy, I have to go to bed. Can you see to Courtney?'

'Yes, love,' I agreed without hesitation. I doubted my helping Jade to parent Courtney now would make any difference to the outcome of Monday's meeting.

So while Jade got ready for bed I changed Courtney, then waited up and gave her the late-night bottle. When I took her up to her cot Jade was in bed with her eyes closed, although I had the feeling she wasn't asleep. I didn't say anything to her, as I could understand why she didn't want to talk, so having settled Courtney in her cot I crept out and closed the bedroom door.

The following morning I was woken by the sound of Courtney crying. I stayed in bed, expecting Jade to get up and give Courtney her bottle, which she had been doing straightaway recently. But when Courtney's cries continued I threw on my dressing gown and went round to Jade's room.

'Jade, Courtney needs her bottle,' I said, going to the cot and picking up Courtney to stop her from crying.' It was 6.00 and a Saturday morning, and Adrian and Paula were still asleep.

There was no reply from Jade, so I went over to the bed and gently shook her shoulder. 'Courtney needs feeding, love,' I said.

'You do it,' she said groggily from beneath the duvet.

'Why? Are you ill?'

'No. I just don't want to feed her.'

I hesitated, wondering if I should insist, but Courtney was fretting for her bottle, so I carried her downstairs to the kitchen, where I warmed the bottle, and then went through to the sitting room, where I fed her. She grinned and gurgled as she suckled, her clear blue eyes lighting up with pleasure. She was such a happy and contented baby and so easy to look after. I felt the emotion rise within me and knew I needed to start distancing myself too. She took the bottle of milk quickly and I returned upstairs to Jade's room. Part of Courtney's morning routine was that once Jade had fed and changed her she kept her amused until she gave her some solid food for breakfast at about 8.00 a.m.

Jade was still in bed when I went into her room, facing away and under the duvet. She made no attempt to get up as I entered. 'I've fed her,' I said. 'Are you going to get up now and look after her?'

There was silence and I waited by the bed. Then Jade said: 'I don't want to look after her. I can't bear it. She's not my baby any more.'

I heard Jade's rejection and understood what she meant. I sat on the bed, with Courtney on my lap, and placed one hand on Jade's shoulder. I was thinking fast, trying to find the words to help.

'Jade, love,' I began gently, 'Courtney will always be your daughter, even if she doesn't live with you and is adopted. You and Tyler will always be her natural parents, and be part of her. No one can change that. She will grow up to look like both of you, and many of her characteristics will be yours and Tyler's. I know it's difficult now, love, I really do. I've fostered children before who've had to say goodbye to their parents. I've seen the pain and anguish of those parents, their suffering, when they have to say goodbye to their children. I know. But try to take some comfort, as they did, from knowing that Courtney will be loved and cherished. She will be well looked after and want for nothing.' I stopped and swallowed hard. Jade didn't move or say anything.

'I don't know what else to say,' I said. 'But I think you should get up now and look after Courtney. Lying here won't help. You have the whole weekend with Courtney, so try to make the most of it.' But my words sounded as flat to me as they must have done to Jade.

'There's no point,' she said after a moment, from beneath the duvet. 'I'm not going to see her grow up, so she may as well go now.'

'Courtney wants you to get up,' I tried. She was reaching out and trying to grab hold of the top of the duvet and pull it from Jade's head.

'I don't want her,' Jade said, her voice breaking. 'Take her away, please, and leave me alone. I've been up all night watching her sleep. I can't take any more. Please do as I say, Cathy, please.'

Overwhelmed and fighting back my own tears, I stood. 'All right, love. I understand,' I said quickly, and began towards the door. Courtney gave a little cry at leaving her mother. 'Come down when you're ready,' I said. 'Don't stay up here all by yourself.'

Leaving Jade, I felt utterly wretched, upset and at a loss to know how to help her. I went into my bedroom, where I laid Courtney safely on my bed so that I could dress. I'd have a shower later when Courtney had her nap, but for now I needed to get the day started and continue as normal as far as possible for Adrian's and Paula's sakes.

Once I was dressed I gave Courtney her bath and then took her downstairs for her breakfast. Adrian and Paula joined me shortly before 9.00 and, expecting to see Jade, asked where she was. I said she wasn't feeling well and that I was looking after Courtney until she felt better, which wasn't so far from the truth.

Jade finally left her room when it was time for Courtney to go into her cot for her morning nap, not because she was feeling 'better' but because it was too painful for her to be in the same room as Courtney now that their days together were limited. Downstairs, Jade sat on the sofa and stared out of the open French windows to where Adrian and Paula were playing in the garden. I tried to talk to her about how she was feeling but she didn't want to, so I tried to make light conversation just to break the silence – wasn't it nice to see the sun, etc. – but she wasn't interested in my chatter, and who could blame her?

Jade refused lunch, saying she wasn't hungry, but made herself a sandwich in the afternoon while Courtney had her afternoon nap. Indeed the only time Jade was downstairs was when Courtney had her two naps; the rest of the time she was in her bedroom so that she didn't have to see her daughter. I suggested to her we could all go to the park, as it was such a nice day, but she said: 'You go if you want and take Courtney but I'll stay here.'

I wasn't going to leave Jade alone in the house when she was so clearly depressed, so Adrian and Paula continued to play in the garden while I looked after Courtney. I thought again it would have been better if Rachel had taken Courtney on Thursday rather than prolonging the agony until Tuesday. Jade didn't want any dinner and when I took Courtney up to settle her for the night she asked me if I could put the cot in my room, as she couldn't bear to spend another night watching her.

'If it will help,' I agreed sadly and very worried.

Jade nodded glumly. 'Yes, please.'

I called to Adrian and Paula to help me, explaining that Jade still wasn't feeling very well so Courtney was sleeping in my room for now. Paula sat on the bed with Jade and looked after Courtney while Adrian helped upend the cot so that we could manoeuvre it through the doorway. We carried it round the landing and into my room, where we set it beside my bed, I made up the cot with the sheet and blanket and returned to Jade's room to collect Courtney.

'I hope Jade feels better tomorrow,' Paula said to me as we settled Courtney in her cot.

'So do I,' I agreed, although I couldn't see how she would.

That night Courtney was very restless, probably because she was in an unfamiliar room, and I had to resettle her every couple of hours. She had been sleeping through the night. The following morning she slept later, until 7.00, when I gave her a bottle and then returned her to her cot while I showered and dressed. I checked on Jade. She was awake but didn't want to get up and help. When it was nearly time for Courtney's breakfast I went into Jade's room again and asked her if she wanted to give Courtney her breakfast, but she didn't; so I began a second day of being totally responsible for Courtney's care.

When Adrian and Paula came down to breakfast Paula asked: 'Is Jade still ill?'

'I'm afraid so,' I said.

'What's the matter with her?' Adrian asked.

I felt like saying a broken heart, but instead I said 'upset stomach', to which they could both relate, although I suspected Adrian knew there was more to it than that.

Sunday followed a similar pattern to Saturday, with Jade staying in her room for most of the day to avoid seeing Courtney, which she would have found too upsetting. I appreciated it was Jade's way of coping and trying to loosen the bond between her and her daughter in preparation for her going on Tuesday, and part of me felt that was no bad thing. I had begun to imagine a dreadful, dreadful scene in which Rachel had to forcibly prise Courtney out of Jade's arms, which I knew did happen sometimes when a baby was removed from its mother. I tried to imagine how I would cope in Jade's

227

situation but it was impossible – some things are just too awful to picture.

On Sunday afternoon I suggested to Jade, as I had done the day before, that we all go out for a while, but Jade didn't want to, so as the weather was fine Adrian and Paula played in the garden again. Also, in the afternoon my neighbour's two children, who were a similar age to Adrian and Paula, came in and they all played together and had fun, so I didn't feel quite so bad that I hadn't taken Adrian and Paula out during the weekend as I usually did.

That evening I telephoned my parents – we often spoke on a Sunday if we hadn't seen each other during the weekend. As part of our conversation Mum naturally asked how Jade and Courtney were doing and I had to say: 'Not very good.'

Mum knew that confidentiality forbade me from telling her the details, so she didn't ask any questions. 'Oh dear,' she said. 'I'm so sorry to hear that. Give Jade our love, dear.'

'I will.'

Adrian and Paula spoke to their nana and grandpa, after which I began their bath and bedtime routine, ready for school on Monday, and I was never so relieved that a weekend was finally drawing to a close.

Courtney was restless again on Sunday night and I repeatedly had to settle her. When she woke for her early-morning bottle I didn't wake Jade, for I assumed she would still find it too painful to look after Courtney, so I took her straight downstairs to the kitchen, where I warmed a bottle, and then fed her in the sitting room. When she'd finished I returned upstairs and laid her in the cot while I showered; then I woke Adrian and Paula and our schoolday routine began.

When it was nearly time for me to leave the house to take Paula to school I knocked on Jade's bedroom door and, going in, asked her if she could look after Courtney while I went to school.

'Can you take her with you?' she said from beneath the duvet.

'Yes, I can. If you want me to.'

'I do.'

'I'll see you in half an hour, then,' I said. I came out and closed her bedroom door.

Paula was excited that we were taking Courtney to school with us. We walked and she helped me push the pram. When we arrived in the playground she proudly showed off 'our baby' to her friends. A few parents looked at me oddly, although most knew I fostered so were used to seeing me appear in the playground with a new addition to my family. I waited until the bell rang for the start of school and then I kissed Paula goodbye and pushed the pram home again. I was grateful for the exercise, having been at home all weekend.

Jade was still in bed when I arrived home and despite my encouraging her to get up she stayed there until mid-morning. Only when I'd put Courtney in her cot in my bedroom for her morning nap did Jade get up. She came downstairs in her nightwear, made herself some toast and then took it into the sitting room, where she switched on the television. I don't normally watch daytime television but I didn't say anything; I was relieved she was downstairs and not shut in her room. However, an hour later when Courtney woke from her morning nap Jade returned to her room, only coming down again (still in her nightwear) when Courtney had her afternoon nap. Later I asked Jade if she would like to come with me when I collected Paula from school, but predictably she didn't want to. I could understand why Jade couldn't bear to see her daughter and I was very worried.

'Is Jade still unwell?' Paula asked when I arrived in the playground pushing the pram.

'Yes,' I said.

Paula helped me push the pram home and then kept Courtney amused in her bouncing cradle while I made dinner. I took Jade's dinner up to her room on a tray, as I knew she wouldn't come down while Courtney was there. She thanked me but hardly ate anything and I took the tray away. Jade didn't wash or dress at all that day and had managed to completely avoid seeing her daughter, although she must have heard her sometimes. Before I went to bed I went to Jade's room and asked her if she wanted anything, but she didn't. She looked dreadful, as though she had given up on life, and I tried again to talk to her about her feelings, but she shook her head and waved me away, close to tears. Very worried but aware there was nothing I could say or do to help Jade, I said goodnight and came out, dreading how she would cope with tomorrow.

The professionals meeting had taken place during the day – I didn't know at what time – and I wasn't surprised that neither Jill nor Rachel had telephoned us with news of the outcome. It is considered good practice (rightly so) that when an upsetting decision of this nature is made the parent should be told in person by the social worker and not over the phone or by a third party. In Jade's case, therefore, no news was not good news – just the opposite, in fact.

Courtney was restless again during Monday night but I was awake anyway. I lay in the dark staring at the ceiling, worrying about the following day. I knew I had to be strong for Jade, who would probably be hysterical when Rachel carried Courtney from the house, but I doubted how strong I could be. I was grateful that Rachel was coming at 10.00 a.m. when Adrian and Paula were at school so that they wouldn't have to witness Jade and Courtney's agonizing parting.

I worried too how little Courtney would cope with all the changes, for by tomorrow night she would have lost everything that was familiar to her and be with new carers in a strange house. How can you explain that to a five-month-old baby?

You can't.

Chapter Twenty-One

Tuesday

It was like waiting for the executioner to arrive. Jade was sitting on the sofa with a screwed-up tissue in one hand and crying quietly, while I was on the sofa next to her, a reassuring hand resting impotently on her arm. Courtney was in her bouncing cradle on the floor on the other side of me and thankfully oblivious to the fate that awaited her. All that could be heard for some time was the ticking of the clock, Jade's snuffling and Courtney's occasional gurgle.

It was 9.50 and part of me thought that Jade had done well to get this far. She was washed and dressed, and while she couldn't bear to look at Courtney she was at least in the same room as her, and hadn't run away. It had crossed my mind that had I been in Jade's position I would have fled the house rather than stay and watch my daughter being taken away.

A couple of minutes more passed and then the doorbell rang. Jade started and gave a little gasp.

'It's all right,' I said soothingly, patting her arm. 'Calm down.' Although I was feeling anything but calm.

With my stomach churning and my mouth dry, I went down the hall and answered the front door. Rachel was dressed smartly as she had been on her previous visit and held her briefcase at her side.

'Good morning, Cathy,' she said formally.

'Good morning,' I replied, standing aside to let her in. 'We're in the sitting room.'

I closed the front door and followed Rachel down the hall.

'Good morning, Jade,' Rachel said stiffly as she entered.

Jade didn't answer. She kept her head down and pressed the tissue to her mouth.

'How is Courtney?' Rachel now asked, sitting in the armchair and tucking her briefcase by her feet.

Jade didn't look up or answer. 'Courtney's fine,' I said, returning to sit on the sofa beside Jade.

'Good. And what sort of weekend have you had?' Rachel asked, again looking at Jade.

Jade stared at the floor and sniffed. 'Jade's obviously upset,' I said. 'She's coping as best she can.'

'So you haven't been out partying all weekend?' Rachel now asked Jade, which seemed rather an insensitive comment, although she was waiting for a reply.

Jade shook her head but didn't look up.

'She's been in all weekend,' I confirmed.

'Looking after Courtney?' Rachel asked.

I nodded, for there seemed little point in telling Rachel I had been looking after Courtney all weekend.

'All right,' Rachel said with a small sigh.

Leaning forward, she unfastened her briefcase and took out some papers, and my stomach churned. She set them centrally on her lap and then, sitting upright in her chair, looked at Jade, who still had her eyes lowered.

'As you know, we had a meeting yesterday,' Rachel began, addressing us both. 'It was a difficult meeting and lengthy. We discussed our concerns in respect of you looking after

Courtney and your behaviour in general, Jade. You remember I explained our concerns to you when I saw you last week?' Rachel paused but Jade didn't look up or reply. Rachel glanced at me before continuing.

'My manager and the other professionals present at the meeting felt it was in Courtney's long-term interest to be placed for adoption and I anticipated removing Courtney today. In which case you would have had to leave Cathy's straightaway, as technically you'd no longer be in care. However, also present at the meeting was a lady called Erica Weston, who runs Grasslands. Have you heard of Grasslands?'

Jade shook her head.

'No,' I said.

'Grasslands is a special unit set up as part of a project to help teenage girls,' Rachel continued. 'It's about an hour's drive from here and can take up to twenty-five girls. They are housed in self-contained units with a shower and small kitchen. The girls are given support to help them return to work or studying, but there are strict rules and the girls have to sign a contract to say they will obey the rules. If they break the rules they have to leave Grasslands. I asked Erica to attend the meeting, as I felt she might be able to help you. Not everyone at the meeting felt you would benefit from going to Grasslands, Jade, but I did. I put your case to them and after much discussion we decided it was reasonable to give you the opportunity to go there and try to turn your life around.'

Rachel stopped and looked at us. I had been listening very carefully, following her every word and studying her as she'd been speaking. Grasslands sounded like a type of correction centre, a less severe form of young offenders' institution that might be able to help Jade.

Jade now raised her head and looked at Rachel. 'What's the point if I haven't got Courtney?'

'You will have her with you if you go,' Rachel said. 'Grasslands is a home primarily for teenage mothers. You can both live there for a limited time.'

I hardly dared believe what I was hearing. Was Jade being given another chance to parent Courtney? It was incredible, and I saw Jade was struggling to take in what she was being told too.

'You mean you're not going to take Courtney today?' she asked after a moment, staring at Rachel.

'Not if you agree to go to Grasslands, no. But, Jade, if you do go, you must understand you have to obey the rules and you still need to prove yourself. You will be monitored carefully by the staff at Grasslands and by me. If you give us any cause for concern Courtney will be taken into care immediately for her own safety, and you will leave Grasslands. Otherwise the girls can stay with their babies for up to a year.'

'I want to go,' Jade said, finally appreciating the chance she was being offered.

'You understand Grasslands is out of this area and away from your friends?' Rachel said. The reason Jade had originally come to me was that the only free mother-and-baby carer had been out of the area and Jade had refused to go.

'I want to go,' Jade said again.

'And you understand you will be wholly responsible for Courtney?' Rachel said. 'Staff will be on hand to advise you but it will be down to you to care for your baby and yourself. You won't be able to dump Courtney on the staff and go out with your mates, as you have been doing here with Cathy.'

Jade nodded. 'I understand.'

'Drinking and smoking at Grasslands are strictly prohibited,' Rachel continued. 'All residents have to be in their rooms with their babies by eight o'clock in the evening. It is for the good of the babies. You can have visitors in your room, but they must have left by seven o'clock and no one is allowed to stay overnight. That includes Tyler. Break any of the rules and you will have to leave immediately, and you know what that means for Courtney?' Rachel was speaking firmly to Jade, harshly almost, but I fully appreciated why and I hoped Jade did too. This was Jade's very last chance to prove herself and keep Courtney, and if she messed up now there would be no second opportunity.

'So you agree to all the rules and to sign the contract?' Rachel asked.

'Yes,' Jade said quietly. 'Thank you.'

'I had to fight for this,' Rachel said. 'So don't let me down, Jade.'

'Thank you,' Jade said again. To which I added my own thank-you.

Then for the first time in two days Jade looked at Courtney. Standing, she came round me and picked up her daughter. She took her onto her lap and encircled her in her arms. Closing her eyes, she held her close and cuddled her, as though she would never let her go. I felt her emotion, so sincere and desperate that I could have cried. I think Rachel felt it too.

Looking at me, Rachel asked: 'So Jade's continuing to make good progress with her parenting skills?'

'Yes,' I said. For Jade's rejection of Courtney over the weekend had been understandable and was now history, and I hoped Rachel didn't go up to Jade's room, find the cot gone and in my room; I'd have some explaining to do! I felt my eyes brim at the thought of all Jade had come so close to losing, and might still lose if she didn't change her ways at Grasslands.

'This is a copy of the contract you need to sign for Grasslands, together with a leaflet about the home,' Rachel said, holding out the papers she'd had on her lap. I took them, as Jade still had her arms around Courtney. 'I'm going back to the office now,' Rachel said to me. 'I'll phone Erica and confirm Jade will be taking the place. Then I'll return here at about five o'clock to collect Jade and Courtney.'

'They're leaving today?' I asked, shocked.

'The room at Grasslands is free now,' Rachel said. 'It won't stay free for long. There's a waiting list for this type of home. It's important we get this moving for Jade's and Courtney's sakes. And I don't want to give Jade the chance to go out celebrating tonight.' The faintest smile crossed Rachel's face. 'Can you help her pack, please, Cathy?'

'Yes, of course.'

Rachel said goodbye to Jade and we left her on the sofa, still cuddling Courtney, and went down the hall to the front door.

'Thank you for giving Jade this chance,' I said, by the door. 'Jade's a good kid really. She just lost her way.'

Rachel gave a heartfelt sigh. 'I just hope she doesn't throw away this chance. I do share some of my colleagues' concerns. It would be even more upsetting for them both if this failed and I had to remove Courtney in six months' time. That was one of the arguments raised against giving Jade this opportunity: that the chances of her succeeding were so slim it would be kinder to them both to place Courtney for adoption now.'

I felt an icy chill run down my spine at the possibility.

'Perhaps you could reinforce what I've said to Jade?' Rachel added.

'Yes, I will,' I said sombrely.

We said goodbye and I returned to the sitting room, where Jade was still on the sofa cuddling, kissing and now apologizing to Courtney. 'I'm so sorry. I won't mess up this time. I promise you. I'm so very sorry.' Then to me: 'Thank you, Cathy, for not telling Rachel about the weekend.'

'It's history,' I said, and I returned to sit beside Jade. 'Jade,' I began seriously, 'Rachel wants to make sure you understand that going to Grasslands is your very last chance. If anything goes wrong this time, you will lose Courtney for good. You know that, don't you?'

'Yes, I know,' Jade said. 'I won't mess up this time, I promise.'

I was pleased to hear this, but I'd heard Jade's promises to change before, as Rachel had, and if I was honest I shared Rachel's concerns (and those of the other professionals present at the meeting) that Jade might not succeed and Courtney would have to be removed from Jade's care. I picked up the leaflet about Grasslands that Rachel had left and opened it. Tucked inside was the copy of the contract Jade would have to sign. I read it out loud and as I finished Jade looked dismayed. 'There are a lot of rules, aren't there?'

'Yes, but they are there for the benefit of you, Courtney and the other residents. You will need to make sure you follow them.'

Jade nodded, but in that nod I could see that even she doubted if she was really up to doing all that was being asked of her.

'You'll be fine,' I said, positively. But only time would tell.

That afternoon I packed Jade's and Courtney's belongings into cases and bags, and stacked them in the hall while Jade looked after Courtney. The leaflet about Grasslands had said that each room contained a cot, so there was no need for me to dismantle mine for Jade to take; I doubted it would have fitted into Rachel's car anyway, with all the bags. There was no mention of a pram or stroller in the leaflet, so I told Jade she could take mine. That was already in the hall. By the time I left to collect Paula from school the packing was done. I had no qualms about leaving Jade alone in the house with Courtney, for she had no reason to run away or harm herself now.

When I met Paula in the playground I explained to her that Jade and Courtney were leaving us and that Rachel would be collecting them at about five o'clock to take them to a new home – a special flat where Jade would be given help to look after Courtney.

'But we can help them,' Paula said, not wanting them to leave. 'I like helping Jade look after Courtney.'

'I know you do, love. You've been very good at helping. But Rachel felt it would be better if they went to Grasslands.' Then, anticipating Paula's next question, I added: 'We'll be able to visit them.'

'Good. I'm excited. Is Jade?'

'Oh, yes,' I said. 'Definitely.'

* * *

However, excited wasn't the best choice of word, for when we arrived home Jade came into the hall in floods of tears. Coming up to us, she threw her arms around Paula and then me, even before I'd closed the front door. 'I'm going to miss you guys,' she sobbed. 'I love you all so much. You've become my second family.'

'We're going to miss you too, love,' I said hugging her. 'But we'll still see you. Where's Courtney?'

'Having her afternoon nap.'

'Good girl,' I said. 'Well done. You remembered.' Usually I had to remind Jade about Courtney's routine; that Jade had remembered seemed to bode well for their future together.

Jade played with Paula while I made an early and quick dinner, for I thought Jade should eat before she and Courtney left on their journey to Grasslands – about an hour's drive away. I was in the kitchen when Adrian arrived home and, as usual, he came straight into the kitchen in search of a snack.

'We're eating early tonight,' I said. I explained why.

'Is Tyler going to live at Grasslands too?' he asked, biting into an apple he'd taken from the fruit bowl.

'No, but he can visit Jade and Courtney, just as we will be able to.'

Adrian nodded and disappeared up to his room until dinner was ready.

A little after 4.30 I called everyone to the dining table, where I served the quick dinner of sausages, mashed potatoes and baked beans. They enjoyed the reprieve from green vegetables, which I usually included in the evening meal, and ate enthusiastically. Jade also spoon fed Courtney her baby food and then gave her some milk from a trainer beaker.

Towards the end of the meal Jade received two text messages. One was from Tyler. 'He says to thank you for all the meals,' Jade said, reading it. 'And to tell you he's doing OK with his exams.'

'Good,' I said. 'Hopefully we'll see him again when we visit you.'

Jade texted a reply.

The second text was from Meryl, the teacher from Jade's school who'd taken an interest in Jade. I hadn't seen Meryl since Jade had first arrived, although I knew she phoned and texted Jade. Jade read out her message: 'Good luck, Jade. I know you can do this. I'll visit you and Courtney.' I was pleased Meryl was going to keep in touch with Jade, for having come through her own problems as a teenager Meryl was a fine example of what could be achieved.

I hadn't had time to buy Jade a leaving card or present as I usually did when a child I'd been fostering left, so I gave her some money and told her to buy something for her and Courtney.

'Thanks, Cathy,' she said. 'That's really nice of you. You've all been so good to me. I'm sorry I was such a pain in the arse.'

Paula giggled at the word arse and Adrian smiled.

'You weren't a pain,' I said. 'Well, maybe a little,' I added with a smile.

When the doorbell rang shortly after five o'clock Jade answered it. As anticipated, it was Rachel. 'All ready?' she asked.

'Yes,' I said, going into the hall. 'Would you like a tea or coffee first?'

'No. I'd like to get going. Thanks anyway.'

Adrian, Rachel and I then loaded Rachel's car while Jade and Paula looked after Courtney. It was a lovely summer's evening, still warm and bright, with the birds singing and children playing outside. Once all Jade's and Courtney's belongings were in the car Adrian – not one for emotional farewells – said a quick goodbye and went up to his room. Then Paula and I hugged and kissed Jade and Courtney, and by the time we'd finished we were all dewy eyed.

'Well, thanks for everything,' Rachel said as we walked with them to the car. 'I expect I'll see you again sometime.'

'Yes,' I said.

Paula and I stood on the pavement as Jade strapped Courtney into her car seat in the rear of Rachel's car. Then Jade straightened and hugged and kissed us goodbye again. She climbed into the car beside her daughter and closed the door. As Rachel started the engine and the car pulled away, Paula slid her hand into mine and I gave it a reassuring squeeze. Jade turned and waved through the back window; then we all waved until they were out of sight.

It was a strange parting and not like the ones of the children we usually fostered. In their cases the court had made its decision and the children were either going home or to an adoptive family, their stories having a happy ending. But Jade's and Courtney's fate still hung in the balance; their long-term future together undecided. As Paula and I turned and began walking silently up the garden path I hoped and prayed that Jade and Courtney's story would eventually also have a happy ending, but that would be up to Jade.

Chapter Twenty-Two

Last Chance

Usually when a child leaves a foster carer, the social worker and the permanency team decide what, if any, contact the foster carer can have with the child. This is based on what they consider to be in the best interest of the child and can range from no contact (the reminder of the foster family could be unsettling for the child) to regular contact (a child can never have too much love). Attitudes towards post-permanency contact vary from one social services to another, but whatever the decision, as a foster carer I have to abide by it, whether I believe it is the right decision or not. However, because Jade was a teenager and deemed capable of making her own decisions it was her choice how much contact, if any, she had with me.

When I switched on my mobile at 7.00 the morning after she'd left us a text message from her came through: *Wz up aL nyt w C.* ☹ Which to my bleary eyes made no sense at all until I translated it as: *Was up all night with Courtney.*

I texted back: *Hi, love. Good 2 hear from u. C will b unsettled for a few nights – strange room etc. She'll b ok soon.* ☺

I hOp so, Jade texted back. *Miss u xxx.*

For the rest of the week I received regular text messages from Jade, upwards of five a day, most of which were worryingly negative:

d nu routine iz straNg = The new routine is strange.

d othR girls don't spk 2 me = The other girls don't speak to me.

som of d staff R horrid = Some of the staff are horrid. Which I guessed was because Jade was having to obey the rules and do as she was told.

I replied positively to all Jade's messages. Then on Thursday morning she texted: *I wsh I cld hav stayed w U xxxx.* ☹ Followed almost immediately with: *cn U vzit DIS weekend?* ☺ = *Can you visit this weekend?*

I couldn't visit Jade that weekend at such short notice, as Adrian and Paula had activities arranged for Saturday and we were going to see my parents on Sunday. So I texted back explaining this and saying that I could visit her with the children the following weekend or by myself during the week. Jade replied immediately: *Monday?* ☺ To which I returned *Yes. I'll be there about 11am.* ☺ I hoped her urgency in wanting to see me wasn't an indicator of bad news.

Following correct procedure, the next time Jill telephoned I told her I was going to visit Jade and Courtney on Monday, and she said she would inform Rachel, which was normal practice. I also told Adrian and Paula that I was going and that they could come with me when I saw Jade at a weekend or during the school holidays. Paula was disappointed that she had school and couldn't come with me on Monday, while Adrian shrugged and said, 'No worries. I'm not really interested in babies.' I didn't have a new foster child that first weekend after Jade and Courtney had gone, so I made the most of my time with Adrian and Paula and gave them lots of one-to-one attention, which was always very limited when I was fostering, and we had a nice weekend.

* * *

On Monday morning, having taken Paula to school, I returned home for a quick coffee and set off in the car to Grasslands. On the passenger seat beside me were my route instructions and a carrier bag of shopping for Jade. One of her last text messages had asked if I could bring her a 'few things': ginger cake, chocolate biscuits, a bag of assorted crisps, lemonade and a brown mascara. I guessed her new budget meant there wasn't much left over for non-essential items. I'd bought everything on her list, together with some essential items that would be useful: nappies, nappy wipes, toothpaste, tissues and toilet paper. I was looking forward to seeing Jade and Courtney again, although of course it was barely a week since they'd left.

Following the instructions, I found Grasslands easily. It was the only building at the end of the B road, a small block of brick-built flats three storeys high. It was surrounded by grass meadows, from which I assumed it had taken its name. I parked in one of the visitors' bays at the rear of the building, picked up the carrier bag and climbed out. It was another beautiful summer's day and out of town the air smelt fresher and sweeter. As I crossed the car park and headed towards the main entrance at the front of the building, I could see a fenced garden at the rear of the flats with a neatly cut lawn and a play area for children. Two young mothers were sitting on the grass with their prams beside them. They glanced up as I crossed the car park and then resumed chatting. Grasslands was situated in a lovely part of the country and I thought that the girls who lived here were very lucky to be given this chance. One of Jade's gripes in her text messages had been that Grasslands was in the middle of nowhere. In fact it was about a mile from the nearest village and there was a bus stop right outside the building.

Jade had already texted me that there was a security lock on the front door of the block of flats and that when I arrived I had to key in the number of her flat – twelve. I did this and almost immediately her voice came through the intercom: 'Is that you, Cathy?' So I thought she must have been watching out for me.

'Yes. Hello, love.'

'Come up. I can't come down because Courtney's asleep and we're not allowed to leave our babies alone.' Sensible rule, I thought.

The lock released, the door opened and I went inside. To my right on a low desk was a signing-in book with a notice asking all residents and visitors to sign in and out. Using the pen provided I printed and then signed my name, together with the time and date of my arrival. I glanced around the reception area. There was a noticeboard for residents, announcing meetings and get-togethers and reminding them to be quiet when entering and leaving the building, a couple of armchairs and a large potted fern in one corner. I couldn't see anyone and the building was quiet, save for the distant crying of a baby. Double doors left and right opened into corridors and a printed sign on the wall in front showed that flats 1–5 were left and the staff area was right. Jade was on the second floor. In front of me was the lift with a staircase to one side and I decided to take the stairs.

A lady appeared through the doors from the staff area. 'Can I help you?' she asked with a cheerful smile.

'I've come to see Jade in flat twelve,' I said. 'She knows I'm here.'

'That's fine.' She smiled and disappeared back through the double doors.

The stairs, like the reception area, were light, spotlessly clean and painted a neutral magnolia colour. At the top of the first flight of stairs was a sign on the wall showing that flats 6–10 were left and 11–15 were right. I turned right and saw Jade standing by her open front door.

'Hello, love,' I said, going over and giving her a big hug. 'You look very well.'

'Thanks. I don't feel it,' she said despondently with a shrug. Then, turning, she led the way into her flat.

I followed her in. 'This is lovely,' I said, closing the front door behind me.

We were now in a small entrance hall, painted the same neutral colour as the corridor. Three partially open doors led off the hall.

'I can't wait to have a look around,' I said enthusiastically.

'There isn't much to see,' Jade said in the same flat voice, pushing open the first door.

I took a step into the bedroom. It was small but had everything she needed: a single bed, where Jade's soft toys sat on the pillow, a built-in wardrobe, a chest of drawers and a cot in a recess, where Courtney now slept.

'How lovely,' I said quietly and, not wanting to wake Courtney, I stepped out again.

'That's the bathroom,' Jade said equally despondently, pushing open the second door.

I put my head round. 'Very nice,' I said. Again it was compact but had a bath with a shower attachment, hand basin and toilet, all in white.

I then followed Jade into the lounge-cum-dining room, the one main room. It was carpeted, painted a light beige and furnished with a sofa, wall unit, small dining table and two chairs. It even had a small wall-mounted television.

'How wonderful,' I enthused. 'And the kitchen is through there?' For I could see what looked like a kitchenette through the open door at the end of the lounge.

'Yeah,' Jade said, with as much enthusiasm as a wet lettuce leaf, and led the way into the kitchen.

'Very nice,' I said. Although the kitchen was compact, the layout had made the best use of all the available space and contained a built-in oven, microwave, fridge-freezer and storage cupboards, with a hob mounted on the work surface. 'Where do you do your washing?' I asked, for I noticed there was no washing machine.

'Downstairs, in the laundry room,' Jade said, pulling a face. 'I've only used it once.'

'It's a lovely flat with everything you need,' I said, staying positive. 'Oh yes, and here's the shopping you wanted.' I passed her the carrier bag.

'Thanks,' she said. As she peered in her expression lost its lethargy and for the first time since I'd arrived she smiled. 'Great!' she said, her hand diving into the bag. 'Chocolate biscuits! Thanks, Cathy.'

'You're welcome. They're your favourite ones.'

She dumped the bag on the floor and tearing off the top of the packet began eating the biscuits, one after another.

'Have you had breakfast?' I asked.

'Sort of.' She poured herself a glass of water to wash down the biscuits. 'Do you want a drink?' she asked. 'I haven't got tea or coffee, only water or squash.'

'No, I'm fine, thank you,' I said. 'Shall we go through to the lounge and have a chat while Courtney is asleep?'

'Yeah, sure,' Jade said, peeling off another couple of biscuits to take with her.

In the lounge I moved some discarded baby clothes from the sofa so that we could sit down. I thought the whole flat could do with a tidy-up but I didn't say so; I was here to visit Jade, not criticize her.

'You seem to be doing well, love,' I said positively, as we sat on the sofa.

Jade shrugged and then, finishing the biscuits, began complaining about Grasslands, much of which she'd already said in her text messages of the previous week. The first complaint was about the staff: 'They watch me the whole time. I feel like I'm being spied on. They tell me what to do and they can come into our rooms even if we're not here.'

'They're only doing their jobs,' I said. 'Rachel explained to you before you came here that the staff would monitor you as well as help you.'

Jade shrugged and continued with the next complaint, which was that Grasslands was in a remote spot, miles from anywhere. 'It's a dump,' she said. 'What am I supposed to do here all day? I can't see me old friends because they might get me into trouble, but the girls here are stuck up. So I haven't got any friends.' The complaints continued and I listened as Jade grumbled and got them off her chest. They weren't allowed to put up posters in their rooms in case it damaged the walls. 'How sad is that?' she said. And her mother could only visit every other weekend because of the lengthy bus journey. I replied to all her complaints positively and constructively and explained the reason for the situation that had given rise to her complaint, or made a suggestion as to how Jade could improve things.

Jade finished with: 'And Rachel's coming on Thursday! She's got a meeting here with the staff and I've got to go.' She pulled a face, folded her arms and flopped back on the sofa.

'The meeting is nothing to worry about,' I reassured her. 'Social workers have lots of meetings. And of course you want to be included: the meeting is about you and Courtney. You wouldn't be very happy if you thought they were talking about you without you being there, would you?' But I could see Jade was unconvinced, just as she had been by all my other positive suggestions that could help her settle more easily at Grasslands. 'Has Tyler been to see you?' I asked.

'Yeah, but he had to leave by seven o'clock. It's not fair. I wish I was still with you, Cathy.' Her face clouded and she looked close to tears.

'Oh, love,' I said, putting my arm around her shoulders and giving her a hug. 'It's bound to be strange here at first. You've only been here a week. You've got to give yourself time. Try talking to the other girls. I expect many of them feel the same as you do. You could suggest going out with your babies, or just go and sit in the garden on a nice day.'

Jade gave a nod but it was half-hearted and uncommitted, and I was concerned. Her negative attitude meant that she wasn't putting the effort needed into settling at Grasslands and making it work. And of course if it didn't work there was no alternative. I continued in the same positive vein, reassuring her that she would be fine if she gave herself time and made a big effort.

Then Courtney woke and Jade immediately stood and went into the bedroom, returning in a few moments with Courtney in her arms. As soon as Courtney saw me she grinned and gurgled.

'She remembers you,' Jade said, setting her in my lap.

'She does.'

I kissed and cuddled her and smelt that delicious baby smell. I'd missed her more than I'd cared to admit. 'She's grown,' I said as she smiled and tried to grab my hair. She was a gorgeous baby and it saddened me that Jade didn't appear to be making the effort that was needed to remain at Grasslands.

'You're going to have to make a big effort,' I said more firmly. 'You need to do all you can to make this work. Remember how you felt a week ago when you thought you were going to lose Courtney? It could still happen.' I thought that Jade might have grown complacent now the immediate danger of losing Courtney had passed.

'I know,' Jade said, lethargically. 'I just wish I hadn't ballsed it up at your place. Then I could have stayed with you and the kids. I feel so alone here. Will you visit me every day?'

I took Jade's hand in mine as Courtney gurgled and grinned at me. 'I'll visit you as often as I can, love,' I said. 'But it won't be every day. I'll be fostering another child before long and really it's up to you to make this work. I can stay in contact, but there's a limit to what I or anyone else can do. You have a lovely daughter. Do whatever it takes to keep her, for both your sakes.'

I stayed while Jade gave Courtney her lunch and then I said I had to go to collect Paula from school. I needed to make sure I allowed enough time for any delay I might meet on the road. It was difficult leaving and I could see Jade would have liked me to have stayed longer. I hugged and kissed them both and said I'd definitely visit again the following week, if not before. I said I'd phone during the week and of course Jade could text or phone whenever she wanted to. Apart from my own commitments I knew I should be careful and limit my involvement with Jade, as she was being assessed to see if she could cope with parenting Courtney alone; my being there too often wouldn't count in her favour.

'Say hi to the kids and your parents,' Jade said, as she came with me to the door with Courtney in her arms.

'I will, love. Take care and look after yourself.'

Jade smiled. 'I'll try. Will you bring me another bag of goodies next time you come?'

'Yes, of course, love. Text me with what you want.'

We hugged and kissed goodbye again and then Jade stood in the corridor just outside her flat, holding Courtney, while I walked to the top of the stairs. I turned and waved before I began down the stairs and they both waved back, Courtney happy and smiling and Jade looking sad and alone. I knew their future together was far from certain and I wished I could have done more to help.

Chapter Twenty-Three

Broken Rules and Promises

That evening I told Adrian and Paula that Jade and Courtney were well and that Jade sent her love. I'd decided on the drive home that I wouldn't take them to visit until the outcome for Jade and Courtney looked more positive. Bad enough if Jade and Courtney were eventually separated but if Paula and Adrian maintained a close bond with them, they would feel their separation even more acutely.

Jill phoned the following day and among other things asked how my visit to see Jade and Courtney had gone. I said I thought it would take Jade a while to settle into Grasslands but she was coping. As I had thought she would, Jill said she would pass this on to Rachel, although my role as Jade's foster carer was finished. And because I was no longer Jade's carer I wouldn't receive any feedback from Rachel (or Jill) on her progress. In line with normal practice I'd sent my fostering notes (in respect of Jade and Courtney) to Rachel to place on file at the social services. As there was no requirement now for me to keep any formal record of my visits to Jade, now she'd left, I just made a note in my diary that I'd visited her. Jill phoned again the following morning in respect of a child the local authority were about to bring into care, and by the evening I was fostering another child, who fortunately attended school, which meant I would still be able to visit Jade as planned on a weekday.

I was very busy with the new child that week and I also had to attend a day's foster-carer training, so I didn't manage to visit Jade for a second time that week, but I went as promised the following Monday.

Unfortunately my time with Courtney and Jade was cut short because I was delayed by a traffic jam. We had an hour and a half together, and Courtney was her usual bubbly self and Jade seemed a bit more positive. She said she'd made friends with a girl in the flat next door. Her name was Tracy and she was the same age as Jade and had a six-month-old son. I was pleased Jade had made a friend, although I was a little concerned that, from what Jade told me, Tracy, like Jade, was anti-Grasslands. They seemed to see themselves as inmates in a penitentiary rather than lucky girls being given a lot of help and a second chance to keep their babies.

'But we escape sometimes!' Jade announced proudly, referring to when she and Tracy left Grasslands. 'Once we've done all our chores we go into the village.'

'That sounds nice,' I said, bouncing Courtney on my lap. 'I drive through the village on my way here. It's very pretty. Have you seen the duck pond and those lovely little thatched cottages?'

'Nah,' Jade said. 'We go to the village shop for our fags.'

'Fags?' I asked in dismay, glancing up from Courtney. 'Jade, you're supposed to have stopped smoking and you're not allowed to smoke here.'

'We don't smoke in the building; it's fire-alarmed,' she said, surprised I should even think this. 'But they can't stop us outside.'

'Do Rachel and Tyler know you've started smoking again?' I asked.

Jade shook her head. 'Nah, and don't tell them, will you?'

'Exactly, Jade!' I said, not pleased. 'The reason you don't want me to tell Rachel and Tyler is because you know they'd be very disappointed. Why start again? It's bad for your health and very expensive. Your budget is stretched to the limit as it is.'

'I know,' Jade said, with a small down-hearted shrug. 'But it's only a packet a week and I need something to keep me sane here. We're not allowed to go to the pub or bring back drink here.'

'No, and don't be tempted to break that rule or you will be in trouble,' I warned.

'Of course I won't.' I hoped she was telling the truth.

'Jade, Tracy is a nice girl, isn't she?' I asked. 'I mean, the two of you are not going to get into trouble, are you?'

'That's what Rachel asked,' Jade said indignantly, a little angry. 'Why don't any of you trust me?'

'We do,' I said. I left the rest of my thoughts unspoken.

Until school broke up for the summer holidays I continued to visit Jade every Monday. Sometimes we stayed in the flat and other times, if the weather was good, we went for a walk or sat in the garden with Courtney. I always took a bag of 'goodies', as Jade called them. As well as the biscuits, cakes and choco-late Jade ordered by text, I added some essential items like nappies and tissues, and also some fruit and vegetables, which seemed to have disappeared from Jade's diet. I met Tracy briefly a couple of times on my way in and out of Jade's flat and she seemed a pleasant girl, although a little immature. She giggled a lot and on one occasion seemed to think it was funny that she'd spent the last of her allowance for the week on having her tongue pierced, and therefore didn't have enough for nappies or food. Jade seemed to be managing on her budget (helped by the 'food parcels' from her mother and me) and she gave some of the nappies and food I'd brought to Tracy. I didn't mind; I felt sorry for Tracy. Jade had told me she'd been abused as a child by her stepfather, and when her mother and her new partner had found out she was pregnant they'd thrown her out of her home, so she was now completely alone in the world.

Jade also told me that Tyler was now working two days a week on a market stall. He was hoping to be taken on as an apprentice mechanic in September, if he got the exam results he needed. I'd always felt Tyler was a good influence on Jade and the fact that he was now seeing Jade and Courtney three times a week seemed to bode well. Sometimes he went to Grasslands, where he and Jade made lunch together, and sometimes they met halfway – between Grasslands and where he lived. A couple of times Jade took Courtney on the bus to see his mother, whom Jade had now forgiven for not being able to adopt Courtney. Jade also visited her own mother, but usually Jackie came to Grasslands; sometimes she brought one or more of Jade's siblings with her, but never all four at once.

When school broke up at the end of July I visited Jade on the Sundays Adrian and Paula were out with their father – two in August. The child I was fostering had weekend contact at that time. At the end of August I took the children on holiday to the coast and we had a lovely time. The first weekend in September, just before the schools returned, I suggested to Adrian and Paula they might like to come with me to see Jade and Courtney. I was more confident that Jade was on track for completing a successful parenting assessment and therefore being able to keep Courtney. Paula was delighted at the prospect of seeing Jade and Courtney again, and Adrian was amenable to the idea. I suggested to Jade we go out for Sunday lunch – my treat – and she asked if Tyler could join us. I said of course he could, which resulted in Adrian being as enthusiastic at the outing as Paula was. I said I would arrange to collect Tyler in the car en route to Grasslands.

Sunday was another lovely sunny day and Tyler was as pleased to see us as we were to see him. He sat in the passenger seat in the front of the car but spent most of the journey swivelled round talking to Adrian and Paula. He asked Adrian and Paula if they'd had a nice holiday, told them about his job on the market, and his apprenticeship; then he talked about school and the new term and how important it was for Adrian and Paula to work hard. I was listening as I drove. He said he'd got the exam results he needed to start his apprenticeship and I congratulated him, saying it was a big achievement considering everything else that had been going on in his life. Tyler said he was going to work very hard in his apprenticeship so that eventually he would be able to earn enough money to support Jade and Courtney so that they could live together as a family.

When we arrived at Grasslands Jade was already waiting outside, at the front of the building, with Courtney. She was pleased to see Adrian and Paula and let Paula push the stroller. I didn't know if Courtney remembered Adrian and Paula, but she might have done for she kept staring at Adrian, although that could have been because of the funny faces he and Tyler were pulling to make her chuckle. We walked in pairs along the narrow country path into the village, where we had lunch in the garden of the pub. Tyler and Jade ordered soft drinks as I did and I was pleased that Jade didn't creep off for a cigarette after we'd eaten. It was a lovely day and I left feeling very positive.

School began again in September and I resumed visiting Jade on Mondays. With no feedback from Rachel I could only assess Jade's progress on what I saw and from what Jade told me, and I thought she was doing well. She'd been cooking regular meals for her and Courtney and had taken Courtney to the clinic regularly to be weighed and measured. There had been a few minor incidents at Grasslands when the staff had had to speak to Jade, but it was no more than typical teenage behaviour. A couple of times she was told to turn down her music, as it had woken the baby in the flat above, and on other occasions she'd been asked to tidy the laundry room after using it. I guessed the laundry room probably looked like my bathroom after Jade had been in there. Jade also told me that she'd received a caution from the police in respect of the previous shoplifting incident at the mall and she appreciated how lenient they'd been as she could have received a custodial sentence. Possibly leniency had been shown because she was trying hard to be a reformed character and had a baby, but I didn't know.

However, at the beginning of October – by which time Jade had been at Grasslands for three months – the optimism I had increasingly been feeling was shattered.

I arrived at Grasslands on Monday morning with the usual bags of goodies for Jade and Tracy, and pressed the security button. I expected Jade to answer more or less straightaway, for I'd got into the habit of texting her an estimated time of arrival and updating it by text if I was delayed. Today she didn't answer straightaway, and I pressed the bell again and waited some more. Then a voice came through the grid and it wasn't Jade.

'Hello, Cathy. It's Rachel. You can come up.' The intercom switched off and the door clicked open.

I immediately knew something was wrong. Rachel wasn't due to see Jade again until the following week, and since Jade had been at Grasslands she hadn't made any unannounced visits, as the staff covered that role. Rachel's voice had sounded flat and serious, and I thought there must have been an emergency of some kind. With my heart pounding and my fears for Courtney's and Jade's safety mounting, I ran up the stairs and round the corner to Jade's flat. I knocked on the door and a few moments later Rachel opened it.

'Come in, Cathy,' she said sombrely. 'It's nice to see you again.'

She disappeared into the lounge. I closed the door and followed her in. Erica, who I knew to be the manager of Grasslands, was sitting on the sofa. As I entered, she looked up and smiled a weak hello. Jade was sitting beside her in tears and Courtney was nowhere to be seen. 'Where's Courtney?' I asked anxiously, looking around.

'Having a sleep,' Erica said, nodding to the closed bedroom door behind me. 'Don't worry, she's all right now.' The 'now' did nothing to reassure me.

'What happened?' I asked, as Rachel pulled up a chair for me.

'There was a bit of an upset here last night,' Erica said. 'It resulted in Courtney having to go to hospital.'

'But she's all right?' I asked, very worried. Jade had her head down and couldn't bear to look at me. She was sniffing and wiping her eyes with a tissue.

'Do you want me to tell Cathy?' Erica asked Jade. 'You said Cathy could come up and join us, so I'm assuming you don't mind her knowing?'

Jade shrugged. 'If you want to.'

'I'll take that as yes,' Erica said formally. Then looking at me: 'Late last night Courtney fell off the work surface in the kitchen and cut her forehead. She needed two stitches and the hospital checked her for concussion. I collected them from the hospital and we got back here just after five o'clock.'

'But Courtney is all right?' I asked again.

'It could have been worse,' Erica said stiffly.

'What was she doing on the work surface?' I asked, for clearly it was an odd place for her to be, especially at night.

'I put her there,' Jade said, finally looking at me, and clearly annoyed with her own stupidity. 'It's my fault. I put her there and she fell off. I didn't know she was going to move, did I?'

I looked from Jade to Erica and Rachel. Although it was a silly thing to do, the atmosphere in the room suggested there was more to it than an unfortunate accident. There was silence before Rachel spoke.

'Jade put Courtney on the work surface while she opened a can of beer,' Rachel said evenly. 'Tracy and she had been drinking and when Courtney woke Jade took her out of her cot and carried her into the kitchen. With her judgement impaired by alcohol, she sat Courtney on the work surface while she opened another can of beer. As a result Courtney tumbled off and was injured.'

I stared in silence at Rachel as the wider implications of what had happened hit me.

'And Jason, Tracy's son,' Rachel added, 'was left alone in his cot in the flat next door.'

'Tracy checked on him!' Jade blurted angrily, her eyes flashing. 'He was asleep.'

Fear gripped me as I looked from Jade to Rachel and then to Erica. The girls knew the rules at Grasslands and they knew they were in place for everyone's safety. They'd broken the rules and Courtney had been hurt.

'We never leave our babies unattended in our flats,' Erica said seriously, turning to look at Jade. 'These flats represent independent living and you never leave a baby or young child alone in a flat or house – here or anywhere.'

'They're going to take Tracy's baby,' Jade blurted through fresh tears. 'They're taking Jason and it's not fair.'

I stared at Jade and hoped she was wrong. Then Rachel spoke: 'Tracy has already left Grasslands. A member of staff here is looking after Jason until the foster carer arrives.'

I went cold and saw the pain and fear on Jade's face. I'd got to know Tracy through visiting Jade and my heart ached for her. She had no home of her own to go to, no parents to support her, and now she'd lost the one person who mattered in her life – her son. And while I knew the decision to remove her baby wouldn't have been taken lightly, I feared for Tracy's safety; she'd confided in Jade that if she ever lost Jason her life wouldn't be worth living.

'Tracy's social worker will be seeing Tracy later today,' Rachel added, by way of reassurance.

I nodded dumbly. I could see that Erica and Rachel were struggling with the decisions they were having to make, and I knew I had to stay focused on Jade and help her all I could.

'Until now Jade's been doing very well at Grasslands, hasn't she?' I said, looking at Rachel and Erica. 'She's established a good routine for Courtney; she's taken her to the clinic regularly, and Courtney is always clean and nicely dressed.'

'Jade has been making progress, yes,' Rachel said. 'It's a pity she's so easily led.' Which of course had always been Jade's problem.

'I'm sorry,' Jade said through more tears, all anger now gone. 'I'm sorry. I won't do it again, I promise. I know I acted stupidly. Please give me another chance?'

I heard the desperation in her plea and, not knowing what had been said before I'd arrived, I looked at Rachel. The hairs on the back of my neck stood up as I asked: 'You're not going to take Courtney into care now, are you?'

Rachel took a deep breath. 'Not now. I'm meeting my manager this afternoon.'

'Grasslands doesn't suit everyone,' Erica added. My fears grew, for I knew that Jade losing Courtney had just taken a big step closer.

'Oh, Jade,' I said quietly under my breath, feeling my eyes mist.

No one said anything for a while and an eerie silence weighed heavily on the room. My thoughts circled as I tried to think of suggestions that might help Jade to keep Courtney, maybe a possible alternative to living at Grasslands, but Grasslands had been the only alternative and Jade's last chance. And Jade knew that.

The silence was broken by the bleep of an incoming text message. Erica took her phone from her pocket and, having read the message, looked at Rachel. 'I have to go now,' she said. 'The foster carer has arrived for Jason.'

My heart clenched and Jade's tears flowed.

'I'll see you downstairs in a minute,' Rachel said to Erica.

Erica stood and nodding a goodbye left the room, presumably to supervise the handing over of Jason to the foster carer. I thought of Tracy and swallowed hard.

We were silent again; then, without looking up, Jade said quietly, 'I want you to go now, Cathy.'

I didn't think she meant it. I thought she was embarrassed by what she'd done and was really asking for a hug, and reassurance from me that I would stand by her. I didn't move, but then she said: 'Go now, please.'

'Jade, if you really want me to go, love, I will,' I said.

'Yes. I do,' she said, still not looking at me. 'I don't want to see you any more, ever again, so go.'

Stunned, I looked at Rachel, who nodded for me to leave. 'Don't worry, Cathy,' Rachel said. 'I'll stay with Jade for a while and make sure she's all right.'

There was nothing else I could say or do and I had to respect Jade's wishes. Standing, I said to Jade: 'Shall I phone you later?'

'No,' she replied without looking at me.

After placing the carrier bags of 'goodies' I'd brought beside the sofa, I crossed the room and let myself out. Hurt and hurting for Jade, Tracy and their babies, I went slowly down the stairs and into reception. Erica, together with another member of staff and a foster carer I didn't know, were standing in a small group facing each other. The foster carer had Jason in her arms and was asking Erica about his routine. When a baby or child is taken into care as an emergency, it is often the foster carer who has to find out all she can about the baby or child. The three of them glanced over as I crossed reception. As I opened the outer door I heard the carer say: 'We're new carers. This is our first placement. My husband and I are very excited.'

And I thought of Tracy and what she must be feeling, having just lost her baby: certainly not excited. But that's the nature of fostering: one family's gain is another family's loss and misery.

Chapter Twenty-Four
Moving On

Jade had said that she didn't want to see me again and that I shouldn't phone, so I didn't – for the rest of that week. I thought she might have felt she'd let me down (as well as herself and Courtney), and also that she needed time alone. Although I didn't hear from her she was never far from my thoughts. I hoped against hope that the future wasn't as bleak as it appeared and a way could be found that would allow Jade to keep her baby. I thought about texting Tyler to see if he had any news but I decided if he wanted to be in touch with me he would.

Finally, on Friday, I texted Jade, saying simply: *Thinking of you, love Cathy x.*

She didn't reply.

A month went by and I heard nothing from Jade, although I knew that she and Courtney were still at Grasslands. Jill, whom I saw regularly in connection with the child I was fostering, saw Rachel at the council offices between meetings, and Rachel told Jill that Jade was still at Grasslands, but she didn't say any more. I cautioned myself not to read too much into what appeared to be good news, and that I should try to distance myself from Jade and Courtney, but it was very difficult. As a foster carer I'm often asked if I get attached to the children I look after. Of course I do. Foster carers couldn't properly nurture and care for the children we look after if we didn't get attached, and it didn't matter that Jade was nearly an adult. I was attached to her and Courtney and I worried about them and missed them just as I would a much younger child.

Then in the second week of November I was shopping in a department store in the mall. Christmas gifts were starting to appear in the shops and some shops even had Christmas music playing. I was examining a box of holly-scented candles when my phone bleeped with a text message. Returning the box to the display, I took my phone from my bag and was amazed to see a text message from Jade: *u cn ph f u stil wn2. Jade x.* Which took me a moment to translate into: *You can phone if you still want to. Jade x.*

Thank goodness, I thought, relieved I had finally heard from her. I left the store and went into the high street to phone her where the reception was better and my conversation couldn't be so easily overheard.

Jade answered her phone immediately.

'Great to hear from you, love,' I said. 'How are you?'

'OK,' Jade said. 'How are you and the kids?'

'We're all very well, thank you.'

There was a long awkward silence, so I began talking – telling Jade that I was shopping with Christmas in mind, and snippets about Adrian, Paula, my parents and our cat – in fact anything that filled the silence and avoided me asking Jade if Courtney was still with her. Then, to my utter relief, I heard a baby in the background.

'Is that Courtney?' I asked.

'Yes, and I'd better go. She's just woken from her lunchtime nap. Cathy, will you come and visit me?'

'Yes, of course. Are you still at Grasslands?'

'Yes. Same flat.'

'So is everything all right, then?'

She hesitated. 'I won't know for a while yet. They've done me a contract. I'll explain when I see you.'

'OK, love. I'll check in my diary and text you a date.'

'Thanks.'

The phone went dead and I stood for a moment in the high street considering what Jade had said. While Courtney was still with her, which was clearly good news, whether they could remain together apparently still hung in the balance. Once home I would check in my diary and text Jade the first date I was free. I returned to the shop but my heart wasn't in shopping any more and I was soon driving home again.

Two days later I arrived at Grasslands, carrying a bag of 'goodies'. I was nervous; it had been over a month since I'd last seen Jade and we hadn't parted on the best of terms. If Jade had been a younger child who'd rejected me on a previous visit I'd simply have forgotten it, but with someone of Jade's age I had to respect the fact she was an adult, with a personality of her own, and might not be ready to completely make up and move on.

I pressed the buzzer to her flat and a minute later her voice answered: 'Come on up, Cathy.' It was lovely to be there again.

When I turned the corner at the top of the stairs Jade was waiting by her open flat door with Courtney in her arms. I went over and hugged and kissed them both. Jade turned and led the way into her flat. But while she was pleased to see me, once inside I thought I detected a certain reserve in her manner, as though she was putting some distance between us.

Courtney, of course, was her usual chirpy self and seemed to remember me. Now ten months old and standing, she was very inquisitive of everything around her. Jade said she was into everything and she couldn't let her out of her sight even for a moment. I was more than happy to sit on the floor and keep Courtney amused while Jade talked to me.

Jade talked generally about her and Courtney, and amongst other things told me that now Tyler had started his apprenticeship he could only get over to see her and Courtney at weekends, but he phoned on the other nights and Jade sent him pictures of Courtney on her phone. Jade said she'd made a new friend at Grasslands, a girl called Sapphire. Perhaps my expression gave away my apprehension, for she quickly added: 'Don't worry, Cathy. She's sensible. We won't get into trouble.'

I nodded: 'So you've been allowed to stay at Grasslands?'

Jade then explained about the 'contract' Rachel had drawn up and which Jade had had to sign. It was essentially a set of expectations (rules) that the social services had set out in respect of Jade's behaviour and her parenting of Courtney, to which she had to adhere in order to stay with Courtney at Grasslands. These included Grasslands' rules as well as some extra undertakings: for example, that Jade stopped smoking so that she could better manage her budget. The contract was similar to a 'home-rules contract' with which I was familiar and which is sometimes used by parents and foster carers to modify unsafe behaviour in teenagers. The consequence of breaking a home-rules contract is usually loss of a privilege: for example, the teenager is stopped from going out in the evening. The consequence of Jade breaking the contract was far more serious, for Rachel had made it clear this really was her very last chance.

As Jade talked, I realized that the reserve in her nature was more a matter of maturity. She appeared less impulsive and seemed to be finally growing up and accepting her responsibilities as a parent. She admitted: 'Seeing Tracy lose her baby did it for me. I never thought they'd take her but they did. Mum says that was my wake-up call.'

I thought Jackie was right. I asked Jade if she'd heard from Tracy, but she hadn't and she said she was worried about her. I reassured her that Tracy's social worker would make sure she was all right, but that was the only reassurance I could give her, for I didn't know what had become of Tracy.

Jade made us a sandwich for lunch, which to my surprise had lettuce and cucumber in it. 'Very healthy,' I said.

She laughed. 'Yeah, the staff here are impressed too, but I still like my fry-ups, and chocolate biscuits.'

When it was time for me to leave, I didn't simply assume Jade wanted me to visit her again; I asked her. She said she did but not every week. 'I need to do this alone,' she said. 'To prove to them' – the social services – 'and me I can do it.'

'I understand,' I said. 'Text me when you want me to visit. You're doing very well.' But how many times had I praised her before and then been disappointed?

I hugged and kissed them both goodbye at the door and I came away feeling fairly positive, although I cautioned myself on being too optimistic. I subsequently told Jill of my visit but not Adrian and Paula. I was protecting them again, just in case the worst happened.

* * *

At the end of November I received a text message from Jade asking if I'd visit again, and I went two days later and stayed for a couple of hours. She still seemed to be making good progress and I allowed myself a little more optimism.

I visited her again a week before Christmas, when I took presents for her, Tyler and Courtney, and included in the bag of goodies sweet mince pies, a chocolate Santa and a chocolate yuletide log. Jade was thrilled with all the chocolate and thanked me. She'd decorated her living room festively with a small artificial Christmas tree with lights and had hung some garlands from the ceiling. It looked very nice. Jade told me that all the girls at Grasslands had been given some extra money towards Christmas decorations for their flats, although apparently some of the girls had spent the money not on decorations but on make-up, so I was pleased Jade (and Sapphire) had used their money correctly.

'The room looks lovely,' I said again. 'You've done a good job.'

'Thanks. I did it while Courtney was asleep, so it was a surprise for her.'

Jade was excited and looking forward to Christmas, which would be Courtney's first. They were spending Christmas Day at her mother's and then on Boxing Day, Tyler was coming to Jade's flat. 'Tyler and me are going to make sure Courtney has a proper family Christmas,' Jade said. 'Just like the ones you see on the television.' And from the way she said this I thought that perhaps her Christmases as a child hadn't always been everything she'd hoped.

* * *

Moving On

On Christmas morning Jade texted me, wishing us all a very merry Christmas or rather *a vry mrry xmas xxx*. The next time I saw her was near the end of January, a couple of days before Courtney's first birthday. I took presents and a card for Courtney, as well as the usual bag of goodies, and Jade hid the presents away until it was Courtney's birthday. I also gave Jade some new clothes for Courtney; she was growing so quickly that Jade was struggling to manage on her budget (even though she had stopped smoking). She'd been buying second-hand clothes for Courtney and herself from charity shops. Encouraged by the staff at Grasslands, Jade was planning a little birthday party for Courtney and had invited six other mothers and their babies to come to her flat at two o'clock on the afternoon of Courtney's birthday. Jade told me the staff were going to help her make some fairy cakes and jellies for the party, and there'd be sandwiches and soft drinks too. She also said that Meryl, the teacher from her old school, was going to visit the following week.

I saw Jade once in February for a couple of hours and everything seemed fine; then in March I received a text message: *I'm MovN*: which meant *I'm moving*. My heart sank until I understood the rest of the message – *We're bn givN a fl@. wl txt wen settld. tnx 4 evryting. lov Jade x* – which meant: *We're being given a flat. Will text when settled. Thanks for everything. Love Jade.*

I knew that being given a social-housing flat was a big step forward. This was independent living for Jade, so the social services must be confident enough that she could parent her baby without the supervision that Grasslands offered. But I also knew that after moving, Courtney would still be monitored by the social services and possibly stay on the child-protection register until the social services were certain she was no longer in any danger. I told Jill of this new development and she was pleased. I also told Adrian and Paula, for although they were now involved with the new child we were fostering they still talked about Jade, Courtney and Tyler, and from time to time asked how they were, just as they did with most of the children we'd fostered. While a child might leave a foster family, they never leave our hearts or memories.

Two months later – in May – I received a text from Jade: *cum n vzit wen u wnt* which I easily translated as: *Come and visit when you want.* She'd included the address of her new flat, and when I looked at the postcode more carefully I thought it must be on the estate where her mother lived. I texted back: *I'd luv to visit. R u lving close 2 ur mum?*

Yes. 5 mins wlk frm mum's, she replied, which was fantastic for Jade.

I decided not to take Adrian and Paula on my first visit, so I chose a weekday when they would be at school. There would be plenty of opportunity in the future for them to see Jade and Courtney when I knew for certain they would stay together.

Jade didn't text me a list of items she'd like in her 'goody bag' as she usually did, so I included her favourite crisps, chocolate biscuits and cake and the essential nappies, fruit, etc. I usually put in. I found the road where she lived easily and parked the car in one of the designated bays at the rear of the flats. I went down the walkway and to the front. It was 11.25 a.m. and Jade was expecting me at 11.30. Jade had already texted me that her flat was on the third floor, and I took the stairs, which smelt vaguely of disinfectant but were clean and freshly painted.

Arriving at the top, I went part way down the corridor until I came to flat twenty. I pressed the bell and waited, nervously twiddling the carrier bag at my side. The door opened and to my astonishment Tyler greeted me.

'Hi, Cathy!' he said, stepping forward and throwing his arms around me in a big hug. 'Welcome!'

'Tyler, how nice to see you,' I said as he released me and I could breathe again.

'Come on in,' he said. 'I took the day off work so I could see you. Do you like our flat?'

'So you live here too?' I asked, surprised.

'I do,' he said, jumping around me like an excited puppy. 'This way!'

He pushed open the first door that led off the hall and I followed him into the lounge, where Jade was sitting on the floor showing Courtney how to do a large-piece jigsaw. Jade immediately stood and came over and kissed my cheek; then she said to Courtney: 'Look who's come to see us. It's Aunty Cathy.'

Courtney looked up at me, made a good attempt at saying Aunty Cathy, and then, standing, toddled over. 'Hello, darling,' I said, picking her up and hugging her. 'Aren't you a big girl now?'

'Mummy,' she said pointing to Jade.

'That's right. Clever girl,' I said.

'And who's this?' Tyler asked, grinning and pointing to himself.

'Daddy,' she said clearly, which obviously pleased Tyler. He clapped, grinned and danced around her, which made Courtney chuckle. I put her down, as she wanted to be on the floor.

'Would you like a cup of tea?' Tyler asked me as Courtney went to the bookshelf and began pulling off the magazines.

'Yes, please,' I said.

'Do you want one?' Tyler asked Jade, who was now redirecting her daughter's attention back to the jigsaw.

'Please,' she said.

'There are some biscuits in there,' I said, passing the carrier bag to Tyler.

'Thanks, Cath.' He disappeared into the kitchen to make the tea while I joined Courtney and Jade on the floor with the puzzle.

'This is a lovely flat,' I said.

'Yes, we're lucky. We decorated it all ourselves.'

The lounge was freshly painted in off-white and had a new carpet and curtains. There was a sofa, which I guessed was good second-hand, and a small coffee table, on which stood some framed photographs of Jade's and Tyler's families and a large one of Courtney. Against one wall was a television on a unit that contained DVDs and CDs. Beside the television were more family photos and a stack of teenage magazines. Pushed against another wall was a large plastic toy box containing Courtney's toys.

'You didn't tell me Tyler was living with you,' I said to Jade as the clink of crockery came from kitchen.

'I wanted it to be a surprise. He's been great. The flat was left in a disgusting state. No one on the housing list wanted it but we jumped at it. Mum looked after Courtney while we cleared out all the rubbish and then cleaned and painted it. We've done well, haven't we, Cathy?'

'You certainly have, love. Do you see your mother more often now?'

'Oh yes, and my brothers and sisters. It's great living here. They're all just round the corner.'

I was pleased Jade seemed so settled and the support from her mother would be invaluable. As we talked, Jade told me her mother had changed her working hours so that she was free to help Jade more, and that they were closer now than they'd ever been and had stopped all the arguing.

We finished the jigsaw and Tyler appeared, carrying two mugs of tea and one of the packets of biscuits I'd brought.

'Goody, my favourites,' Jade said, standing and taking the packet. Opening it, she peeled off two and then offered the packet to me. I took a biscuit and sat on the sofa beside Tyler, so that my hot tea was away from Courtney on the floor.

'So how is work?' I asked him.

'Good,' he said. 'The governor's pleased with me. He says I'm the best apprentice they've had at the garage in a long while. He says I don't mind getting my hands dirty.'

'Yeah, his overalls are filthy and I have to wash them,' Jade said, throwing him an indulgent smile.

'Comes with the job,' Tyler said. Then to me: 'How's the kids?'

'Adrian and Paula are fine,' I said. 'Looking forward to the end of term and the long summer holidays.'

'Bring them next time,' Tyler said. 'We'd like to see them and we're a good example now, aren't we? Rachel said so.'

I smiled, while Jade pulled a face at the mention of Rachel. 'She keeps coming here,' she moaned. 'Sometimes we don't know when she's coming. She can see we're doing well. I'm fine now with Tyler here.'

'It's her job,' Tyler said, and I nodded.

I'd always thought that despite his youth Tyler was a good influence on Jade and this seemed to have been confirmed. As the three of us talked, I could see that Jade relied on Tyler, listened to what he said and respected his opinion, which in my view was no bad thing. Although he was young in many ways he was far more mature than others of his age. He acted responsibly, had sound values and principles, and as far as I knew had never got into trouble as Jade had.

We finished our tea and Tyler suggested he show me around the flat, as Jade was keeping Courtney amused. But when Courtney saw her father about to leave the room she immediately stood and toddled over, wanting to come too, so we all went on a guided tour: the main bedroom, Courtney's bedroom, the bathroom and kitchen, all of which, although sparsely furnished, were clean and very tidy. Jade and Tyler were justly proud of what they had achieved and I admired each room and congratulated them on their achievements. As we went round, Jade also made a point of telling me she never drank or smoked now, not at all.

'Well done,' I said again. But by the end of the tour I was starting to feel that they were trying too hard, as though showcasing their family and wanting to impress me, probably as they did when Rachel visited.

We returned to the lounge and talked some more, and then Tyler offered to make me some lunch, but I said I needed to go and do a few things before it was time to collect Paula from school. I also thought Tyler needed to relax on his day off from work; he hadn't stopped since I'd arrived. I made a fuss of Courtney and then the three of them saw me to the door.

'Come again soon,' Tyler said.

'Thanks, I will,' I said. 'You're all doing very well.'

I stepped out of the flat and into the corridor and was about to head towards the staircase when Jade suddenly said: 'Oh, Cathy! I nearly forgot to tell you. I've got some good news.'

I stopped and turned, thinking she was about to tell me of another home improvement they were planning to make or, heaven forbid, that she was pregnant. But to my delight she said quietly: 'I've applied to go to college in September, to do some exams.'

'That's fantastic,' I said, returning to her. 'What will you study?'

'I'm going to take my A-levels. Then I was thinking of training to be a teaching assistant.'

'Fantastic. How sensible,' I said, truly impressed.

'The college has a crèche and Mum said she'd have Courtney some days,' Jade explained. 'I'm so excited. I can't wait.'

'You'll do very well, Jade. I know you will. You're a clever girl.'

'She is,' Tyler said, tenderly slipping his arm around Jade's shoulders; Courtney was standing between them. 'I'm very proud of my Jade,' he said. 'It'll be hard work but I know she can do this.'

'Absolutely,' I said. 'There's no doubt,' and I kissed Jade's cheek. 'I'm proud of you too, Jade. Let me know if I can help with childcare or even the studying.'

'Thanks, Cathy. I will.'

'And there'll be another piece of news soon,' Tyler added, straightening and puffing his chest out like a proud pigeon.

'Oh yes?' I looked at Tyler, slightly apprehensively. Jade looked at him too, puzzled.

'I wasn't going to say anything just yet,' he said, glancing at Jade. 'But as you're here, Cathy, I'd like you to know. It's Jade's birthday in two weeks and I'm planning on asking her to marry me.'

I could see from Jade's face that she was as surprised by this as I was. Her eyes rounded and her mouth dropped open.

'Well, what a lovely surprise!' I said, recovering first. 'How wonderful.'

Tyler then turned Jade to face him and, taking her hands between his, looked deep into her eyes. 'Jade, will you marry me?' he asked sincerely. 'I hope you will.'

Jade didn't have to say anything; her expression said it all and I felt my eyes mist. As a foster carer I've witnessed many emotional scenes over the years – from the joyous to the dreadfully sad – but never before had I witnessed a young man proposing marriage, and I was delighted.

Epilogue

I love happy endings and none could have been happier than the ending of Jade's story. She and Tyler became engaged two weeks later – on Jade's birthday – when Tyler gave her his grandmother's ring. In September of the same year Jade began studying for three A-levels – a part-time course over two years at the local college.

She and Tyler were married in June the following year (when Jade was halfway through her course), but she kept studying right up to the day before the wedding and then began again a couple of days afterwards. The wedding was small, to keep down the cost – just Jade's and Tyler's families at the local register office. Jade's father and his partner were also there. I saw the wedding photographs the next time I saw Jade, and Courtney looked very sweet as the bridesmaid. She wore a long peach-coloured lacy dress and carried a little bouquet of flowers that matched her mother's bouquet. Jade wore a full-length cream dress and had little white flowers in her hair. She really did look like a fairy-tale princess, and with her prince beside her, looking very smart in a grey suit, the tableau was complete.

Two months after Jade and Tyler were married Courtney was taken off the child-protection register, which Jade said was the best wedding present ever. Rachel's visits then stopped, as the social services were no longer involved with Jade, Tyler and Courtney. On my next visit I was relieved to find that the flat was noticeably less tidy – more lived in – and Jade was far more relaxed now that she felt she was no longer being 'watched'. I was also relieved when Jade told me she had found out that Tracy's baby, Jason, was being brought up by an aunt and Tracy was happy with the arrangement, as she could still see him regularly.

Jade passed three A-levels with good grades, and was then accepted onto a one-year course to train as a teaching assistant (TA). Courtney began school the year Jade qualified and Jade did some voluntary work as a TA at the same school as Courtney, although not in the same class. A year later Jade was offered a part-time teaching assistant post at the school, mornings only, which worked out very well, as Jade could take Courtney to school with her in the morning. Tyler completed his apprenticeship and was awarded a City and Guilds qualification in motor engineering with distinction. His boss gave him a pay rise and, with Jade also working, money at last became less tight. When Courtney was six the three of them went on their first holiday – a week in Majorca. They sent us a postcard and I still have it.

I saw Jade, Tyler and Courtney regularly for four years after they'd moved into the flat. Sometimes I visited them and other times they came to see us – usually at the weekend, as Jade was at college and then working, and Tyler was at work. They often stayed for a meal. I always gave them a 'goody bag', although the contents changed over the years. When Courtney became dry I replaced the nappies, first with pens, paper and vouchers for the books that Jade needed for her studying and then when she qualified with little extras – for example, a potted plant or bunch of flowers – and of course I always included the chocolate biscuits and cake Jade loved. A couple of times we bumped into the three of them while shopping in the mall on a Saturday morning and we went to a burger restaurant for lunch. Tyler said it reminded him of our day out to the castle. The family outing that had been Tyler's first had made such an impression on him that he said he planned to take Jade and Courtney there as soon as he passed his driving test and bought a car.

As time passed we gradually saw less of Jade, Tyler and Courtney, for clearly they had their own lives to lead. But we kept in touch and continued to see each other a couple of times a year, usually around Courtney's birthday and Christmas. I wondered if Jade and Tyler would have another child so that Courtney had a brother or sister, but no baby came along. Then one day Jade confided in me that they'd been trying for a baby and she'd had some tests at the hospital and been told she couldn't have any more children. Thank goodness she had been able to keep Courtney, I thought; what a double tragedy it would have been to lose the only child she could ever have. Jade continued to say that she and Tyler had discussed the possibility of fostering, but they were worried her past would count against her in the assessment for becoming a foster carer. I said I didn't think it would; indeed, the fact that she'd overcome her problems and had turned her life around showed her strength of character and therefore should count in her favour.

'Also, you've had first-hand experience of being in care,' I said. 'You'll have empathy based on your own experience, so you're in an ideal position to help the children you foster.'

'I hadn't really thought of it that way,' Jade said. Then she looked thoughtful for a moment before exclaiming, 'Oh my! I hope I don't have to foster anyone as bad as me. I was awful. I don't know how you put up with me, Cathy.'

I smiled and took her hands between mine. 'Because I saw the person you could become: the person you are now. I'm very proud of you, Jade. Well done, love, you made it through.'

Jade's story had a happy ending but it could so easily have been different. The majority of babies placed for adoption come from young single mothers. More needs to be done to educate boys to take responsibility for their sexual relationships, while girls need to understand that having a baby isn't the answer to their problems. Far from it – a baby is likely to add to them. While I am overjoyed for Jade, my heart goes out to the thousands of other young mothers whose stories can't have happy endings. We still see Jade, Tyler and Courtney and they are all doing very well. There is an update about them on my website: www.cathyglass.co.uk

SUGGESTED TOPICS FOR READING-GROUP DISCUSSION

What reasons could there be for England having one of the highest teenage pregnancy rates in the developed world? Why is this of concern? Discuss what could be done/is being done to change this.

What problems can arise if the teacher-pupil boundary is blurred, even if the intention is well meant? Why does Meryl want to help Jade?

Jade is little more than a child herself. Discuss. How might this contribute to her irresponsible and unsafe behaviour?

Jackie, Jade's mother, is understandably upset, as she wanted better for her daughter. With hindsight, what might she have done differently in parenting Jade?

Although younger than Jade, Tyler could be said to be more mature. Discuss with reference to the text. What role does he play in supporting Jade so that she is able to keep her baby? Would she have managed without him?

Cathy has to accept that she has been helping Jade too much rather than assessing her. Put yourself in Cathy's position. How would you have handled Jade's behaviour?

Rachel, Jade's social worker, gives Jade the time and support she needs to mature and start behaving responsibly. Some might say she allows Jade too many chances. Do you agree or disagree? Give your reasons.

At the very end of the book Cathy says teenage girls need to understand that having a baby isn't the answer to their problems. What do you think she means by this? To what degree is it true of Jade?

Cathy Glass

———

One remarkable woman, more
than **150** foster children cared for.

Cathy Glass has been a foster carer for
twenty-five years, during which time she has
looked after more than 150 children, as well
as raising three children of her own. She was
awarded a degree in education and psychology
as a mature student, and writes under a
pseudonym. To find out more about Cathy
and her story visit www.cathyglass.co.uk.

Girl Alone

An angry, traumatized young girl on a path to self-destruction

Can Cathy discover the truth behind Joss's dangerous behaviour before it's too late?

Saving Danny

Trapped in his own dark world, Danny doesn't understand why his parents are sending him away

Cathy must call on all her expertise to deal with his challenging behaviour, and discovers a frightened little boy who just wants to be loved.

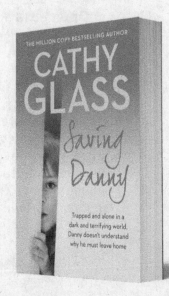

The Child Bride

A girl blamed and abused for dishonouring her community

Cathy discovers the devastating truth.

Daddy's Little Princess

A sweet-natured girl with a complicated past

Cathy picks up the pieces after events take a dramatic turn.

Will you love me?

A broken child desperate for a loving home

The true story of Cathy's adopted daughter Lucy.

Please Don't Take My Baby

Seventeen-year-old Jade is pregnant, homeless and alone

Cathy has room in her heart for two.

Another Forgotten Child

Eight-year-old Aimee was on the child-protection register at birth

Cathy is determined to give her the happy home she deserves.

A Baby's Cry

A newborn, only hours old, taken into care

Cathy protects tiny Harrison from the potentially fatal secrets that surround his existence.

The Night the Angels Came

A little boy on the brink of bereavement

Cathy and her family make sure Michael is never alone.

Mummy Told me not to tell

A troubled boy sworn to secrecy

After his dark past has been revealed, Cathy helps Reece to rebuild his life.

I Miss Mummy

Four-year-old Alice doesn't understand why she's in care

Cathy fights for her to have the happy home she deserves.

The Saddest Girl in the World

A haunted child who refuses to speak

Do Donna's scars run too deep for Cathy to help?

Cut

Dawn is desperate to be loved

Abused and abandoned, this vulnerable child pushes Cathy and her family to their limits.

Hidden

The boy with no past

Can Cathy help Tayo to feel like he belongs again?

Damaged

A forgotten child

Cathy is Jodie's last hope.
For the first time, this abused
young girl has found someone
she can trust.

Inspired by Cathy's own experiences...

Run,
Mummy, Run

The gripping story of a
woman caught in a horrific
cycle of abuse, and the
desperate measures she
must take to escape.

My Dad's a
Policeman

The dramatic short story
about a young boy's
desperate bid to keep his
family together.

The Girl in the Mirror

Trying to piece together her past, Mandy uncovers a dreadful family secret that has been blanked from her memory for years.

Sharing her expertise...

About Writing and How to Publish

A clear and concise, practical guide on writing and the best ways to get published.

Happy Mealtimes for Kids

A guide to healthy eating with simple recipes that children love.

Happy Adults

A practical guide to achieving lasting happiness, contentment and success. The essential manual for getting the best out of life.

Happy Kids

A clear and concise guide to raising confident, well-behaved and happy children.

Be amazed
Be moved
Be inspired

———

Discover more about Cathy Glass
visit www.cathyglass.co.uk